WORK *and* DEMOCRACY
in Socialist Cuba

In the series
Labor and Social Change,

edited by Paula Rayman and Carmen Sirianni

WORK *and* DEMOCRACY
in Socialist Cuba

LINDA FULLER

Temple University Press
Philadelphia

Temple University Press, Philadelphia 19122
Copyright © 1992 by Temple University. All rights reserved
Published 1992
Printed in the United States of America

The paper used in this publication meets the minimum
requirements of American National Standard for Information
Sciences—Permanence of Paper for Printed Library Materials,
ANSI Z39.48–1984 ⊗

Library of Congress Cataloging-in-Publication Data

Fuller, Linda, 1944–
    Work and democracy in socialist Cuba / Linda Fuller.
        p.   cm. — (Labor and social change)
    Includes bibliographical references and index.
    ISBN 0-87722-893-0 (alk. paper)
    1. Management—Cuba—Employee participation.   2. Industrial
relations—Cuba.   3. Trade-unions—Cuba.   I. Title.   II. Series.
HD5660.C9F85   1992
331'.097291—dc20   91-17102

For
Russell Kenneth Olsen and Jeanne Louise Fennell Olsen
and in memory of Betty Quiñones Fernández,
one of many Cubans who have accomplished so much

Acknowledgments

I have many thanks to give for the love and friendship, intellectual guidance, and practical and financial aid I received as I worked on this book. Michael Burawoy, my teacher and friend, comes first to mind. He kept up his enthusiasm for the project when mine waned; he prodded or cajoled when that was necessary, then let me alone when that was best. His own dedication to changing the world as he interprets it is always an inspiration. I also thank Andy Zimbalist and Carmen Sirianni, whose comments at a very early and at a much later stage were encouraging and useful.

Numerous Cubans, who had far more pressing matters to attend to, gave generously of their time and thoughts. I thank each of them, especially Betty and Teresa, whose pampering made my work a great deal easier and whose companionship made it much more fun. Practical help and sound advice along the way were offered by Carlos Forment, Sheryl Lutgens, Rebecca Scott, and Grace Stimson, by Michael Ames, Debby Stuart, and Heidi Trombert at Temple University Press, and by the staff at the Hoover Institution library, especially Andre Pierce and Hilja Kukk. Support during various phases of the project came from the Center for Latin American Studies at the University of California, Berkeley; the Haynes Summer Fellowship and the Faculty Research and Innovation Fund, both at the University of Southern California; and the Joint Committee on Latin American Studies of the Social Science Research Council and the American Council of Learned Societies, with funds provided by the National Endowment for the Humanities, the Ford Foundation, and the Andrew W. Mellon Foundation.

There is no way I could have completed this book without

regular doses of the sanity and insanity, seriousness and frivolousness, cynicism and optimism, sophistication and innocence, and most of all the care and love of my good friends. Special thanks to: Joyce (the Voice) Carrillo, Teresa Cordova, Lew Friedland, Dave (the Brave) Froba, Bob Fuller, Nora Hamilton, Eun Mee Kim, Steve McMahon, Steve McMillan, Jon Miller, Stacey Oliker, Rusty Olsen, Teresa (Slush) Sharpe, Vicki Smith, Carol Warren, Karen Williams, and, of course, Greg McLauchlan.

Contents

Preface

This book originated in my deep dissatisfaction with the shallowness of democratic practice as I had experienced it at the paid workplace in the United States. Reinhard Bendix's (1956:1) short statement describes well my own succession of jobs from salesperson to playground supervisor, teacher, clerk, and interviewer: "Wherever enterprises are set up, a few command and many obey." I began to wonder if people had ever challenged the pervasive absence of democracy at work, and later, after studying the topic as a graduate student, I learned they had. I began to question how social thinkers had resolved the striking contradiction between the widespread and passionate support for the idea and practice of democracy in the political realm and the authoritarian and hierarchical arrangements at work, and I found they had not. Finally, I began to calculate how many hours of our lifetimes most of us would likely spend working for pay, and it struck me that there were probably few areas of life where democracy could be as important.

Prompted by these experiences and concerns, in this book I ask two major questions about the relationship of the many to the few in the process of production. The first is: What would production actually be like if it were controlled more democratically? My initial problem was where to research this question in a world so poor in examples of democratized production relations. After a number of detours into the literature on Yugoslavia, Peru, Nicaragua, and collectives and cooperatives in the United States, I eventually settled on postrevolutionary Cuba. I had been enticed by fleeting references to some changes there that seemed to portend well for enhanced democracy at work. As it turned out, Cuba was an even better choice than I had imagined, because a period of increased democratization at work (roughly 1970 through the mid-1980s) had been proceeded by one from 1959 to 1970 in which democracy had been far more circumscribed. Cuban history thus offered a good way to grapple with the first question I had posed. Contrasting these two periods helped illuminate the main factors that were essential to but also detracted from the democratization of work. The second major question I address in this volume followed logically on the first: How and why had such a change toward greater democratization of production relations taken place in Cuba?

Roughly coinciding with the completion of research for this book in the mid-1980s, the socialist world began to undergo significant changes. Most of these could be characterized as attempts to reform existing socialism, and while such attempts had occurred before, this time they were more thoroughgoing and widespread. Glasnost, perestroika, and Solidarity became household words. The 12th Party Congress in China approved increased reliance on markets, and Hungary resuscitated earlier decentralization plans. In 1986 Cuba too embarked on a series of changes under the label *rectificación*. All this gave impetus to a new interest in the dynamics of reform in socialist countries, long constrained by dominant academic paradigms that had stressed the uniformity and continuity of socialist societies. As a result, reviewers of my research suggested that I revise my work in order to situate it within this growing reform literature and that I include a discussion of the Cuban *rectificación* campaign.

By the time I began to undertake these suggested revisions, however, far more dramatic changes had occurred in numerous socialist countries. These were sparked (or attempted) by mass protests in most countries in Eastern Europe and in China, and have resulted, everywhere except in China, in the total transformation, not just the reform, of existing socialism. In many countries the transformation has meant steps, albeit of varying lengths, back in the direction of capitalism.

In the aftermath of these revolutions, many now question whether there could be anything at all to learn about democracy from an existing socialist country like Cuba. The revolutions of Eastern Europe have been read as evidence that capitalism has all the solutions to the democracy puzzle. I find this position untenable. In my view, rather than offering assurance that capitalism is the "end of democratic history," the 1989 revolutions in existing socialist countries underscore the importance of the search for more deeply democratic alternatives to the previous ways humans have organized their societies, alternatives that expand democracy into all areas of social life, including production, and drastically transfigure its content.[1] The revolutions of Eastern Europe were, in large part, indigenous reactions to undemocratic systems that erected rigid barriers before people's attempts to shape their own social arrangements. This being so, why does it make sense to turn to an existing socialist society to investigate what more thoroughly democratic production arrangements might look like and how they might be achieved? The reasons are fourfold.

The arguments and evidence that capitalism is incompatible with extensive and thoroughgoing democratization of production are powerful. I will not review these in detail, but instead will underscore the principal point on which most hinge: Private ownership of productive property—arguments that ownership and control can be separated notwithstanding[2]—bears a definite, empirically demonstrable connection to undemocratic production relations. The two have been the closest of historical partners, such that attempts to alter authoritarian production arrangements in the context of private ownership have nearly always been isolated, incomplete, and fragile.

There are a number of reasons for this. First, private control over decisions about where, when, how, and whether to invest or produce carries an inherent bias against the democratization of production.[3] Second, private ownership translates into a very skewed distribution of power within and over the state, such that owners have been able, both directly (e.g., through their ability systematically to bias election outcomes and legislative, executive, and administrative decisions) and indirectly (e.g., through their control over investment and production) to obstruct public sector efforts to democratize production.[4] Third, the ideology of private ownership legitimizes unequal power over production. Each individual is perceived to have the freedom and an equal opportunity to become an owner. Ending up without control thus becomes evidence that one is less capable of exercising control; ending up with control becomes proof of exceptional ability and, hence, of one's right to assume control. None of this is to belittle attempts that have gone on to democratize production under capitalism or to trivialize the benefits that have accrued to workers as a result of them. It is only to be clear about what I judge to be the ultimately insurmountable obstacles private ownership places in the path of extensive and thoroughgoing democratization of production and, hence, to highlight the importance of seeing what can be learned about the topic in places where productive property is not in private hands.

It is not only capitalism's poor empirical record that prompts us to look elsewhere to further our understanding of the democratization of production. In contrast to capitalist ideology, the ideals of Marxism, upon which existing socialist states were founded, are strongly democratic in their implications for how production should be controlled and organized. It is not, however, merely the abstract content of socialist ideology that is of importance here. In Cuba I saw how gaps between ideology and practice helped keep the issue of how and by whom production was controlled a live one, at the forefront of social discourse. The ideals of socialism could be used as a yardstick by which to judge its practice, and, if practice were found wanting, the contrast could help focus direct producers' attempts to democratize the production process. I observed, for instance, how base-level union leaders cleverly used the ideal-real discrepancy and the uneasiness it caused, to bolster the control claims of their members before enterprise managers. This pressure for the democratization of production generated by contradictions between ideology and reality has been noted in other socialist countries as well.[5] And, as its form and intensity appear unmatched outside this context, these countries bear watching if we are to understand when and why the emancipatory potential of this contradiction is realized and when and why it is not.

Yet the reasons for studying existing socialism to learn about the democratization of work go beyond the content of socialist ideology and its contrast with practice. Despite their systemic economic and political failings and the variations among them, socialist societies have provided ordinary working people with important services and guarantees that most capitalist countries have been unable to offer. These include affordable health care, basic foodstuffs, education, housing, childcare, transportation, and recreational opportunities, together with job and old-age security, and access to reproductive alternatives and job training. Moreover, despite the undeniable material privileges enjoyed by a small upper strata, it has been politically possible to distribute these benefits, and income as well, far more equitably in socialist than in capitalist countries. As David Held (1987:285) has argued, and common sense suggests, the lack of such services and guarantees together with a highly skewed income distribution voids discussions of democracy. Without "equal rights to enjoy the conditions for effective participation, enlightened understanding and the setting of the political agenda," minority control of production will continue.

Finally, as an epistemological matter, we must ask ourselves if it is sensible to close off *any* options for learning about deeper democracy when our knowledge in this area is so undeveloped, our empirical examples so sparse, and the problem so complex. I am convinced it is not. These options certainly include the theory and practice of feminism, the ecology movement, and groups world over dedicated to ending racism, ethnocentrism, homophobia, militarism, and violence. And they include existing socialism as well. To ignore existing socialism's record on democracy—what it has accomplished and what it has left undone, where it has succeeded and where it has failed and why—would be shortsighted and premature.

I base the analyses contained in this book largely on field data gathered on three visits to Cuba in 1982 and 1983, totaling two and one-half months, and on primary written sources consulted throughout much of the 1980s. Gathering and interpreting these data presented certain problems of which readers should be made aware. The problems stemmed from the three-decade-long hostile relationship between the United States and Cuban governments. In various, sometimes subtle, ways, my own research activities, as well as those of all the postrevolutionary Cuban and non-Cuban sources I consulted, were charged with the emotional and intellectual fallout from this relationship, which not only has fostered ignorance, misunderstanding, and prejudice on both sides but also has discouraged many U.S. researchers from studying Cuba at all.[6] The dissuasions were especially pronounced for me because my project dealt with the contemporary period, with living individuals, and with substantively and ideologically controversial topics.

Before I ever set foot in Cuba, this context complicated my research efforts. Some well-endowed funding sources discouraged or even disallowed field research in Cuba; telephone and postal contact with the island was frustrating, slow, and uncertain: Cubans in positions to provide information about their country to U.S. audiences had regularly been denied U.S. visas; U.S. citizens and institutions had been able to import postrevolutionary Cuban publications only with great difficulty. The cumulative effect of this more than a quarter century of stifled communication, encumbered travel, and restricted availability of printed materials was a severe erosion of the personal, professional, and institutional contacts between Cubans and North Americans that were critical for arranging to conduct research in Cuba.

Once I was in Cuba it was clear that the long-standing acrimony between the U.S. and Cuban governments would continue to affect my work. In the midst of my first visit, travel to Cuba by U.S. citizens was severely restricted.[7] Moreover, many Cubans felt understandably insecure in their ability to judge the credentials or the intentions of a U.S. scholar. My vita, for example, listed membership in such organizations as the American Sociological Association and the Guatemala News and Information Bureau, none of them familiar to most Cubans who reviewed it, and some of them, by their titles alone, sounding suspect to others. Nor had most Cubans heard of the U.S. academics, well known in their fields here, who had written letters of introduction for me. In addition, the politically imposed separation of Cuba and the United States has given rise amongst some Cubans to what Medea Benjamin, Joseph Collins, and Michael Scott (1984:xiii) describe as a "siege mentality." The "siege mentality" has found expression in an uncooperative, defensive, and distrustful posture among some Cubans in both official and unofficial capacities, in the denial of entrance visas and access to certain data, and in various forms of harassment of outside scholars.

Even after I had returned from Cuba, Cold War–inspired geopolitics continued to interfere with my research. Surveillance of individuals and organizations communicating with Cuba began as early as 1962.[8] Suspicions that it continues have not been allayed by U.S. researchers' and journalists' reports of U.S. Customs delays and confiscations, or by the U.S. government attempt to subpoena travel agency records containing the names and addresses of most of the people who journeyed from the United States to Cuba since 1982. During the period when I traveled to and from the island, I was distressed by the disappearance of mail sent me by individuals and organizations with knowledge of my research in Cuba and by a barrage of telephone calls to my home (up to five or six on some days and continuing for nearly six months). No one ever spoke on the other end of the line, but sometimes crackly or mechanical noises were audible.

The data from which I learned about work and workers in postrevolutionary Cuba had to be collected and interpreted within this context. My primary data are mostly of two kinds—interviews and documentary materials. Additional data were collected from informal observations at eleven Cuban worksites[9] and from secondary sources representing divergent perspectives on the revolution. Because the data I incorporate into my analysis are varied, I was continually afforded opportunities to cross-validate information derived from one source against that derived from others.

The interviews, an unusual source of data on postrevolutionary Cuba (Roca 1986:155), were with twenty-nine people, currently working in Cuba, which I arranged and conducted on my own, and with an additional eight people, which I also conducted but which were arranged for me by a government bureau.[10] I followed an open-ended interview format; nearly all the interviews were conducted in Spanish; they ranged in length from one-half hour to over three hours, the average being approximately two hours.

As I traveled to Cuba on three different occasions over a nineteen-month period, I was able to re-interview, once and sometimes twice, many of the twenty-nine respondents I had found on my own. Thus, in all, I conducted forty-three interviews with these twenty-nine workers. Re-interviewing turned out to have unanticipated advantages. The most obvious was that as workers got to know me better, many of their suspicions about my motives as a North American scholar asking some politically sensitive questions were dispelled. They were able to speak more frankly in repeat conversations, enabling me better to handle interpretive problems posed by disjunctures between theory and reality (e.g., the difference between what unions actually did and what workers knew they were supposed to do). Re-interviewing also provided insight into the internal consistency of respondents' reports and allowed workers opportunities to verify their recollections against what co-workers or family members remembered. And, over the nineteen-month period, some respondents changed jobs, and I thus had the benefit of their comparisons of different worksites.

When re-interviewed, many also came to reflect more deeply

about what happened at their worksites. It is difficult for people to answer questions about their day-to-day activities, because they take them for granted, and because their continuous involvement in them affords no perspective from which to ponder daily routines. By the second or third interview, however, many workers were able to offer insights about their work that they could not have articulated during our first meeting. Often it was workers who reintroduced topics covered in earlier sessions. On further consideration, they discovered they had much more to say.

Aware early on that to insist on a random or even slightly more scientific sample would have meant no interviews at all, I developed my sample through a procedure commonly called snowballing. Comparing my respondents with relevant populations on characteristics likely to bear a systematic relationship to relevant aspects of work yields the following: Women made up 38 percent of the workers I interviewed; in 1984 they made up 36 percent of the paid workforce (Padula and Smith 1985:88). The 1981 census reported around 33 percent of the population were not of European descent (Domínguez 1988:7); my sample contained 43 percent respondents of African descent.[11] Based on 1979 data roughly comparable to my own (Pérez-Stable 1985:295), clerical and service workers were underrepresented in my sample by 4 percent, and high-level administrators were overrepresented by 3 percent. The widest discrepancies, however, appeared among production workers (54 percent of the labor force and 38 percent of my respondents) and professional and technical workers (18 percent of the labor force and 35 percent of my respondents). The skewing of my sample toward the higher-paying end of the occupational scale owed mostly to the fact that the people I interviewed worked in and around Havana, the educational, scientific, commercial, and political center of the country. Workers I interviewed were members of twelve of the eighteen sectoral unions existing in the late 1970s. The unions unrepresented by my respondents also reflected the Havana bias of my sample. Last, based on general impressions from the interviews and from additional, sometimes lengthy, discussions with twenty-one of my thirty-seven respondents, I would classify 30 percent as either hostile to or indecisive about the revolution, and the other 70 percent as either favorably or very favorably disposed toward it.[12]

It would be foolhardy to maintain that neither workers' suspicions of a North American academic lacking official Cuban credentials nor their worries of reprisals from the authorities could affect the quality of my interview data. Indeed, before beginning this project, I was uncertain, for precisely such reasons, whether interviews in Cuba would yield useful information. By the end of my fieldwork, however, I felt confident that neither eventuality had colored my interview data in a serious way.

My confidence can be justified on a number of counts. To begin with, my requests for interviews were almost always responded to with friendliness and eagerness. Only one person declined to be interviewed, and none of the respondents whom I asked for re-interviews refused. In the interviews, most respondents proved candid, often outspoken.[13] Respondents who held positive views of Cuban socialism nevertheless felt little hesitation in criticizing some of its aspects, and many people who were hostile to the revolution expressed their negative evaluations in unguarded terms. Both types of respondents, venturing beyond topics broached in the interviews, offered opinions on issues as controversial as hard currency stores, Cuba's presence in Africa and its relationship to the Soviet Union, and the status of women and people of African descent in Cuba.

I also made deliberate efforts to assuage any fears workers had about being interviewed and to detect any responses that might be problematic or disingenuous. I always assured respondents of anonymity. I asked them to choose interview locations, some preferring their homes, others my apartment, and still others a restaurant or a hotel lobby. Finally, I soon became aware of a tendency, particularly among the revolution's most ardent supporters, to respond to some of my questions in near-identical, stylized, politico-cultural phraseology and symbolism, not in their own words. Liberal probing was therefore necessary to determine whether such commonly used words and phrases were hollow repetitions or meaningful and expressive shorthand and, if the latter, precisely what was being communicated by respondents who used them.

Documentary materials were my second major source of primary data. The Cuban acquisitions of the major university libraries to which I had ready access (Stanford and Berkeley) have been sporadic over the past quarter century. I was, however, able to supplement these with a variety of primary documents gathered in

Cuba. The single most useful primary documentary source was the newspaper *Trabajadores*, published by the CTC (Central de Trabajadores de Cuba). Its publication history parallels the growing visibility of the unions in postrevolutionary Cuba: In 1971, when it first appeared, it was published twice a month; by 1982 and 1983 it was being published daily (except Sundays) and sold on the streets of Havana.

Many issues of *Trabajadores* published before 1976, however, were barely readable or not available, even at the Biblioteca Nacional José Martí. The Hoover Institution library at Stanford has been receiving *Trabajadores* since 1976, though with occasional gaps. There, I read every available issue from 1976 through 1979. Of the months for which issues were available between January 1980 and June 1989, I read every issue of the paper for thirty-seven months and seven or eight issues a month randomly for an additional forty-four months. Further, whenever any of these issues revealed that items of particular interest would soon be or had already been published or when I knew an important event had occurred on or near a particular date, I also consulted the relevant editions of the paper. Aside from news reports about the CTC and the sectoral unions, *Trabajadores* regularly published the following informative items: union news from outside Havana; worker education articles (e.g., columns explaining how to calculate bonuses or conduct union elections); interviews with rank-and-file workers and union and political leaders; question-and-answer columns in which workers sought advice on arranging transfers, health and safety issues, worksite disputes, and so forth. Finally, *Trabajadores* published, very often in their entirety, numerous laws, regulations, decrees, and commission reports affecting workers, as well as internal union documents.

Information from informal interactions also proved quite valuable for my work. Taking advantage of Cubans' gracious invitations, I spent hours eating, talking, arguing, and sharing stories in their homes, attending sports and cultural events, going to beaches and restaurants, shopping, and participating in voluntary labor and block events of the CDR (Committees for the Defense of the Revolution). Time spent in these pursuits provided a context within which to situate people's interview responses and the information contained in documentary materials, allowing me to grasp their multiple meanings more fully.

WORK *and* DEMOCRACY
in Socialist Cuba

Chapter 1

WHAT MIGHT DEMOCRATIZATION AT WORK ENTAIL?

Democratization, as I employ the term, refers simultaneously to political practice and political structure. Judging the extent of democracy in production relations thus involves analysis of political form *and* political activity. Political practice occurs within structures that provide opportunities for, not guarantees of, democracy. These structures themselves, however, are crafted through political practice shaped both by ideas and by material circumstances.

Below I explore seven major issues pertinent to the democratization of practice and structure in the realm of production: economic decision makers, the nature of production decisions, workers' collective organization and action, the worksite and supraworksite arenas where practice occurs and structures are located, multiplicity, size and democratization, and democratization as empowerment. My primary purpose is to provide some guideposts for analyzing what changes in Cuban production relations between two historical periods signify for democratization. The considerations raised in this chapter will thus resurface repeatedly in Chapters 2–8. Because democratization is a multi-layered and ideologically charged concept, not ordinarily considered relevant to what happens at work, they prove useful in systematizing and clarifying the discussion in these chapters and in helping discriminate between more and less significant aspects of the changes that occurred.

I do not, however, understand these seven considerations, taken together, to constitute a normative blueprint for the democratization of production, an abstract ideal that can be used to determine whether production relations in Cuba, or anywhere else, are "really" democratic or not. This said, I must say also that, inso-

1

far as the discussion in this chapter prompts readers to expand their vision of what an alternative, more deeply democratic system of production may be, it is also of value. "Radical imaginaries" (Laclau and Mouffe 1985:190) remind us, boldly and insistently, that what exists is not all that is possible. They inspire us to action. They challenge us. Sheila Rowbotham (1986:98) says it best: "Visions of what might be are precious, for they sustain hope and humor; without these qualities democracy becomes far too difficult for must of us to bother with."

Nonetheless, the real problem is ever practical. "What happens," writes Rudolf Bahro (1978:348), "will depend also on the conditions under which [you] take up the struggle, and not simply on [your] 'ultimate' goals and values." Whether significant moves in the direction of increased economic democracy are made, who will make them, how they will work, and whether they will endure are contingent upon real social, political, and economic conditions, real opposition, and the real strengths and weaknesses of those who undertake the struggle.

ECONOMIC DECISION MAKERS

According to C. Wright Mills (1959:40), the "basic problem of power" concerns the identification of those involved (and those not involved) in making decisions. As I understand it, this "basic problem of power" has three components: the proportion of worker to non-worker participants in decision-making forums or processes, the inclusiveness of decision-making procedures, and the question of whether participation in decision making is direct or indirect.

Worker compared to non-worker involvement is the least complex of the three, reminding us, as Rosabeth Kanter (1977) has, that proportions matter in social life. Ordinary workers may be totally excluded from a particular decision-making process; they may constitute the majority or the minority (sometimes the extreme minority) of participants; workers and non-workers (under socialism typically mid- and upper-level managers or party people) may share equally in decision making; or, unusually, an entire decision-making apparatus or procedure may be in workers' hands. The issue of proportions is important because the power balance at work is typically skewed by the relative disadvantage of workers in terms of time, skills, contacts, and so on. Producers can offset some of these disadvantages through a greater relative presence in decision-making arenas; alternatively, the power imbalance at work is protected wherever their proportional involvement is reduced.[1]

A second matter is inclusiveness. At issue here is the extent to which decision-making processes and forums involve *all* workers. The exclusion of some workers may be formal or informal, intentional or inadvertent. While the vast majority of workers are formally excluded from most decision making at traditional workplaces, informal exclusion, which has raised more complicated theoretical and practical problems for democratization, has been the focus of much recent attention. Feminists concerned with democracy have shown special concern for this form of exclusion from economic decision making. How, they have asked, could women workers, saddled with the major responsibility for child and parent care, household tasks, and maintaining family social ties, ever be expected to become as involved as men if decision making at work were democratized? Why, in Carole Pateman's words (1989:221), should women who are already burdened with at least two jobs "be eager to take on the new responsibilities, as well as exercise the opportunities, that democratization [of production] would bring"?

Besides gender, exclusion can also be based on other ascribed characteristics like race and age. In addition, it can be tied to acquired traits such as workers' education or knowledge levels, skill differences, length of employment, employment status (e.g., seasonal, temporary, and contract workers have been excluded from unions and workplace decision-making structures in China), and to variables such as self-confidence, verbal agility, and even voice tone and speaking style.[2] Suggestions for minimizing both formal and informal exclusion range from provision of child care and transportation, improved information distribution, ambitious and extensive educational programs, and alternating and maximally convenient meeting times and places to chair and task rotation, compulsory participation, and leadership selection by lot.[3]

Traditionally, one of the most widely debated topics in the democracy literature has been whether involvement in decision making should be indirect, through representatives, or direct, through such varied mechanisms as surveys, petitions, referenda, direct voting, and face-to-face assemblies. Reflecting serious short-

comings in both existing capitalist and socialist democratic practices, recent thinkers are nearly unanimous in stressing the need to
supplement and invigorate indirect democratic forms with direct
ones.[4] Displeased by the "political wasteland stretching between
the individual and the state" (Bowles and Gintis 1986:140), commentators forward a long list of reasons for increasing direct democracy in the political as well as the economic arena. Most commonly, they argue that people's preferences and interests would be
reflected more accurately, inequalities would be lessened, and political involvement would increase as alienation from politics decreased.

Despite what comes close to a universal yearning for the expansion of direct democracy, its shortcomings, some easily remedi-
able and other less so, lead most to caution that indirect representative forms must not be scuttled en masse.[5] Nevertheless, they
must be carefully rethought. Special attention has been devoted to
the problems of ensuring that representatives accurately represent
their constituents' needs and opinions. Are representatives elected
or appointed and what are the details of the process? Is representation based on what Raymond Williams (1983:112–14) terms typ-
icality (sharing characteristics like gender, race, or political ideology with your constituents), or diversity of opinions (representing
the plurality of different interests within your constituency), or
neither? How do representatives assess their constituents' preferences and inform them of their activities? Is recall practically possible at any time? Are representatives bound by formal constituent
instruction, as Marx preferred? Are representative proceedings
public and publicized? Do representatives have personal and regular contact with their constituents? Here Stan Weir (1983:183), for
example, argues that union officers should not be full-time professionals. Instead, they should continue to work at their regular jobs
so they can maintain frequent face-to-face contact with the membership, in the context of production.

THE NATURE OF PRODUCTION DECISIONS

A second consideration draws attention to the nature of production decisions themselves, rather than to who makes them.
Considerations here include: the stages of decision making, the
character of insertion into the decision-making process, and the
content of the decisions taken.

Decision making is a process rather than a single act at a discrete point in time. At the least, the process incorporates the following stages: formulation, implementation, and evaluation, with decisions of different types made in each. Although rarely discussed by people whose interest is democracy in the state arena, the decision-making process has occasionally received attention from those whose primary interest is the economic realm.[6] To the extent that workers are involved in all stages of the process, democratization is advanced. Job rotation or other schemes that break down the rigid division of labor between planning and execution have been proposed in an effort to accomplish this. Often, however, decision-making stages have been strictly compartmentalized and democratization confined to the implementation stage (Grenier 1988:128).

Concern over the character of workers' insertion into decision making recognizes that involvement can be in one of three forms: advisory or informational, negative, or positive. When workers are consulted on upcoming decisions, ultimately made by someone else, or when they are informed about past, present, or future activities of decision makers, involvement is advisory or informational. The International Labour Organization (ILO) (1969:14, 118, table 1; Espinosa and Zimbalist 1978:3) recognizes an increase in workers' advisory or informational involvement, which clearly entails only minimal democratization, as the "striking feature" of the development of labor relations in the score of years following World War II.

The nature of involvement in decision making is negative when workers have the right and ability to veto, resist, or dispute decisions that have already been made. The strike is one familiar example. Negative involvement is also in evidence when workers approve managerial appointments or remove managers they do not like. By contrast, positive involvement is assertive rather than reactive. Workers so engaged can raise issues and determine agendas and have the power to push for resolution of problems they identify and for adoption of ideas they forward. Because positive involvement supposes the capacity not only to propose but also to impose, it carries the assumption of responsibility for consequences. Some who have written about democratization in the state arena have pointed to positive worker involvement in decision making as by far the most consequential of the three forms. "When values have been named, issues identified, agendas set, and options delineated," writes Benjamin Barber (1984:157, 180–81), "most of what is meaningful in politics has already taken place."[7]

The content or substance of production decisions is a last matter to be considered. The number of different kinds of decisions that affect production is so immense that some system of classifying them is in order. In Table 1 I have grouped decisions according

---

Table 1
Categories of Production Decisions

Category 1: Relationship of the Workplace to its External Environment (e.g., Other Workplaces or the State)

Investment
Financing
Budgeting, expenditures, and purchases
Pricing
Distribution of earnings among investments, dividends, reserves, bonuses, and so on
Wage, salary, and benefit policies
Production planning (quantity, quality, and type of product)
Research and development
Product and service distribution
Staffing levels and distribution of workforce

Category 2: Relationship of Workers to Owners and Managers within a Workplace

Hiring and firing
Discipline
Promotions, evaluations, and training
Transfers and leaves
Internal information and communication systems
Administrative procedures and rules
Organizational form
Wage and salary structure
Extent and nature of supervision

Category 3: Relationship of Workers to One Another and to the Physical Features of Work

Quality control
Working conditions
Methods of remuneration
Maintenance of machinery and equipment
Work methods, work speed, task ordering, job division, job rotation, variety of tasks, and so on
Scheduling
Work distribution and assignments
Type and level of interaction among workers
Employment of technology
Incentives

---

to one of three production relationships to which they are most relevant.[8] Table 1 implicitly orders decisions from the least (category 3) to the most consequential (category 1). That is not to imply, however, that if workers participate in making decisions of the most important kind, they will necessarily be making lower-category decisions as well. The real world is by no means so orderly. Nor is it to suggest that decisions falling into category 3 are unimportant to workers or to the democratization of production. Indeed, in the final passage of *Labor and Monopoly Capital*, Harry Braverman (1974:445–46) chastises those whose demand for democratization would overlook the importance of workers' command over the immediate action of production. Still, the inability to grasp the connection between Braverman's "degradation of labor" and workers' lack of power over such matters as investment and discipline is a major obstacle to achieving more just production relations.[9] Democratization demands that producers have input into decisions that fall in not just one or two but all three content categories.

COLLECTIVE ORGANIZATION AND ACTION BY WORKERS

Unfortunately, a sustained discussion of the importance of collective action and organization for democratization is muted in many radical democratic, participatory, and even feminist writings.[10] In the realm of production, collective organization and action might take a number of forms, but historically the most prominent has been unionization. Unions are pivotal in efforts to initiate, expand, and protect democratization efforts because, as noted above, in terms of money, time, certain skills, status, contacts, training, education, and so forth, the majority of workers are disadvantaged relative to most managers, state functionaries, and owners. Many of these inequalities are imported from outside the workplace; however, these are always exacerbated, and others are reproduced, in the production process itself.

If these manifest inequalities are to be countered and production reordered, workers' ability to organize into unions and to pursue democratization goals collectively is a necessity. "It makes no sense," David Harris (1983:232) reminds us, "to think of things working out; one must think of them being brought about." Organized, deliberate, and militant collective action from below has repeatedly proven effective in the state, but also in the economic arena when democracy has been at issue. In concert, through unions, workers have been able to overcome formidable obstacles and to make notable strides toward this goal—strides that could never have been made by isolated producers acting individually. Ellen Wood (1986:187), in her critique of those who would excise "class and class struggle from the socialist project," makes the larger theoretical point: "Failing a collective agent, history must be made by individuals acting independently, or by Great Men and/or Great Women, or else there are no human agents in history at all—in which case *any* political movement is clearly a delusion and a waste of time."

Collective action and organization through unions, though indispensable, is not, however, a guarantee that production can be democratized. The many examples of minimal democratization in workplaces with unions and of situations where producers had to oppose unions in order to expand democracy attest to this. For unions to be able to promote democratization, they too must be democratized. In other words, union practice and structure must itself be scrutinized in the light of other considerations raised in this chapter and, where necessary, altered. The more unions themselves are democratized, the better they are able to protect past gains in, exploit opportunities for, and fashion new mechanisms of economic democracy.

LEVELS OF PRODUCTION: WORKSITE AND SUPRAWORKSITE ARENAS

The micro or worksite and the macro or supraworksite levels are crucial to the analysis of how production is controlled and organized. In both sites activities occur and structures exist that, in large measure, determine the course and character of production. The macro level is roughly analogous to the varied combinations of plan and market, and the politics distinctive to them, that characterize the political economies of different nations. The micro level is coterminous with the politics of workplace structures and processes.

Although it is not difficult to separate the worksite and the supraworksite levels conceptually, the separation is artificial, because each arena has demonstrable effects on and connections to the other. Moreover, in terms of democratization, these are rarely simple, direct, immediate, or identical from one time and place to the next. Nor are they symmetrical. Evidence from different world contexts reveals two common patterns of interconnection, both of which point to the primacy of the macro level. First, political and economic activities and structures at the macro level have often limited, and sometimes decisively halted, efforts to democratize the workplace.[11] Second, democratization attempts originating in the worksite have been largely unsuccessful in prompting democratization of the supraworksite political and economic arena.[12]

In the light of these two prominent patterns, the hopes Samuel Bowles and Herbert Gintis (1986:212) raise at the end of *Democracy and Capitalism* appear unrealistic: "But why should not the workers who have won control of their workplaces also want to make good the promise of democracy writ large? Would the capacities and sentiments fostered in the democratic workplace not seek to range more widely and more effectively over the terrains of finance and investment?" A more historically grounded reading of the interaction between micro- and macro-production politics indicates that sustained and thoroughgoing democratization of production will be much more difficult to accomplish than Bowles and Gintis imply, for two reasons. The micro and macro levels are both central to the control and organization of production, and therefore democratization of one level, but not the other, is inadequate. Also, the fact that the effects of developments in one level on developments in the other are asymmetrical portends difficulty for the democratization of production. In the absence of any attention to macro-level politics, which have often doomed efforts to democratize the micro arena and which have so far proven impervious to democratic impulses emanating from it, fervent hopes, even astutely executed plans for economic democratization, are not likely to be realized.[13]

MULTIPLICITY

The number of different avenues through which the nature of production is determined is a fifth relevant consideration. In my view, a multiplicity of avenues is crucial to the democratization of production. Production in the contemporary world is normally a complex undertaking. Daily and concurrently, it requires that numerous political, economic, technological, social, psychological,

and organizational calculations be made. Democratization therefore demands that producers be involved in decision making
through a myriad of structures and practices at many different
levels. Workers' inclusion in some of these may be more crucial
than in others, but to the degree producers can exercise power
through a multiplicity of activities and structures, democratization
is advanced. But more than the democratization of existing practices and forums is at issue. Additional avenues of influence over
production, in which workers also take part, must be opened. In
this I concur with those, such as Ernesto Laclau and Chantal
Mouffe (1985:178), who argue that "the multiplication of political
spaces" is a precondition "of every truly democratic transformation
of society."[14]

There are at least two justifications for increasing the number
of "political spaces" through which power over production is exercised, the first suggested by Laclau and Mouffe. The expansion of
multiple democratized forums and practices, offering workers a variety of opportunities to influence various aspects of production,
makes it less likely that a reduced number of people will be able to
monopolize the control and organization of economic life. Multiplicity would mean that the power of each political forum and
activity would continually be counterbalanced by that centered in
alternative sites and associated with alternative activities. Second,
multiplicity creates participatory opportunities for larger numbers
of individuals. It grounds democratization, in a manner that
less plural forms and practices cannot, in the "authentic diversity
and complexity of any peoples" (Williams 1985:304). Individual
workers differ greatly along a host of often cross-cutting dimensions—values, interests, affiliations, identifications, time commitments, talents, and expertise. As a result, the degree to which they
display an ability and a willingness to participate in organizing and
controlling production is quite varied. The existence of a variety of
distinct participatory opportunities is the most sensible way to see
that workers' involvement is broad-based, rather than limited to a
few whose personal characteristics happen to match the particular
demands of a narrowed range of participation options.[15]

SIZE AND DEMOCRATIZATION

A sixth matter to consider in thinking about democracy and
work is size. For Václav Havel, the first president of postrevolution-

ary Czechoslovakia, size is a central problem of modern civiliza-
tion: "Mega-machines, large scale enterprises, faceless governments and other juggernauts of impersonal power represent the
greatest threat to our present-day world."[16] While it would be impractical to insist that the democratization of production be built
exclusively around small-group activities and forums, many have
argued that significant amounts of small-group interaction are required for democracy to flourish.[17]

Suggested democratic advantages associated with small size
include the limits small numbers place on the development of hierarchy and the centralization of power and the superiority of small
numbers for theoretical and practical problem solving (Kanter
1977:8; Bahro 1978:298). Most democratic advantages accruing to
smallness, however, can be traced to the face-to-face, body-to-
body, interpersonal communication it allows. For Barber (1984:
173–78), the salient characteristics of small-group communication
include its listening as well as its speaking requirement, its affective
as well as its cognitive character, and its active as well as its reflec-
tive qualities ("Political talk is not talk *about* the world; it is talk
that makes and remakes the world").[18]

Small groups offer participants opportunities, unavailable
through political forums and practices embracing larger numbers,
to communicate subtly yet directly and to develop deeper and
more complete knowledge and understanding of one another.
Through face-to-face interaction, compassion, empathy, caring,
and respect for co-participants are nurtured rather than stunted, as
they are by larger, less personal forms and practices. As a result,
because it is grounded in more accurate perceptions of problems
and players, small-group decision making is fast, flexible, and creative. Participants assume greater responsibility for their opinions,
actions, and decisions; group and individual accountability are
strengthened. In addition, the difficulty of "differential preference
intensities" is resolved: Decision making on the basis of a majority
vote, in the absence of face-to-face communication, furnishes only
a quantitative measure of preference or opinion. Small groups provide a way for the intensity of interest, position, conviction, and
feeling to figure into the decision-making equation.[19] Feminists
also remind us how face-to-face communication characteristic of
small groups has expanded the content of the political to include
emotions, "private" life, "personal" issues, "the new terrain of sub-
jectivity" (Rowbotham 1986: esp. 87–92). This expansion is espe-

cially important for women as it has opened areas of human life where their subordination finds deep roots to "public," political consideration. Last, the kind of interaction allowed by small size bears on one of the most enduring and prominent themes in political theory and philosophy—the relationship between democracy and community. Numerous authors have argued that the quality of interaction allowed by small groups helps overcome the isolation, distance, and alienation exacerbated by democratic forms and practices encompassing large numbers of people. In contrast, smallness helps people maintain *and* create communities based on shared interests, identifications, histories, goals, and commitments.[20]

DEMOCRATIZATION AS EMPOWERMENT

A final consideration apposite to the democratization of production is empowerment. Claims that democratic practices and structures empower the people participating in them are not easy to assess empirically. Indeed, the data I have on postrevolutionary Cuban production relations will allow me to do no more than speculate on what impact changes in production relations had on this facet of democratization. Nevertheless, discussions of democratization as empowerment are both theoretically interesting and philosophically and politically important and so should not be ignored when considering how democracy might apply at work.

The argument that democracy empowers people rests on two major pillars. The first is the contention that all human beings have important potentials and abilities, the realization of which are thwarted by the social arrangements under which they live. We are capable of producing and creating far more than is ever asked of or allowed us. This optimistic view of human potential is in opposition to the "low conception of humankind underlying conservative political theory and political science," which Graeme Duncan (1983:203), for one, insists is "nowhere confirmed by argument and evidence."

The second underpinning of the idea of democratization as empowerment is well stated by Bowles and Gintis (1986, esp. chap. 5).[21] For them politics, democratic or otherwise, produces people, not just decisions. In other words, we are formed by the political practice and activities in which we engage. Our needs and preferences, our relations with others, the ends we pursue, our identities, and—very important sociologically—our interests, do not exist apart from and prior to what we do in the world. Instead, all are formed as we act in it. And, as Bowles and Gintis (1986: 131) recognize, the arena of paid work is one in which a large, though variable, portion of human activity occurs. Its politics thus have a great impact on who we become: "The experience of individuals as economic actors is a major determinant of their personal capacities, attitudes, choices, interpersonal relations, and social philosophies. Individuals develop their needs, powers, capacities, consciousness, and personal attributes through the way they go about transforming and appropriating their natural environment."

In the light of arguments about undeveloped human capacity and the idea that we are products of the kind of politics we participate in, how could the democratization of production be seen to empower people? How would the democratization of work make us different? What would we be able to do that is now beyond us? Answers given to these questions are wide-ranging and not often well grounded in empirical observation, mainly because examples of democratized production relations are so few.[22] Still, many of the answers offered seem quite reasonable. To begin, people could expand their intellectual, cognitive abilities. Were production democratized, they would gain knowledge about complex organizational, economic, and technological topics and have the opportunity to use this knowledge to help solve difficult problems involving complicated judgments.[23] As important, their political skills and abilities would be developed. As they participated in the control of production, they would learn to interact with others more effectively and productively. Both cognitively and affectively, people would display more creativity and imagination. As a result of acquiring such new powers and skills, people would develop more self- and collective respect, confidence, and pride. Their uniqueness would be strengthened at the same time they became more public minded, socially responsible, and politically active outside the workplace.[24] The focus on activity and potential when considering democracy casts notions of power and leadership in a new light. "Power to" and "power along with" are valued, rather than merely "power over" and "power as coercion." Leadership as ordering, commanding, and directing is replaced by an understanding of leadership as engaging, enabling, teaching, inspiring, and developing other's leadership skills.[25] Eugene Debs is reported once to have said, "Too long have workers of the world waited for some Moses to lead them out of bondage. I would not lead you out if I could; *for if you could be led out, you could be led back again"* (Barber:1984:242).

In the following chapters, the seven considerations discussed above reappear as measures against which to evaluate the claim that, compared to the previous decade, the control and organization of production in Cuba after 1970 was more democratic. As we move from the more abstract discussion here to the more historical and concrete ones later in the book, it becomes apparent that none of these seven dimensions can stand alone or above the rest as *the* measure of democracy. Nor can we always be certain what constitutes the most democratic alternative within any of these dimensions. For example, the multiplicity consideration suggests that unions that are independent of political parties advance democratization furthest by providing workers a greater plurality of avenues through which to exercise power over the production process. Yet unions have sometimes been most successful in advancing their demands for greater democratization where they have been closely aligned with a political party. Sweden is a good example. Nor are these seven considerations discrete. Change along one dimension of democracy is commonly associated with change along another, but the latter may not necessarily enhance democracy. Thus, for example, the introduction of more direct, as opposed to indirect, representative workers' involvement in decision making could spell its confinement to the deliberation of less consequential matters.

Chapter 2

CHANGING UNION FUNCTIONS

It is often argued that the role of unions in furthering the democratization of production, whether under capitalism, under socialism, or in a transition phase, has been largely negative.[1] Unions in Cuba, however, were indispensable to the advances made in the democratization of production between the first and second decades of the revolution. Clearly, this progress cannot be attributed to unions alone; indeed, their relationship to democratization had many ambiguous aspects. Nonetheless, workers' collective action and organization at both the worksite and supraworksite levels have been essential to the process. When unions were weakest, democratization was minimal; when they became stronger, democratization advanced. Unions were important to democratization because they provided the vehicle through which isolated, individual, and sometimes unmotivated producers scattered around the island were mobilized, educated, organized, and coordinated to take full advantage of existing control opportunities and to bring pressure for their expansion. If workers had not been brought together in this fashion, it would have been less likely they could have made as significant inroads against the inequitable distribution of power over production as they were able to make after 1970.

UNION FUNCTIONS BEFORE 1970

In the first decade after the ouster of Fulgencio Batista, the unions' principal function was unquestionably to support government efforts to develop the economy. As a prominent Cuban Communist explained in 1962: "If previously, the fundamental function of the unions was to fight for the partial and immediate demands of each labor sector . . . today the fundamental task of the unions is to fight for an increase in production and productivity."[2] The primacy of this task was stipulated repeatedly during these years and illustrated by actions taken at the 10th and 11th National Congresses of the Central de Trabajadores de Cuba (CTC), the country's union confederation. At these meetings in 1959 and 1961, the unions, as their part in the effort to increase production and hasten industrialization, pledged to forego certain sick-leave and holiday bonuses, renounced the right to strike, and agreed to a 4 percent payroll deduction.[3] To encourage workers to produce more and better goods, the unions undertook activities designed to mobilize the workforce to support and implement the production decisions made by their superiors, that is, they tried to create and ensure workers' fervent cooperation in the performance of the production tasks assigned them. The quality of this cheerleading approach was captured in some workers' recollections of planning discussions at the time: "What is sought now is no longer the patriotic appeal, the revolutionary sloganeering after a figure. . . . In those days it was *Patria o Muerte*! as we used to say" (Harnecker 1980:11).

In their role as mobilizing agents, Cuban unions expended a great deal of energy on two particular activities: emulation and voluntary labor. Socialist emulation campaigns began in Cuba in the early 1960s, with local unions publicizing the program among the workforce, helping management check the fulfillment of emulation goals, and assisting in the preparation of reports for upper levels of union and state administration.[4] Yet, despite the unions' energetic pursuance of these tasks, "socialist emulation was at least a partial failure" in the 1960s, because workers' involvement was only indirect (O'Connor 1970:205); the rank-and-file participated neither in organizing nor in administering the campaigns. As voluntary labor was deemed the simplest and most easily realized form of emulation, the unions in the first postrevolutionary decade also assumed major responsibilities in this area (Vilariño 1980:86–87). In 1962 the CTC absorbed the Organization of Volunteer Workers, founded in the first year of the revolution, and thereafter assumed the major responsibility for recruiting volunteer workers and for organizing, directing, and evaluating their activities. Indeed, many of the workers whom I interviewed recalled the unions' participation in voluntary labor campaigns, especially during the sugar harvests, as their main responsibility during the decade.

Unions were little concerned during this early period with encouraging workers to take a prominent part in any of the three stages of decision making, as an alternative way of securing their cooperation in the fulfillment of production goals. Although unions sometimes held production meetings, attendance was poor, according to Adolfo Gilly (1965:40, 42); in 1966 the secretary-general of the CTC described them as gatherings "where cold figures are released by officials without any participation or lively discussion among the workers" (Hernández and Mesa-Lago 1971: 239). In 1982 a CTC official explained to me that "the union didn't have a very important role in [these] assemblies, which were much more informal then. Generally, we didn't insist that they even be held at all."[5] Nor, according to an official description of meetings of the base-level union structures (secciones), was workers' participation in decision making occurring in this forum, beyond a minimal advisory or informational role.

> The meetings of the local unions are predominantly meant to activate and inform. They are not devoted to examining and discussing labor matters. There is generally little time between the notice of meeting and the date it is held, which consequently limits the possibility of preparing matters for discussion. . . . The speaker generally talks at great length. He ends with verbal propositions that are approved without discussion—or at most discussed slightly—and *ipso facto* the meeting is dissolved.[6]

Neither were the unions in the 1960s deeply involved in defending workers' rights.[7] Consistent with the prevailing idea that workers' interests were identical with those of the state, unions were hesitant to give public support to members who disagreed with management, politicos, or bureaucrats. Union reluctance in this respect is well illustrated by Barry Reckord's (1971:101–6) description of a workplace assembly he attended in the late 1960s and by Gilly's (1965:20, 22) recollections from his stay in Cuba in the early part of the decade. Moreover, as Maurice Zeitlin points out, the lack of an organization that would advance workers' positions and protect their interests was apparent at all levels in the

1960s—individual plants, industries, the country as a whole (Hernández and Mesa-Lago 1971:213). Workers thus had no effective way to defend their rights in either the micro or the macro arena. The practical benefit of the many formal guarantees and protections granted workers by the young revolution was diminished because producers had no organization to insist on their enforcement.[8]

ORGANIZING AND PREPARING WORKERS FOR PARTICIPATION IN WORKSITE MANAGEMENT AFTER 1970

How can the worker be made to feel more involved
with his workplace, with his production goal if he is
only a producer who never has any opinion, who
cannot make any decision, who is never consulted
about factory management?
—JORGE RISQUET, MINISTER OF LABOR

Without a doubt, the increased production of goods and services continued to be of prime importance to Cuban unions after 1970 and was stressed in virtually all official statements on the unions during the period. No Cuban I spoke with in 1982 or 1983 failed to mention it as a central union task.[9] Although this goal remained, however, the unions' method of pursuing it changed noticeably. No longer was it considered sufficient merely to mobilize the rank-and-file, through emulation and voluntary labor campaigns, to implement policies developed by the country's economic and political leadership. Reaching beyond such means for involving workers in production, unions began to organize and prepare their members to take part, in various stages of the decision-making process, in a variety of forums both at the worksite and above it.

Production and service assemblies (*asambleas de producción y servicios*) were an important worksite body through which unions attempted to do this. They had existed in Cuba in the 1960s, but in the early 1970s attempts were made to convene them more regularly. In 1973, the 13th National CTC Congress suggested a bimonthly schedule; ten years later all but one of the individuals with whom I talked said they were held every month at their worksites. The 13th Congress also proposed that the government promulgate a law concerning the establishment and conduct of the assemblies. Five years later the 14th National CTC Congress requested that managerial responsibilities in regard to the meetings be specified, partly because of problems with some managers who did not bother to attend the meetings or sent underlings in their stead.[10] In 1984 the 15th National CTC Congress suggested that decisions in the assemblies be made by vote (*Trabajadores* 1 Apr 85:4).

Production and service assemblies were held during working hours; most lasted between forty-five minutes and one hour, although many workers told me that when discussions got "heavy" the meetings might go two or three hours.[11] Several workers said the assembly discussions helped them grasp the overall functioning of their workplaces. As a tobacco worker nearing retirement explained:

> The assemblies help build our understanding of production and work in the factory. Before 1959 many things were done to try to lessen each individual worker's knowledge of what went on in the rest of the factory. For example, the *patrón's* machines were kept in a separate part of the factory, and no workers aside from the few who tended them were allowed to go into that room.[12]

Cuban unions took primary responsibility for conducting the production and service assemblies, though management assisted in their preparation. Workers told me that it was up to the unions to ensure that the assemblies were lively. Careful preparatory work by union officers—including developing and posting the agenda in advance, participating in CTC training seminars, ensuring that people pertinent to the discussion attended, and working with management to see that its reports were neither excessively detailed nor lacking in substance—was essential to forestall a common complaint that the meetings could be mechanical, formal, and uninspiring. Union officials chaired the assemblies, and many workers felt that the chair's conduct was an important determinant of their quality. The executive officer of one union section concurred: "Our assemblies used to be pretty poor. But they've improved now that I chair them. I organize them well, and I'm a firm chair, and I really try to tell it like it is when I'm directing the meeting."[13]

The agenda of the assemblies seemed fairly standard. First

came reports, always from worksite administrators, sometimes from workers, and occasionally from the party as well.[14] Management reports detailed the current state of production or service delivery at the worksite and, very important, discussed the fate of recommendations and resolutions—which were put into practice and which were rejected and why—made by workers at previous meetings. Since managers had the authority to act as they saw fit on such proposals, workers were keenly interested to know what actions, if any, management had taken on their suggestions.

Although surveys have found that the majority of workers saw improvements in problems brought up in the *asambleas* and that workers did consider their input in the meetings influential,[15] technically, their participation was only advisory. This reality contributed to a climate of indifference and cynicism among the workforce and was the basis of the most commonly voiced complaint about assemblies: Managers did not take workers' suggestions seriously enough or act on them regularly enough.[16] In the words of one disgruntled worker:

> We call the production and service assemblies *las asambleas de no se puede* [it-can't-be-done assemblies], since we bring up suggestions and issues over and over again and this is often the answer. This is the main thing that discourages workers from participating in the assemblies. Over and over again they speak up, but nothing is ever done.[17]

A union could play a crucial role in improving this situation because it was the body expected to bring pressure on management to consider and implement workers' assembly proposals. Beginning in 1981, in some five hundred of the country's most important worksites, the unions instituted a new procedure designed to improve responses to workers' proposals originating in assemblies. Suggestions were to be forwarded directly to the national office of the CTC, which would then discuss them with the appropriate ministry, state committee, industrial or sectoral unions, or party office. Not long afterward, all union sections began regularly to inform higher-level union officials of the problems brought up by workers during the assemblies, and in 1986 the CTC unveiled a plan to conduct provincial- and national-level production and service assemblies every trimester to review proposals made in the analogous meetings at the base.[18] These new procedures may have evoked more administrative responsiveness to workers' proposals, yet they could also have conflicted with the goal of greater enterprise autonomy outlined in the SDPE (El Sistema de Dirección y Planificación de la Economía), the new management and planning system implemented in the late 1970s.

After hearing reports, the union opened the assembly to discussion. Any topic related to production or to service delivery at the worksite could be introduced. With the SDPE, the list of topics that could meaningfully be considered at the worksite level expanded. The progress of plan execution, workers' dining rooms, lighting, uniforms, the fulfillment of inter-enterprise contracts, discipline, and raw materials and supplies were all subjects broached by workers at the meetings. One of the most popular topics, I was told by workers, was administration performance: "The production assembly is your chance to throw mud at the administration. When I get up and complain, the administration gets real nervous," explained one worker somewhat gleefully. Another asked: "Aren't strikes an accumulation of complaints against management? That's what the assemblies are mainly for here, so workers can bring up their complaints against management on a regular basis."[19]

Understandably, it was not easy for workers to complain about managers and managerial procedures in so public a forum as an assembly, and it could also be risky.[20] Yet most of the workers with whom I spoke reported a high level of participation in their assemblies, a statement corroborated by the findings of Antonio José Herrera and Hernan Rosenkranz (1979:48). There were exceptions, however: worksites where workers' interventions were minimal and perfunctory. Here, again, the unions could be an important force for improvement. First, union officers could take advantage of their status as workers' leaders to set an example of critical intervention in the assemblies. An articulate and combative local union leadership encouraged other workers to speak up; if the union leaders hung back, the rank-and-file could consider it wise to follow suit. As a CTC official explained, "A good union leader has to be ready to speak up without thinking about personal considerations."[21] Second, the union as an organization had to be ready and willing to close ranks behind individual workers who publicly stood up to managers in assemblies. When the unions failed in these two respects, the contribution of the production and service assemblies to the democratization of Cuban production was sharply curtailed.

In sum, production and service assemblies were an important component of increased democratization in the revolution's second decade. The issues deliberated in them covered the full spectrum of production-relevant topics; workers expanded their knowledge of work and production through their discussions of these issues in the *asambleas de producción y servicios*; the *asambleas* were usually, though not always, held at the shop or department level. Consequently, most meetings were not mammoth, and thus might have been accompanied by some of the democratic advantages conferred by small size. Moreover, the *asambleas* were held monthly and during working hours. This distinguished them from the production conferences in Czechoslovakia, held outside work, and from the work collective meetings in the USSR and the Workers' Congresses in China, held no less than twice a year (Porket 1986:94; Belousov, Gritsenko, and Shkurko 1988:194; Wilson 1987:309). It also allowed for greater inclusiveness. The *asambleas*, again in contrast to production conferences in the USSR, Chinese Workers' Congresses, and permanent production councils in the GDR (German Democratic Republic) (Ruble 1986:33; Wilson 1987:309; Rueschemeyer and Scharf 1986:72), provided workers an opportunity to participate in discussing production matters *directly*, rather than through representatives, and in a setting where they were the numerical majority. Finally, despite the fact that workers' input during assemblies was technically only advisory, the assemblies represented a focal point of the unions' efforts to organize and activate the Cuban workforce.

A second important forum through which unions organized workers for participation in worksite-level decision making was the management council (*consejo de dirección*). Management councils, which as far as I know did not function before the early 1970s, existed at various levels of the production organization, from the department to the enterprise. As the top administrative forums at different structural levels of the firm, the *consejos de dirección* considered all production-related topics: health and safety, discipline, quality, the operations plan, personnel, budgets, and so on. As with production and service assemblies, the implementation of the SDPE increased the number of substantive issues taken up by management councils. In addition, it expanded the areas in which the councils had positive, rather than just negative or advisory, authority and broadened their activities to include more phases of the decision-making process. The councils convened whenever necessary—monthly, weekly, or even more frequently.

The management councils were attended by top managers and technical personnel, department heads, and local party and Communist Youth League (UJC) leaders. Workers' involvement was indirect, occurring through the executive officer of the parallel-level union body who was clearly in a minority on the *consejo*. Also, political and union representatives were permanently invited and thus were only advisory members of management councils, which meant, according to one worker, that "neither has a vote."[22] My impression from discussions with other workers, however, was that voting was not the most common method of arriving at decisions on the relatively small councils. More often, members attempted to reach a decision through consensus. I was told that in some production and service delivery units management councils sometimes met without their party and union members, but I do not know how frequent or widespread this practice was.

It is difficult to ascertain the overall contribution union inclusion on the management councils made to the democratization of production in Cuba. Most workers, of course, had never attended a management council meeting and, although many said they regularly received updates on its activities from the union, workers' information about the councils was often limited to knowledge of their existence and their composition.[23] Yet, in general, workers emphasized the value of union presence on the councils as a guarantee that "another point of view be represented." A cultural worker, for example, said her union representative's attendance was invaluable when the council addressed such issues as individual and collective performance evaluations and rehearsal scheduling.[24] Some workers, however, expressed doubts about union effectiveness in this largely management forum: "Union participation on the *consejo de dirección* is only very minimal. The union has a kind of rubber-stamp function. That's all. They are informed after the fact and automatically give their approval."[25]

Here, as in so many other areas, democratization appeared firmly tied to the overall quality of union performance explored here and elsewhere: the mix of union functions and the methods through which they were carried out, the effectiveness of union organization, and the character of the union's relationship with party and management. The *consejos de dirección* were likely to make the greatest contribution to democratization when, for instance, unions actively defended workers' rights and organized their participation in making decisions about production, when union leaders genuinely represented the rank-and-file, and when unions exhibited a degree of independence from worksite management and political leaders.

DECISION MAKING AT THE SUPRAWORKSITE LEVEL AFTER 1970

In socialist societies in particular, many major decisions about work and production are made, not at worksites, but outside and above them by various political, administrative, and technical bodies. Hence, workers cannot expect to exercise much control over production so long as they are excluded from these forums.[26] Observers of Cuba in the 1960s have noted that workers had minimal, if any, influence over decisions made at the supraworksite level. They had little to say, either directly or indirectly, about what and how much was produced, how work was organized, how the social product was divided between consumption and investment, or what investment priorities, work quotas, or wage scales were.[27] After 1970, however, workers' participation in supraworksite decision making was expanded. Of necessity, the changes that accomplished this relied heavily on indirect procedures.[28] Through union representatives, workers were linked to a variety of macro-level political and economic bodies that were involved in the formulation of many of the country's production policies.

Preliminary suggestions for union participation in high-level decision making were put forward by the unions around the time of the 13th National CTC Congress in 1973. Lázaro Peña, then secretary-general of the organization, in his main report to the Congress called for more direct union involvement in determining social security policies, setting prices, and distributing goods. The Theses of the Congress also called for a union role in planning, in investment, and in determining wages, hours, norms, and workers' rights and obligations. The Theses further argued that, in order to affect decision making, workers, through their unions, had to "have access" to and be members of state organs that dealt with such issues.[29]

After the 13th National CTC Congress a number of steps were taken to formalize union involvement in decision making above the worksite. One of the first and most widely publicized of these was the inclusion of the secretary-general of the CTC on the Council of Ministers and its Executive Committee, a move subsequently written into the Cuban Constitution.[30] The Council of Ministers was the top administrative and executive organ of the Cuban government. Among its forty-five members were high-ranking political figures and the heads of all state committees and ministries. The Executive Committee included about one-fourth of the Council's members (Domínguez 1982:27; Álvarez Tabío 1981:301–13). Fidel Castro referred to union representation on these two bodies as the fruition of "an old revolutionary desire to give organized workers the maximum participation in economic management" (*Cuba internacional* 1974:17). Union participation, however, was interpreted to mean having an active voice, but no formal vote, in the proceedings of the two bodies (Álvarez Tabío 1981:313–15).

Union attendance at meetings of the Council of Ministers and its Executive Committee allowed them a voice in discussions of issues of major, though sometimes indirect, importance for the character of work: The Council of Ministers developed the country's budget, directed its economic activities,[31] oversaw foreign trade, regulated and coordinated all ministries and state committees, and revoked or nullified regulations issued by them or by the local organs of People's Power (OPP). The Council also approved decrees relevant to work, such as the 1979 regulation governing the conduct of production and service assemblies.[32] As the sole worker representative on the Council, however, the secretary-general of the CTC entertained little hope of securing policy decisions opposed by many other Council members. Still, CTC representation on the Council's Executive Committee, whose membership did not even include the president of the Central Planning Board (Junta Central de Planificación [JUCEPLAN]), the National Bank, the state committees, or any of the ministers, demonstrated the eagerness of Cuba's political leaders to involve organized labor in the highest levels of decision making. The Executive Committee rendered decisions on all issues addressed and decided by the Council of Ministers. One decree it issued, for instance, established

a national system of remuneration when production was interrupted for reasons over which workers had no control; another
transferred responsibility for employing redundant workers from
central state organs to local OPP bodies.[33]

Also beginning in the 1970s, the unions began to participate
in decision making at supraworksite levels below the Council of
Ministers and its Executive Committee. For example, a 1976 law
granted the secretaries-general of Cuba's seventeen sectoral unions
the right to take part in meetings of the management councils of
central administrative bodies, especially ministries and state committees that dealt with labor issues. Although union officials were
technically not full-fledged members of these councils (Hernández
González 1980:18–19), by 1978 Roberto Veiga (1978:16) noted
that they regularly attended management council meetings at all
levels. It would be a mistake to assume, however, that formal participation in high-level management councils provided the sectoral
unions with their only opportunity to influence decisions of the
ministries and other government bodies. There was also continuous informal interaction between the two groups, as explained by
an official of the Education and Science Workers' Union.

> The relationship between the Education and Science Workers'
> Union and the Ministry of Education is close and amply devel-
> oped. We have tight relationships with those in charge of ev-
> ery sphere of educational activity at the ministry. Every time
> there's a problem or a certain matter needs to be attended to,
> we're in contact with them and we discuss the best way to
> deal with the situation.[34]

Through their participation in the formal and informal decision-making activities of the ministries and certain state committees, Cuban unions had input into deliberations that often directly
affected workers. For example, the ministries and state committees
supervised planning at the intermediate level between the JUCE-
PLAN and the Council of Ministers, on the one hand, and individual enterprises on the other. Ministries and state committees elabo-
rated and oversaw the execution of the general plan for the sector
on the basis of guidelines, proposals, and suggestions coming from
both above and below (López Coll and Santiago 1975:21–22).
Aside from facilitating union participation in mid-level planning
activities, union attendance at the management sessions of these

state bodies, together with their informal contacts, resulted in their inclusion on commissions that worked out the details of state committee and ministerial resolutions and decrees. For example, CTC provincial officers sat on committees that implemented the 1980 salary reform (Comité Estatal de Trabajo y Seguridad Social 1980: 138–44), sectoral unions cooperated with the central state administrative organs that set rules for distributing enterprise reward funds (JUCEPLAN 1980a:128–35; *Trabajadores* 16 Aug 79:1), the CTC worked with the State Committee of Labor and Social Security (CETSS) on guidelines for implementing a new social security law (*Trabajadores* 31 Mar 79:3), and the national office of the CTC and the Sugar Workers' Union cooperated with the CETSS and the Sugar Ministry on a National Commission of Health and Safety in the Sugar Industry (*Trabajadores* 9 Jan 80:1).[35]

A final mechanism for union participation in supraworksite decision making was created when the electorally based political system of People's Power (OPP) was established in the mid-1970s. By nominating *candidates* for the Executive Bureaus of the municipal and provincial OPP assemblies, and *candidates* for delegates to the provincial and National OPP assemblies, the unions became indirect participants in yet another macro-level decision-making forum.[36] Although final selections were made by members of the relevant OPP assemblies, unions worked with representatives of other mass organizations and the party to make up lists of candidates for these posts. The National OPP Assembly had the power, among other things, to pass legislation and to revoke or modify any law, executive order, or decree; it also approved economic and social development plans, the state budget, and the basic principles governing economic planning and management. Some observers have argued, however, that the Assembly's de facto powers in these areas fell short of those granted in the Constitution.[37] Finally, it is noteworthy that municipal, not national, union leaders named the union representative to the commission that nominated candidates for delegates to the National OPP Assembly.

Because the involvement of municipal and provincial OPP organs in mid-level planning received special emphasis in the 1980s, union influence over nominations for provincial OPP assembly delegates and the Executive Bureaus of both the provincial and municipal OPP assemblies afforded the workers' organization an additional avenue of input in the process.[38] Moreover, OPP assemblies and Executive Bureaus exercised jurisdiction over all enterprises that produced goods or delivered services consumed primarily within their local areas. Local governments in Cuba were thus the immediate superiors of the top administrators of a wide range of worksites including schools, repair shops, hospitals, bus lines, bakeries, and post offices. Although the day-to-day job of overseeing these worksites belonged to the OPP administrative bureaucracy, the assemblies' Executive Bureaus, elected, as explained above, from a list of nominees selected in part by the unions, had direct authority to hire and fire managers at the worksites subordinate to them (Álvarez Tabío 1981:354–55).

DEFENDING WORKERS' RIGHTS AFTER 1970

During the 1960s Cuban unions were little concerned with defending workers' rights. They focused almost exclusively on increasing production and, concomitantly, on enforcing workers' obligations to their collective employer, the revolutionary government. At the beginning of the 1970s, however, this began to change. While increasing production remained a primary union function—though there were major changes in how this was carried out—workers' organizations began to assume the additional task of protecting workers from abuses suffered in the process of fulfilling their productive obligations.

The first inkling that Cuban unions were expected to be more vigorous in this respect came in a series of public statements by government officials in 1969 and 1970. In August 1970, for instance, the Minister of Labor, after lamenting the deplorable state into which the unions had fallen, suggested that they begin to play "their natural role." The unions' primary duty, he argued, should be to see that labor legislation was enforced and that workers' rights were protected.[39] After so long a period of inactivity in defending workers' rights, however, the unions were ill prepared to heed advice of this kind. Thus, by 1975 Marifeli Pérez-Stable found that only 18 percent of the workers she interviewed mentioned defense of workers' interests as an obligation of local trade unions.[40]

In contrast, by the early 1980s every worker I interviewed mentioned the defense of workers' rights as an important task for the unions. The following are typical of comments I heard.

Workers *must* be able to call on their union leaders when their rights are being violated, and the union leaders *must* help them. The union has to protest if, in the course of doing its work, the administration breaks a law protecting workers.[41]

The union has to watch out for the worker's welfare. It has to confront management when workers are being shafted.[42]

These responses suggest that, in terms of workers' expectations, Cuban unions now had a new function to perform, a task that, because it often entailed reacting to a management decision or behavior, well exemplifies negative involvement in decision making. It was no longer acceptable for union officers to sit quietly by—as they often had in the 1960s—when a worker was "being shafted" by a superior. Nor was it enough for a union to act as a neutral intermediary in a conflict over workers' rights. Instead, Cuban unions were expected to act as workers' representatives and advocates, to defend their members' rights and interests when the occasion arose.

Because Cuban workers seemed so adamant about the unions' role in the defense of their rights, it is reasonable to ask what rights workers thought it important to protect, how unions tried to perform this function, and, finally, to what extent unions satisfied this widely held expectation among Cuban workers. The most common responses to my question about workers' most important rights fell into four categories. Workers often mentioned the right to have a job. Here they referred to the availability and permanence of employment, protection against layoffs and dismissals, and equal access to jobs for Blacks and women. The right to a fair wage or salary was also commonly mentioned. Probing revealed that "fair" referred to the level of remuneration, equal pay for equal work, acceptable norms, and reasonable income differentials among jobs in various categories. A third right workers mentioned was the right to upgrade or improve their skills and abilities through general education and job-training programs. In speaking of this right, workers exhibited both pride and emotion: "Our chief writer on military affairs used to be a secretary! Our receptionist used to be a cleaner! We have teletype operators who started out working in the cafeteria!" boasted one respondent.[43] Finally, many workers mentioned the right to paid vacations and holidays.[44]

Some also included the right to union representation on their list of the most important rights of Cuban workers. "The right to protest and make demands through the union is a very critical right for us workers," said a former agricultural worker who was then a cashier.[45] "For me," explained a bank clerk, "the right to the protection and counsel of the union when we need it is one of the most important we have."[46]

Unions had to be prepared to operate at many levels in order effectively to defend these rights. For example, the interests of workers as a class could need to be defended when they conflicted with those of planners, managers, or consumers in supraworksite decision-making forums. The unions might also defend the rights of workers at a particular worksite through, for example, their participation in management councils and their role in the yearly planning assemblies. Finally, individual worker's rights had also to be protected, something the unions might do through the work councils. When I asked workers how their unions attempted to defend the rights they deemed important, however, they seldom spoke of these formal structures and did not usually mention their defense at the supraworksite level. A union leader, respondents ordinarily replied, first talked a problem over with the administration, either alone or accompanied by several rank-and-file members. In other words, the union was likely to begin by taking an informal approach, which many argued was a swifter, more circumscribed and more amicable way of settling disputes over workers' rights.

According to workers I spoke with, unions often succeeded in resolving disagreements in favor of individual workers or groups of workers via this informal method. One worker described three such instances at her worksite. In one of them, an administrator had tried to change a work schedule in several departments for what the worker described as "arbitrary" reasons. In the second instance, a job opening was filled without consideration of an internal applicant's qualifications, and in the third the discretionary powers of the personnel director were trimmed after many workers expressed dissatisfaction to the union over his treatment of them. "We complain to the union here when our rights are overlooked because they fight a good fight. They have influence up there," the same worker explained.[47] Another worker, the executive officer of her union section, succeeded in having a woman's vacation rescheduled to coincide with that of her son, who was studying in the countryside. "I stood up for the worker even though the administration and the party were against me. You see, they don't always get what they want"![48] If a union failed to convince management to change its mind through informal discussions at the section level, the next step, according to many of my respondents, was to solicit the aid of successively higher levels in the union hierarchy. These higher-level union officers then engaged in informal discussions with the administrators concerned or, if need be, with their superiors.[49]

Besides these informal mechanisms for defending workers' rights, unions had additional ways of performing this function. Some of these alternate methods relied somewhat less on the capabilities and initiative of individual union leaders, and more on the power of the union as an institution. At times they also entailed a more positive type of involvement in decision making. One good example concerned the protection of workers' health and safety. A major piece of legislation passed in December 1977 detailed the variety of ways in which unions were to defend these rights.[50] For example, they were to assist in preparing health and safety plans for each enterprise; ensure that new workers received safety training and that disabled workers were retrained and suitably placed; and conduct on-site health, safety, and accident investigations and inform workers of the results. Moreover, union health and safety technicians could order the shutdown of a worksite if it were unhealthy or unsafe. Finally, if management disagreed with a worker's decision to refuse potentially life-threatening work, the union was called on to determine whether the worker's decision was justified.[51]

Union powers in protecting other types of workers' rights have not been legally specified in such detail.[52] Yet, despite the absence of any legal mandate, in 1980 all Cuban unions launched a massive campaign to uncover infractions of labor legislation. Through union inspections carried out over a two-month period, the labor records of every worker in the country were reviewed.[53] The inspections revealed an average of 1.5 infractions per labor record. Among the abuses uncovered were many in areas workers had indicated to me to be of particular importance to them: wage and salary violations; job evaluation, promotion, and hiring irregularities; infringements of social security, maternity, and vacation laws; illegal or incorrect application of disciplinary measures.[54] After completing the inspections, the unions prepared reports of their findings and met with worksite managers in an effort to rectify the violations in a timely manner. Some administrators were eventually penalized for infractions discovered during the investigation.[55]

My interviews with workers in the early 1980s revealed that most expected unions to defend their rights using an assortment of methods.[56] Moreover, examples they related to me, which I am convinced were not anomalous, indicated that unions had some degree of success in fulfilling these expectations. This situation was in sharp contrast to the 1960s, underscoring the change in union functions that had taken place. Although this conclusion indicates a trend toward greater democratization of production in Cuba after 1970, unions after that time were still not always willing or able to defend members whose rights were violated. For example, a woman working in a light industrial plant (see nn. 20 and 49) saw her position eliminated because she frequently spoke up in production assemblies. (She claimed this was a common way to get rid of a worker in Cuba, where firing an employee was relatively difficult.) Her interventions in the assemblies, as she described them, were frequent, demanding, and forceful—precisely the kind of behavior unions were expected to encourage among their members. Yet, when this woman protested her firing, neither the union leaders from the section nor the enterprise would, or perhaps could, do anything for her.[57] Another example comes from a woman I interviewed both in 1982 and in 1983. In 1982 she worked at one location, but, when I spoke with her a year later, she had been temporarily transferred to another worksite and, after working there a few months, had been asked to remain. Her reply: "Absolutely not!" because the union at the second site "existed on paper only." She was adamant that the union there would not defend her, or any other worker, against unjust actions by the administration. "Without that, a worker could be out in the cold!" she exclaimed.[58]

Why did unions in some places and situations not play the role officially ascribed to and commonly expected of them by many Cuban workers? When asked this question, workers often blamed their union leaders, sometimes for insufficient education or incomplete knowledge of the relevant laws. "Our section and _buró_ [enterprise level] leaders mean well," commented one worker who had formerly been a section official himself, "but they're not too good. They don't have a full understanding of the legal rights of the workers, and so they are easily intimidated by administrators or the *empresa*'s lawyers."[59] Cuba's continued emphasis on raising the population's general educational level and the unions' efforts to provide their officials with special legal training could bring improvements here. Many base-level union leaders stressed the value of these training programs, viewing their expansion as an important reason for the unions' greater ability to defend workers' rights after 1970. Other workers who faulted union leaders for failing to defend workers' rights emphasized the issue of personal ambition: The strongest, most combative leaders were those who harbored no desires to move up in the ranks and therefore identified totally with producers. One of the most important protections workers had against careerists assuming union posts were the electoral procedures the unions began to follow in the early 1970s.

Poor leadership, however, was not the only or even the main reason why Cuban unions sometimes faltered in defending workers' rights. Knowledgeable leaders with strong worker consciousness could still fail to counter infringements of workers' rights because their position, like that of the unions as a whole, was rife with the contradiction. The contradiction stemmed from the ever-present tension among the varied functions unions were expected to perform in Cuba, and the effect it had on the unions' contribution to the democratization of production could be substantial.

CONCLUSION: INHERENT CONTRADICTIONS IN UNION FUNCTIONS

The democratization of production was advanced during the second decade of the Cuban revolution, in part because unions took on new functions and began to fulfill prior ones in new ways. This created tensions and conflicts, however, rooted primarily in the unions' simultaneous attempts to serve as workers' defenders and advocates before managers, state representatives, and politicos and as collaborators with these same people in decision making at the worksite and beyond. These tensions and conflicts afflict unions in capitalist countries as well, but they are more prominent and more widely recognized as symptomatic of their work under socialism.[60] Although their expression, intensity, and prevalence differ in the two kinds of societies, in both contexts they are grounded in a stark division between the many and the few, who organize, plan, and supervise their work.

The contradiction among union functions was expressed in a number of ways in post-1970 Cuba. To the individual worker it usually manifested itself as a tension between the defense of workers' rights and the enforcement of workers' productive obligations. Workers frequently enunciated this in their responses to my question, What is the role of unions in Cuba? All the workers I interviewed said it was the union's job to defend their rights, yet many, without hesitation, added emphatically, "¡*Siempre que tenga razón!* [Provided the worker is right!]." Although succinctly expressed, it is easy to imagine how difficult this formula could be for base-level union leaders to implement. In what situations and with what workers should expected rights take precedence over acknowledged obligations, and vice versa? What should unions do when defending a worker's rights and enforcing a worker's obligations called for opposing actions? Interestingly, in Cuba, as elsewhere, the conflict between workers' rights and workers' obligations was often played out in interactions between rank-and-file union officials and those from mid and higher levels in the organization.

The same contradiction between advocacy and collaboration surfaced not only at the individual but also at the worksite level. To what extent and under what circumstances did union activities in planning, organizing, and conducting production assemblies and encouraging and preparing workers to participate in these meetings ensure workers' docility rather than direct serious attention to their points of view? Was it workers or managers who stood to gain the most as a result of union representation on management councils? Could workers really participate in management without simultaneously jeopardizing their own rights? Where was the line between empowerment via participation and disempowerment through complicity at the point of production?

The same kinds of questions could also be asked about the interests of the working class as a whole and the unions' role as its representative in supraworksite decision-making forums. Did union representation on powerful bodies such as the Council of Ministers and ministry management councils exemplify inter-class collusion rather than working-class power? Was it more an example of the corporatist approach to control than an attempt to democratize socialism? To what extent did it encourage overcentralization of the union apparatus, reducing its accessibility to the rank-and-file? With ownership and appropriation public, how could high-level workers' representatives determine what position on an issue best served and most empowered their constituency?

The more actively and aggressively unions carried out their new and redefined tasks, the more apparent it became that union activity would continue to be characterized by contradiction and tension. The ambiguity inherent in Cuban union work was not completely resolvable, because union activities in one area often limited or conflicted with union activities in another. Should the unions therefore have abandoned some of the functions they assumed after 1970? In my opinion, no. Despite the contradictions between defending workers' rights and collaborating with management in the direction of the economy, production became more democratic, in part, because unions simultaneously undertook both tasks. In post-1970 Cuba it would make no more sense for unions to cease preparing workers to participate in worksite decision making or to stop representing workers in decision making at the supraworksite level than it had for them to neglect the defense of workers' rights in the 1960s. Strong unions performing both kinds of functions are necessary for continued democratization in Cuba.

Chapter 3

CHANGING
UNION ORGANIZATION

Without substantial organizational changes Cuban unions would not have been able to handle the expanded functions they assumed after 1970. The following changes were crucial: Union structures were modified, unions became mass organizations, union financing was altered, and methods of selecting union officers were democratized. Those unconvinced that post-1970 changes in union functions contributed to democratization are likely to interpret these organizational changes as efforts to facilitate union control over the working class:[1] Restructuring made more direct supervision of workers possible; the drive to expand membership meant compulsory affiliation; elections legitimated authoritarian leadership; individual dues collection allowed frequent checks on the rank-and-file. My own interpretation of these organizational changes, however, stresses different outcomes. Cuban unions could hardly have been expected to do a thorough job defending workers' rights if many producers were not even members—hence their transformation into mass organizations. The workforce could not have been adequately represented on decision-making bodies if union structures had remained undeveloped and unresponsive to shifts that occurred in the economic and political system—hence the changes in this area. Unless unions had an independent financial base and leaders responsive to the rank-and-file, their advocacy of workers' rights and their ability to organize and prepare workers to participate in management would have been weak at best—hence the post-1970s emphasis on balanced budgets, democratic elections, and individual dues collection.

RESTRUCTURING FOR ACTION AND EFFICIENCY

A distinguishing feature of Cuban union structure before 1959 was dualism, a characteristic preserved and even strengthened immediately after the victory over Fulgencio Batista. Dualism was evident in the parallel structures of the CTC (Central de Trabajadores de Cuba) and the sectoral or industrial unions (Sindicatos Nacionales) operating at municipal, provincial, national, and, at one time, regional levels. From the Cuban perspective the dual structure had two advantages: Workers and union leaders had more forums to which they could submit problems; and the industrial unions, by focusing on specific economic sectors, left the CTC free to concentrate on broader questions of concern to the entire workforce.[2] This dual and multi-tiered structure, however, complicated the relationship between the CTC and the sectoral unions; periodically it was blamed for a degree of inertia, for a pass-the-buck mentality, and for confusion over the division of union responsibilities.

The victory of the July 26 forces also gave impetus to a second distinguishing feature of Cuban union structure. Instead of organizing workers by trade, the industrial unions brought together all workers in a particular economic sector, regardless of occupation. In this way all workers at a given worksite were represented by one union.[3] Twenty-five of these industrial unions existed throughout most of the early 1960s. At that time the lowest-level union structures, called sections (*secciones*) and roughly corresponding to establishments, departments, areas, and sometimes shifts in an enterprise, were affiliated with the sectoral unions. Although critics have argued that organization by economic sector rather than by occupation weakened the unions' ability to defend their members' interests,[4] many Cuban workers I spoke with who had been represented under both systems did not agree. They felt that a single union at worksites had increased, not diluted, their bargaining strength.[5] An analogous point can be made regarding the protection of workers' interests at higher levels. The Cuban economy is largely organized and administered by sector (e.g., by Ministries of Agriculture, Construction, Education, Sugar, etc.). The representation of all workers in a particular economic sector by one instead of several different unions would therefore minimize the opportunity to pit one group of workers against another at supraworksite levels.

In the mid-1960s Cuba embarked on an anti-bureaucracy campaign that ended abruptly after the 1970 sugar harvest. In the heat of this campaign the number of industrial unions was reduced by nearly half (down to fourteen) and, simultaneously, they were stripped of their provincial and municipal branches. These developments effectively eliminated the dual structure of Cuban unionism and lessened the influence of sectoral unions for a time. Union structures at the base were severely weakened. Although the CTC may have retained some structures at the rank-and-file level, *secciones* probably became inoperative in many work centers (Pérez-Stable 1975:66, 69; Hernández and Mesa-Lago 1971:215–17). As one commercial worker recalled: "Our unions just weren't organized then, and a revolution means getting organized, doesn't it?"[6] The number of union meetings and conferences at all levels was reduced. The interval between national CTC congresses, for example, lengthened throughout the decade. Union posts were lost, full-time CTC personnel being reduced by 53 percent (*Granma* 26 Aug 89:3). Organizational decline was paralleled by a constriction of union functions; in fact, the two trends reinforced each other. Fewer functions meant that fewer union leaders, structures, and meetings were required. As organizational life atrophied, as structures were dismantled, and as leadership posts were lost, the unions were increasingly incapable of performing even their dwindling number of functions (Pérez-Stable 1975:67).

The structural alterations wrought under the banner of anti-bureaucratism proved disastrous for the unions. Fortunately, however, they did not stand; they were one of the first casualties of a wave of reforms that substantially altered the character of Cuban socialism after 1970. By late 1970 the CTC had already decided on a procedure for structural revitalization of the industrial unions, and by 1973 their number had jumped back up to twenty-three. At the same time, their intermediate (i.e., municipal and provincial) branches were reformed, meaning that the dual structure of union organization was reestablished. Sectoral unions convened meetings in the early 1970s,[7] and in November 1973 the CTC held its 13th National Congress, the first in more than seven years. In the same period union bodies at the grass-roots level received more attention: By mid-1972 approximately thirty-seven thousand union sections had been created (Pérez-Stable 1975:69), and by the beginning of 1973 the number had grown to almost forty-one thousand.[8] The minimum number of members per section was reduced from fifteen to ten, allowing workers in the smallest work centers to form their own locals.[9] In 1973, the average union section had about fifty members and in 1978 about fifty-four members (Veiga 1978:5; *Trabajadores*, 1st half Dec 73). Although there was apparently wide variation in section size across the country, *secciones* with an average number of workers would have been fairly certain to benefit from democratic advantages accruing to small size. The 1973 CTC Statutes placed union sections within the industrial unions, rather than the CTC, further boosting sectoral union organization.

The structural modifications of the early 1970s pre-dated by several years the implementation of the SDPE (El Sistema de Dirección y Planificación de la Economía), the introduction of the OPP (People's Power), and the administrative reorganization of the island, all moves that necessitated further changes in union structure during the latter half of the 1970s. An important feature of the SDPE was the devolution of economic decision-making power from the center to individual production and service delivery units. In part, the OPP was an attempt to accomplish a similar goal in the political arena; it increased the authority of local and intermediate political bodies over work and production in their immediate geographical areas. Finally, the new administrative system shared with the OPP and the SDPE the aim of streamlining Cuban economic life.[10] These consequential shifts in the loci of decision making required that the unions redesign their structures in order to handle their expanded functions effectively. In the process, the dual and sectoral character of Cuban union structure was retained, though in some instances the latter was slightly modified.[11]

Perhaps the most significant structural change of this period was the strengthening, or often the introduction, of a second base-level industrial union structure, the bureau (*buró*).[12] Nearly three thousand bureaus were established before the 14th National CTC Congress met in 1978 (Veiga 1978:4, 6). The average bureau, comprising all union sections within a given enterprise, included approximately eight hundred fifty workers. Sections were subordinate to their corresponding bureaus. Although the bureaus were seen as important base-level structures, they were not intended to replace sections, which still maintained direct relations with higher union bodies.[13] Rather than decreasing after the introduction of the bureaus, the number of sections rose in rough proportion to the increase in the size of the workforce.

The main reason the introduction or strengthening of the *buroes* was so important related to the SDPE. For unions to participate effectively in decision making at the newly important enterprise level, they had to create a structural counterpart to enterprise-wide management. For example, if workers' involvement in post-SDPE planning were to be influential, an enterprise-level union body was needed to coordinate workers' input from the various parts of the enterprise and to help workers in its many subdivisions consider the plan from the perspective of the whole enterprise. Moreover, in the absence of any union officers who could claim to represent the entire workforce in management councils and other enterprise-level deliberations, it would have been easier for managers, using the familiar justification that they alone could evaluate matters from the perspective of the organization as a whole, to dismiss workers' input as parochial. In sum, besides strengthening sectoral unionism and grass-roots organization in Cuba, the bureaus helped workers capitalize on the democratic potential inherent in the decentralization of economic decision making. Indeed, one might well have discounted Cuban leaders' public support for the democratization of production in the 1970s if some union structure like the bureaus had not been activated along with the implementation of the SDPE.

CREATING MASS ORGANIZATIONS

One measure of the legitimacy of any union movement's claim to speak on behalf of working people is the number of workers it organizes.[14] Numbers alone, however, are not sufficient to indicate how well, or even whether, workers' true interests are being represented. To answer this pivotal question other things must be considered, such as how union leaders are selected, the union's influence in the national arena, the definition of its functions, and so on. Still, the degree to which the labor force is organized cannot be overlooked in any discussion of union power in a given society.

Before the revolution Cuba boasted more organized workers (more than 1.2 million in 1955) than any other Latin American nation except Brazil, Mexico, and Argentina, all countries with considerably larger populations (Manitzas 1973:36). Union membership was therefore a part of many workers' experience long before January 1959. The victory that year provided a slight impetus to further union growth. In 1961, for instance, civil servants gained the right to organize for the first time (Hernández and Mesa-Lago 1971:214), and retired workers could join unions. Professionals were also incorporated into unions, a move decried by one group of exile scholars as a signal that professionals were being "treated as salaried workers in accordance with Soviet policy" (Cuban Economic Research Project [CERP] 1963:122). In the rest of the 1960s, however, union membership stagnated or possibly declined. By mid-decade, according to Roberto E. Hernández and Carmelo Mesa-Lago (1971:215), about 60 percent of the labor force was organized, a figure only slightly higher than before the revolution.[15]

Union numerical weakness in the 1960s was exacerbated by the growth of the Advanced Workers' Movement (Trabajadores de Avanzada). Advanced Workers, an elite group within the working class, were chosen by assemblies of their peers on the basis of their production performance (e.g., output, quality, attendance), and their activities outside work (e.g., studying and participation in mass organizations or the militia). The Advanced Workers' Movement, to which most working people could never belong, probably comprised only between 10 and 18 percent of the workforce, and thus, as Andrew Zimbalist notes, the majority of workers were simply "left behind" (1975:49).[16] By the late 1960s the Advanced Workers' Movement had become a substitute for unions in many workplaces, and as such it began to assume the unions' already limited tasks. "Everything was centered on the activity of the vanguard workers," recalled a union official, and in 1970 Fidel Castro himself cited the movement's development as one reason for the unions' disarray (Harnecker 1980:19; Domínguez 1978:225).

After 1970, however, Cuban unions moved to become mass organizations. It was not enough, according to the Minister of Labor, for a vanguard of workers to be deciding things for everyone else. All workers had to become involved. Unions would be strong only when they truly represented, included, and mobilized all workers (*Granma* 9 Sept 70:5; *Granma Weekly Review* 24 Oct 71:5). In response to this new emphasis, union membership began to increase in the early 1970s, and the trend continued into the 1980s. Affiliation was a simple process: A worker's application with the executive officer of a section or a bureau was later ratified at a general membership assembly. The new recruit received a membership card and agreed to pay a percentage of his or her monthly salary in dues (CTC 1978:III.6, 7). By 1974, 88 percent of the Cuban workforce was organized. The CTC had set a goal of 97 percent affiliation by the 1978 meeting of its 14th National Congress, but fell short by 3 percent. Undaunted, the Congress resolved to try to affiliate all Cuban workers in the coming years. Most workers I interviewed in 1982 believed that nearly everyone at their work centers belonged to unions. One stated: "It's a nice feeling to have the satisfaction of knowing there are no scabs around." Another commented, "Everybody belongs. The trade union is a collective effort."[17] By the end of 1983, 99.2 percent of the Cuban workforce was reported to be union members.[18]

Few observers would challenge the claim that Cuban unions became mass organizations even if membership figures were 10 or 15 percent lower.[19] Affiliation figures as high as those reported, however, raise the question: Was union membership really voluntary? The interpretation of the CERP—that the "state has developed a system of *pressures* used against the worker, granting *benefits and advantages* to those who affiliate with the union and making it *quite hazardous* for those who do not"[20]—will doubtless sound reasonable to some. Yet in Cuba, as elsewhere, one of the most important things reflected by high membership figures was sustained organizing efforts, efforts that union foes commonly describe as "pressures." One man, for example, who had been in charge of organizing in his section, explained that some workers, needing to feel that the union wanted them as individuals to join, had to be approached personally. Then too, he added, there were the "*medio gusanos*," who required a stronger effort and who even then might not become union members, although "I've even had one or two successes with some of them," he boasted.[21]

Union affiliation in Cuba was undoubtedly accompanied by certain "benefits and advantages," even though all workers, whether or not they were union members, were protected by legislation on health and safety, wages, social security, retirement, and so on. Only members were represented by union leaders in their dealings with supraworksite and enterprise administrators; only members could participate in union educational, cultural, recreational, and sports activities; the union played an important role in the distribution of certain highly desired material goods, which were allocated to individual work units. Still, since nearly every worker was a union member, affiliation, in and of itself, could hardly insure very special privileges. Membership was indeed viewed as an indication of involvement in the revolutionary process. Yet, while it clearly was "quite hazardous" in the 1970s and 1980s for many workers throughout Latin America to affiliate with unions, it would be inaccurate to characterize the position of Cuban workers who did *not* join unions in the same way.

ABOLISHING THE CHECKOFF AND ACHIEVING FINANCIAL SELF-SUFFICIENCY

Immediately prior to the revolution, unions were financed by a method commonly termed the checkoff. Employers automatically deducted 1 percent from the wages of all workers, whether or not they were union members, and transferred the money to the unions. That workers disliked these compulsory contributions was acknowledged by the revolutionary government, which, only twenty days after the July 26 forces entered Havana, adopted a law formally abolishing the checkoff system. According to the CERP, however, the procedure persisted at least through mid-1962.[22]

Two decades later the automatic checkoff had completely disappeared. Cubans claimed, as have many others elsewhere,[23] that this was a good thing, because the checkoff had insulated union leaders from the rank-and-file, whose opinions they were supposed to represent. The monthly payment of dues, which thereafter required personal contact between workers and section officers (often the treasurer), afforded regular opportunities for rank-and-file workers to exchange views with the section leadership individually and in person.[24]

Despite advantages over the checkoff system, direct collection of dues was not free of problems. The unions' financial base was less secure, at least in the short run, and periodic collection of dues from fellow workers was a time-consuming and delicate task that union officials would sometimes just as soon have avoided (and apparently sometimes did). A woman who had formerly been treasurer of her section recalled: "You always have to stay on top of the few who don't pay each month." In her experience, this meant seeking out each person who had not paid in order to find out what was wrong and to devise an individual solution.[25]

In 1978, the eighteen industrial unions collected between 80 and 100 percent of their dues (the average was roughly 93 percent); dues collection in Cuba's fifteen provinces ranged from 75 to 99 percent (*Trabajadores* 27 Jan 79:5). Overall, unions collected over nine million pesos more than they had in 1973.[26] The dues collected in the sections were sent to a superordinate body that distributed them according to budgets submitted earlier by the sectoral unions and the CTC. Eventually each union section received 10 percent of the total dues it had collected for the month (CTC 1978: arts. 82–86). Dues financed nearly all activities at the national, intermediate, and base levels of both the CTC and the sectoral unions, including national congresses and other meetings, publication of the union newspaper *Trabajadores*, operation of a nationwide system of union-run schools, and sponsorship of sports, recreation, and cultural programs. Members' dues also covered the salaries of all paid union officers and employees. Union sections, however, sometimes solicited member contributions to help finance special work-center activities such as New Year's parties and International Women's Day celebrations. Unions also generated extra income by sponsoring recreational and cultural activities, and enterprises began to reimburse unions whose members performed voluntary work, though such funds were earmarked for particular purposes.

Because many unions, including some in prerevolutionary Cuba, have compiled unsavory financial records, it is important to ask what workers knew about union financial affairs. To begin with, no one seemed concerned about the possibility of financial corruption. Workers with whom I spoke did not believe that their local leaders would steal from the union. All members of an executive committee would have to be in collusion, they said, since running a section was a collective endeavor. Workers derived their knowledge of section finances from treasurers' financial reports at general assemblies or from information posted at workplaces. In addition, beginning after the 13th National CTC Congress, every two and one-half years members elected from their own ranks an

Auditing Commission (*Comisión de Glosas*) to review the section's finances and report back to the general assembly.[27] With the formation of the *buroes*, analogous committees were established at this level. At the intermediate and national levels of the CTC and the sectoral unions, seven-member review and control commissions (*comisiones de revisión y control*) were elected by union leaders at the corresponding level. Among other duties, these commissions scrutinized union finances and reported to union congresses, council meetings, and conferences.[28]

Special attention was focused on union finances in the 1970s because unions were expanding their functions and enlarging their structures, and because, after the institution of the SDPE, they were required to perform their new functions and operate their multi-level structures while simultaneously balancing their budgets. "We are self-financing now," explained a national CTC official. "The unions receive nothing from the state."[29] Although this requirement augured well for union independence, it was difficult for the unions to remain solvent while supporting higher levels of activity and expanded structures. Constant monitoring of expenditures, a clear sense of budgetary priorities, and creative ideas about how to increase union income were necessary. Partly to enhance their financial viability, some industrial unions merged.[30] Emulation campaigns focusing on dues collection occurred between and within sectoral unions. Special efforts were made to collect dues from all workers, including retirees and those with irregular work assignments. Individuals who worked in multiple centers were allowed to become members of two union sections simultaneously. Unions enforced austerity measures. Finally, in order to gather workers' suggestions about dues levels and collection methods, union finances were discussed in every section in the first half of 1979. Activities like these improved the financial position of the unions. From a deficit of 6.5 million pesos in 1975, the unions registered a surplus of four hundred thousand pesos in 1976 and 1977, despite a sizable increase in expenditures. Income continued to outstrip expenditures in 1978. In addressing the 14th National CTC Congress, however, Roberto Veiga (1978:29) warned that union expenses would continue to grow: The important activities of the newly created bureaus were not yet receiving adequate financing, and the number of union professionals and employees was expected to rise (*Trabajadores* 3 Dec 78:3, 21 Oct 77:4–5).

SELECTING UNION LEADERS

It is impossible to understand the 1959–61 struggles for leadership of the Cuban unions without understanding how they were rooted in the country's labor history. The Communists had been the major political and organizational force in the labor movement in the 1930s and much of the 1940s. But by 1948 Eusebio Mujal, then allied with the Auténticos, a nationalist, vaguely reformist, middle-class party, had assumed control of the CTC and with it most of organized labor. Few kind words have been spoken about developments in the union movement after Mujal took charge, or about Mujal himself, who retained his post as secretary-general of the CTC until the triumph of the revolution. Described in accounts as venal, ambitious, and opportunistic, Mujal was a well-to-do sugar planter. Throughout his tenure he collaborated closely with whoever held political power. As a result workers came to regard the CTC as an appendage of government rather than as their representative. The union movement, rife with corruption, excluded large sectors of the working class and was top heavy with bureaucrats who had minimal contact with the rank-and-file. The leaders of this nondemocratic organization, most adept at shifting their positions in response to personalistic changes in Cuban politics, retained their posts year after year.

After Batista's 1952 coup against Cuba's last Auténtico president, Mujal and his followers quickly made their political peace with the dictator in return for remaining apolitical and for being allowed to handpick local union officers (Spalding 1977:232). As the opposition to Batista intensified in the late 1950s, high-level CTC leaders never faltered in their support of the beleaguered president. Mujal denounced as Marxist any labor sympathizer of the July 26 Movement and applauded government repression of anti-Batista dissidents within the ranks of organized labor. To a 1957 call by Castro's forces for a general strike, the CTC responded, "People who treat labor well deserve well of labor, and President Batista has done more for labor than any other president Cuba ever had" (Spalding 1977:237).[31]

Given the hostile prerevolutionary relationship between the July 26 Movement and the leaders of Cuban labor, it is not surprising that the early years of the revolution saw a rapid turnover in union leadership under less than optimally democratic circumstances. What occurred was neither proof of the totalitarian predilections of the new government nor unique in postrevolutionary situations, commonly characterized by political and social instability. Although most Cubans had been glad to see Batista go, some still preferred the former president to his conquerors. Others had not been deeply involved in the revolutionary struggle and so could not necessarily be regarded as sympathetic to the new government. Nor was the "poorly organized and ununified" July 26 Movement a cohesive group in terms of either class background or political ideology (Karol 1970:185). The movement comprised students, professionals, middle-class elements, Catholics, members of anti-Batista political parties, some workers, some peasants, as well as a few Communists.[32]

Early struggles for control of the unions cannot be divorced from this volatile social context. Instead, as Paul Baran (1961:17) reported at the time: "The Trade unions reproduced on a smaller scale the tensions and differentiations besetting the nation as a whole." Almost immediately, *mujalista* elements began to be ousted from important leadership positions by the conglomeration of forces that had opposed Batista, moves which often sparked fierce maneuvering for control of the vacated slots. Legal sanction for these actions came with the passage, in the first month of the revolution, of Law 22, suspending union officials who had held office on December 31, 1958.[33] The law also set up a provisional committee, headed by David Salvador of the July 26 Movement, to lead the CTC until elections could be called. Its composition reflected the inability of any faction to achieve hegemony over either the revolutionary process or the union movement.

The first postrevolutionary union elections were held between April and June 1959, as dictated by Law 22 (CERP 1963:107), and apparently filled both section and industrial union positions. Riding the crest of their victory over Batista, the July 26 candidates swept the elections, gaining control of more than 80 percent of the industrial unions. Later on, July 26 candidates also won elections for delegates to the upcoming 10th National CTC Congress, which would select the top-level CTC leadership. The Communists and their supporters won only around 10 percent of the delegates in these elections, a fact that has been subject to divergent interpretations. Some have understood the outcome as a decisive vote against communism. Others have argued that the Communists were denied full participation in union activities at the time and that, therefore, such a conclusion is unfounded.[34] What is clear is that substantial animosity arose during this period between sections of the labor movement primarily identified with the Communists or the July 26 Movement, both of which had set their sights on control of the unions. According to Lionel Martin (1974:29), Castro downplayed political affiliation during the electoral process, emphasizing instead how important it was for workers themselves to choose the unions' leaders. Even Castro, however, was unable to forestall the impending fray.

In November 1959, when the 10th National CTC Congress named the confederation's new officers, the struggle for control of the labor movement reached crisis proportions. The sharply polarized accounts of the Congress attest to this. On the one hand, the CERP (1963:107–9) claims that the new government, realizing that the Communists and their sympathizers could not win control of the CTC in an open election, first tried to cancel the Congress. When labor leaders threatened to resign, the Congress was allowed to proceed on schedule, but the government and the Communists, in the name of unity, pressured, threatened, coerced, and blackmailed the protesting CTC delegates into accepting three Communists as members of the Executive Committee. Other observers, however, maintain that some July 26 labor leaders had joined counterrevolutionary elements in an effort to exclude Communists from leadership positions. Castro, knowing that the Communists increasingly supported the revolution and that many July 26 labor leaders were beginning to oppose it, successfully pressed for a committee that was dominated by July 26 Movement people who were neutral on the issue of communism and that excluded both Communists and vehement anti-Communists (Spalding 1977: 239–40; Pérez-Stable 1975:64).

As the chasm between opponents and supporters of the revolution widened after the 10th National CTC Congress, labor leaders who refused to accept the officials designated by the Congress or who opposed nationalization and other revolutionary measures, were summarily removed from their posts, often being accused of counterrevolutionary, *mujalista*, or pro-Batista activities (CERP 1963:109–11; Thomas 1971:481–82, 496).[35] In May 1960, David Salvador himself, after calling for a 20 percent salary increase, critiquing the continuing anti-*mujalista* campaign, trying to leave

Cuba illegally, and supporting counterrevolutionary activities, was ejected as secretary-general of the CTC (Pérez-Stable 1975:64).

As these events reveal, the process of selecting union leaders in Cuba in the immediate postrevolutionary period was far from democratic. Government interventions were frequent and decisive. Winners of elections for important posts, for example the CTC Executive Committee, often had no opponents. Nor was there any pretense that the membership was consulted before numerous union leaders were dismissed or instated. The new Cuban government realized that the ascendancy in the labor movement of people who preferred the previous social, economic, and political system could jeopardize its attempt to restructure Cuban society. The government's offensive against them provoked the wrath of the United States and of powerful sectors of the Cuban population. But the history of the developing world has shown more than once that to have assumed a defensive, reactive position could have allowed the opposition to set the parameters of the struggle, thereby decreasing the likelihood that the revolution would achieve its most important social goals. What may seem to some a patent disregard for democracy in the Cuban union movement was simultaneously, from an opposing perspective, a necessary step in the arduous process of constructing a new social order under less than ideal circumstances.

After Salvador's ouster and before the 11th National CTC Congress met in November 1961, the CTC was led, de facto, by a "loyal *Fidelista*" (Hernández and Mesa-Lago 1971:211). In the same period a law dealing with union organization was passed; it specified that no one who had committed a counterrevolutionary offense could serve on any executive committee and granted workers the power to nullify elections held at any union level (CERP 1963:97, 100, 111–12). Although 95 percent of the eligible voters participated in the secret ballot elections for delegates to the 11th Congress, the selection of top leadership at the event differed little from the previous Congress (Spalding 1977:241–42). The new secretary-general, Lázaro Peña, was chosen by acclamation and apparently without opposition. His selection, as Adolfo Gilly puts it, "was much more a decision from above than an election from below."[36]

Although elections for delegates to the 12th National CTC Congress, held almost five years later, have been described as "relatively unhindered" (Domínguez 1978:272), questions remained about the selection procedures followed at this Congress for the top CTC leadership. Some observers say that Miguel Martín, the new secretary-general, was properly elected; Jorge Domínguez (1978:2) claims he was appointed (and removed two years later) by the Political Bureau of the party, even though National Committee members were chosen by normal electoral procedures (Pérez-Stable 1975:66). Regulations probably established in 1966 granted the Congress power to elect its own executive officers. Apparently elections were also held at intermediate-union levels the same year. In the elections for base-level leadership in 1966, workers chose their nominees at assemblies attended by local party members, though selection of party people was discouraged. Anyone associated with Mujal and Batista in prerevolutionary union, political, or military activities could not be nominated, and municipal party and union officials could reject workers' nominees so long as the average number of nominees for each position did not fall below 1.25 (Domínguez 1978:291–92).

In sum, the little information available indicates that the spirit of Castro's 1959 promise to bring real democracy into the selection of union leaders was not being fulfilled between 1961 and the end of the decade (Bray and Harding 1974:686). The party and the government were so influential in nomination and electoral proceedings that union leaders, including even those elected in the first place, could be removed or transferred without members' approval. As the decade wore on, union members had fewer and fewer opportunities for meaningful involvement in the selection of local, intermediate, or national leaders: Local elections were held less regularly; many intermediate union structures were abandoned; rank-and-file input into national leadership selection at the CTC congresses, when they were held, was limited. As a result, union leaders tended to be more responsive to outside authorities than to the members of their own organizations. As Gilly observed, strong worker support for the revolution and its leadership coexisted with equally vehement opposition to the unions and their leaders. Such a situation was more understandable before the revolution had been consolidated, but less so once it was firmly on course. By that time organized Cuban workers deserved better, though improvements were nearly a decade in coming.

Changes in union electoral procedures, however, proved one

of the most prominent facets of union revitalization efforts that began in 1970. Castro promised that subsequent elections would be "absolutely free," noting that if a "worker has really been elected by a majority vote of all his comrades, he will have authority. He will not be a nobody who has been placed there by decree" (Zimbalist 1975:50; Mesa-Lago 1978:83; *Granma* 20 Sept 70:2–9). Supervised by electoral commissions made up of workers, the first section elections after revitalization were held in November 1970. Nominations were made at an assembly chaired by a regional union officer; the political restrictions of 1966 had been eliminated, so anyone could be nominated except high-level administrators. Two or three nominees contended for each post, and the number of posts varied from three to eleven, depending on the size of the section. As no campaigning was allowed, assembly discussions served to inform voters about the nominees' qualifications;[37] in addition, the electoral commissions could post information about candidates at workplaces (Mesa-Lago 1978:85–86). Everyone nominated was listed on the ballot; voting was direct and secret. A worker voted for as many candidates as there were openings (one could presumably vote for fewer), putting a double check beside the name of the person she or he wanted as executive officer of the section. In all, 164,367 local leaders were elected in November 1970, an average of about four per section (*Trabajadores*, 2d half Feb 1973). Between 73 and 87 percent of the winners would hold union office for the first time.[38]

Each union section in the country also elected a candidate from the rank-and-file for delegate to the 13th National CTC Congress, the first in more than seven years. The sections could propose nominees for higher-level union posts as well. The delegates were finally chosen at regional and provincial conferences held by the industrial unions. By Domínguez's (1978:293–94) calculations the delegate-to-worker ratio ranged from 1:339 in some of these unions to 1:1,578 in others; about 48 percent of the delegates elected came from the rank-and-file (*Granma Weekly Review* 11 Nov 73:5). In accordance with established procedure, the delegates selected the national leaders of the CTC. No one seems to disagree that the new secretary-general, Lázaro Peña, was properly elected this time.[39] At the close of the Congress, Castro (1973:42–43) stressed the fact that the party had not interfered in the selection of top CTC leaders. Its role, he said, had been to help define the criteria for leadership positions and to ensure that the process was democratic, rather than to tell the Congress who should fill the positions.[40]

Throughout the remainder of the 1970s and into the 1980s, Cuban union members continued to take part in selecting their leaders at the grass-roots, the intermediate, and the national levels of the sectoral unions and the CTC. Although union election processes were complex, workers whom I interviewed in 1982 and 1983 were generally aware of their most important aspects. They also reported that, in the main, these processes were adhered to.

Section elections continued to be by direct and secret vote every two and one-half years. Those in 1977 were preceded by seminars to familiarize union leaders with the electoral process and regulations.[41] As in earlier years, candidates were nominated in a general assembly where their qualifications were discussed.[42] Workers I spoke with said that, ordinarily, they were fairly well aware of the candidates' qualifications before the assembly, because all were fellow workers and the average union section was not a large body. As before, anyone except high-level administrators could be nominated for section office; the names of all nominees appeared on the ballot; voters double-checked the name of the person they wanted as executive officer.[43] Regulations for the 1977 elections stipulated that the nominating assembly had to be attended by at least 75 percent of the section's members.[44] Although the number of candidates for each post was not specified, the ballot was to contain more names than section positions but no more than two nominees per position.[45] The number of offices in a section was still tied to its size, but the upper limit was increased from eleven to thirteen. In 1977, 233,724 section officers were elected, an average of about five per section; 54 percent of the successful candidates were elected for the first time. Of the total Cuban union membership, 87 percent participated in the section elections, which usually took twenty to thirty days in each sectoral union.[46]

Union bureau officers, however, were not elected directly by the rank-and-file. In 1977 they were chosen by all or some of the section officers and by the candidates for delegates to the national congresses of the sectoral unions.[47] The list of candidates for bureau office was presented to the electors by a committee from the next-highest level of the industrial unions, but the electors could nominate additional candidates. This committee also set the number of posts in each bureau, which averaged about eight. Voting was secret, and no candidate who failed to receive a simple majority could be elected. The new bureau officers elected their secretary-general by open vote in a joint meeting with the immediately superior union body (i.e., at the municipal or provincial level). Like section officers, bureau leaders served terms of two and one-half years.[48]

Cuban workers also played a role in the election of municipal, provincial, and national leaders of their sectoral unions at this time.[49] As in bureau elections, however, their participation was indirect. Delegates to the national Congress, held every five years, selected the thirty- to forty-member National Committee of each sectoral union by secret ballot. To be elected to the Committee, a candidate had to receive a simple majority of the votes cast. In an open vote, the members of the National Committee then elected seven of their own number to serve on the union's Executive Secretariat.[50]

How were the delegates to these Congresses, who ultimately elected the national leaders of the sectoral unions, chosen? Before the 1977 Congresses, each union section, in an open vote, nominated one candidate as delegate to their Congress. Later, by secret ballot, each union bureau chose its candidates for delegates to the Congress from among those nominated by the sections. The number of candidate-delegates from each bureau, which depended on the number of workers it represented, varied from two to eight. The final delegates to the Congress were then elected at provincial meetings, again by secret ballot.[51] New nominations could be made at these meetings, but their number could not exceed 20 percent of the total delegates elected from the province. As in bureau elections, a candidate had to receive a simple majority of the votes cast in order to become a delegate. The number of delegates at each sectoral union congress (and thus the number of union members who voted directly for the union's national leadership) ranged from about 140 to more than 400, varying with the union's total membership. Each delegate to a congress from a large industrial union, however, usually represented more workers than did each delegate from a small one.[52] Other information about delegates was scarce. Fifty-one percent came from the grass-roots level in the

Agricultural Workers' Union; about 64 percent of the delegates at the Congress of the Sugar Workers' Union were members of the party or the Communist Youth League (UJC) and about 73 percent were Advanced Workers.[53]

In 1977 the selection process for intermediate-level leaders of sectoral unions was similar to the process for choosing the national leaderships. Members of provincial and municipal committees were elected for two-and-one-half-year terms by delegates to meetings at the corresponding level; to be elected, candidates had to receive a simple majority vote. In that year, 460 municipal committees and 201 provincial committees were elected. Each committee then elected a seven-member Executive Secretariat from among its ranks in an open vote.[54] In 1977 the delegates to the provincial and municipal meetings were the same candidate-delegates for the sectoral union congresses who had been selected at the bureau level. The importance of a particular economic activity in a given geographical area determined the number of delegates attending the provincial and municipal meetings. *Trabajadores* reported that some provincial meetings were attended by only 50 delegates, whereas others comprised as many as 250.[55]

The procedure for selecting the CTC leadership at the national and intermediate levels was similar to the one just described for sectoral unions. National leaders of the CTC were elected every five years by delegates to a national CTC congress. The 1978 CTC Statutes specified that the delegates both elect a National Council by secret ballot and determine its size. One hundred and forty-three members were elected in that year (*Trabajadores* 20 Feb 79:1). Published accounts revealed few specifics of the process, though Castro's closing speech to the Congress gave one small indication of what took place: "Some of our most outstanding and worthy union leaders received a few opposition votes. I remember some murmurs as the vote tally was read and I said, 'Very good, very good!' . . . because the right to cast a vote against someone is one of the most sacred rights of any delegate [applause]" (*Trabajadores* 4 Dec 78:3). Many of the winners were from the grass-roots level, and they reportedly played significant roles in subsequent Council meetings.[56] The National Council in turn elected from among its members the National Committee, its secretary-general and second secretary, the Secretariat, and the president of the Review and

Control Commission.[57] The 1978 CTC Statutes also empowered the National Council to set the procedure for choosing delegates to the national CTC congress. Prior to the 14th National CTC Congress, 45,000 candidate-delegates were selected in work-center general assemblies. Of these, 2,104 were eventually elected as congressional delegates at municipal- and provincial-level meetings. According to Veiga, 68 percent of the delegates came from the grass roots, 20 percent more than the corresponding figure for the 13th National CTC Congress.[58]

Provincial and municipal CTC committees were elected every two-and-one-half years by delegates to conferences at the corresponding level. These committees then elected from among their number a secretary-general, a second secretary, and a president of the Review and Control Commission. Most provincial CTC conferences held before the 14th National CTC Congress were attended by 150 to 350 delegates elected at municipal conferences. These delegates elected provincial committees, whose memberships ranged from forty-five to fifty-five. Municipal committees were probably smaller.[59]

Also worthy of mention alongside post-1970 procedures for selecting union officers are those for removing them, which were instituted during the same period. How this was done provides a good example of a negative form of participation in the evaluative phase of decision making. A union leader could be recalled at any time by a majority vote of the body that originally elected him or her.[60] A leader elected by a council, conference, or congress that would not soon reconvene could be removed by any body charged with running the union in the interim, but previous authorization by the superordinate level and subsequent ratification by the appropriate body of electors were required. A leader who was removed had the right to appeal, even up to a national CTC congress if necessary. When a leader was removed or resigned, a special election could be called to fill the vacancy. A vacancy in any office in a union section, except that of the executive officer, could be filled by a nominee who received votes in the preceding election but did not get elected. New elections had to be called if no such alternates were available or if the position of executive secretary became vacant (*Trabajadores* 14 Jul 79:3; CTC 1978, arts. 9, 89, 90).

CONCLUSION: EVALUATING POSTREVOLUTIONARY CHANGES IN UNION LEADERSHIP SELECTION

Although unions are central to the democratization of production, their contribution is minimized, if not negated entirely, when their own practice and structure are undemocratic. How union leaders are selected (and removed) is an important indicator of how democratic unions are. The kinds of changes in this area that occurred in post-1970 Cuba were both an indication of, as well as an inducement to, advances in the democratization of production. Nonetheless, union electoral process continued to exhibit certain deficiencies that obstructed further progress toward economic democracy.

Prior to 1970, union leaders at both the worksite and supraworksite levels were frequently installed, or installed themselves, in accordance with the political exigencies of the moment. Formal procedures, let alone electoral ones, played a minor role. Likewise, early in the revolution union leaders were sometimes summarily removed from their posts by outside authorities. Beginning in the 1970s, however, all union officers were chosen according to a formalized electoral process that was well publicized and spelled out in great detail. Moreover, union leaders could only be removed by the bodies that elected them, and every deposed leader had the right to appeal.[61] The aprocedural shifts in leadership common at the beginning of the revolution became events of the past.

In addition, especially in the latter half of the 1960s, those union elections that were held occurred with decreasing frequency. We have seen, for example, how the time interval between national congresses was not even specified and kept increasing. Beginning in the 1970s, however, all union officers had to face reelection or replacement on a frequent schedule: every five years for national officers of sectoral unions and the CTC, and every two and one-half years for all others. Frequent opportunities to effect leadership changes allowed and encouraged more people to take part in running the unions, especially since assuming such positions involved substantial time commitments.

Restrictions on eligibility for union office also disappeared, with obvious implications for inclusiveness. Some maintain that in the early postrevolutionary years pressures were exerted to prevent

Communists from running. Later on, counterrevolutionaries, or those with prerevolutionary associations with Mujal or Batista, were excluded, and party and union officials above the section could reject its nominees for office. By 1970 all these restrictions had been removed. The names of all persons nominated for section office appeared on the ballot. The only remaining restriction at this level was the nominee-per-post recommendation, which varied from 1.25 (1966) to two or three (1970) to none (1973) to no more than two (1977). This recommendation, however, has prompted some to conclude that section elections were uncontested or noncompetitive. This charge would be nearer the truth if *each* of the three to thirteen section officers were elected separately, but in fact a *group* of three to thirteen people was elected jointly to lead each section. Varying with the year and the size of a section, workers were thus presented with lists of four to thirty-nine names to fill three to thirteen positions. Domínguez (1978:292) estimates that in 1970, for example, the average number of candidates per section office was 1.6. Hence, ballots in the smallest sections listed five to eight names for three to five posts. In the largest sections ballots contained eighteen names for eleven posts. Workers clearly had some choice when electing their section leaders.

Inclusiveness, however, is not guaranteed by the mere absence of intentional or formal restrictions on participation. It is often difficult for women, for example, to serve as union leaders because of the inequitable division of domestic labor by gender and widely accepted suppositions about their abilities and preferences. Beginning in the 1970s, increased attention was focused on this problem. No major public statement on the unions neglected it, and figures indicate that the attention was accompanied by some noteworthy changes: By 1984, women comprised nearly 46 percent of base-level union officers; in 1986 over 50 percent of the elected *sección* leaders were women (Bengelsdorf 1988b:127; *Trabajadores* 2 Apr 86:1, 9 Apr 86:2). Although women's representation in base-level leadership positions exceeded their rates of participation in the paid labor force (41 percent in 1985 [*Trabajadores* 25 Feb 85:4]), the percentages of women leaders descended at higher levels in the union hierarchy. In 1984 only 16 percent of the municipal and 15 percent of the provincial officers were female. Acknowledging the problem, Veiga announced in 1986 that the proximate goal in a number of sectoral unions with large female memberships was for women to assume the majority of leadership posts at intermediate and national levels.

In the context of growing union membership and increases in the number of union leadership posts, the democratization trend meant union officers were more dependent on, more responsive to, and more representative of the rank-and-file after 1970 than they had been in the early years of the revolution.[62] Nonetheless, in the 1970s and 1980s, unions continued to rely heavily on indirect electoral procedures. The only union leaders elected directly were section officers. No candidate at any other level of the structure need ever have defended her or his record or faced an opponent in a contest decided by the constituency he or she would serve. The outstanding example of indirect voting was the elections of the national CTC and sectoral union leadership. In the 1977 sectoral elections, for example, the highest-ranking national officers were insulated from the direct expression of rank-and-file preference by four procedural stages. The indirectness of elections was mollified by certain facts: A significantly higher percentage of delegates to the 14th, as opposed to the 13th National CTC Congresses came from the base level; most union officers could not be elected without receiving more than half the votes cast; the number of elected union officers was much larger in Cuba than in many other countries. Certainly, it could have been unduly cumbersome to require a direct vote for each of these elective union positions, and no worker with whom I spoke was troubled by the indirectness of elections. Indeed, some favored the system, arguing that workers would be unfamiliar with the candidates for higher offices, whereas the chosen electors had greater interest and made the effort to get information on them. Nevertheless, direct elections would have enhanced union democracy, even while necessitating the utilization of some more traditional campaigning methods.

Equally important, the influence of those delegated to elect union leaders above the section level was diminished insofar as posts were uncontested or nominations originated from above rather than from below. We know that during the 10th and 11th National CTC Congresses top leaders faced little or no electoral opposition, and it is not clear this had changed in the 1970s and 1980s. Nor is it clear how competitive indirect elections at intermediate and *buró* levels were. Moreover, in 1977 nominations for bureau officers were submitted by a superior body of the corresponding sectoral union, though the electors could propose additional candidates. In addition, it is highly possible that nominees for intermediate and national levels of the sectoral unions and the CTC also came from superordinate bodies. Even though most union officers could be elected only by a majority vote, union democratization will be stalled in Cuba in the absence of more electoral competition and of more rank-and-file involvement in nominating procedures.

Chapter 4

THE CUBAN
COMMUNIST PARTY

Much research on work under both capitalism and socialism has underscored the importance of technology, economic processes and structures, firm organization, and ideology for understanding how production is controlled. Often obscured is the fact that the control of production is basically a problem of politics. That is, power over production is both the object and the product of conflict, negotiation, compromise, and collaboration among various social classes and groupings at the level of the workplace and above it.[1]

Under capitalism the control of production has appeared only minimally a problem of politics because the political and economic spheres are relatively separate at both the worksite and supra-worksite levels. Under socialism, however, politics and economics are closely intertwined in both arenas. It would therefore be impossible, in my view, to examine the control of production in Cuba without investigating the country's quintessential political organization, the Communist party. Both changes in workers' relationship to the party and changes in the party's involvement in making decisions about production bear close scrutiny.

EVOLUTION OF THE PARTY SINCE 1959

For important historical reasons discussed in Chapter 9, the Cuban Communist party did not direct the struggle against Fulgencio Batista, nor did it mastermind the seizure of political power in 1959. In fact, the absence of a vanguard party distinguished the revolution long after it had been declared socialist. According to Hans Magnus Ezensberger (1976:136), it was a "shadow of a party that will perhaps never exist." The party was poorly organized during the first postrevolutionary decade: It had no statutes, no by-laws, no coordination and control mechanisms, and virtually no program; its constituent organs met rarely, if ever; and it held no congresses. The party's small membership had few responsibilities, other than those assumed on individuals' initiative. Its performance of administrative tasks was both a cause and a reflection of its weakness. Overburdened, especially at the end of the decade, with the detailed and massive task of day-to-day administration, the party could not assume the leading role associated with most ruling Communist parties. In short, the party did not have *political* power in Cuba; it did not and could not govern the island.[2]

Following a decade of semi-dormancy, the Cuban Communist party began a slow process of change. Eventually it came to behave more in accordance with the classic tenets of Marxism-Leninism. By the mid-1970s, no major policy decision was made without its participation, and the more important the decision, the more central the party's involvement in making it. To qualify for this new role, the party had, first, to create an organizational structure able to carry out its expanded functions and, second, to lighten its administrative burden.[3] Advances were made in both areas after 1970. Two party congresses had been held by 1980; new party structures began to function at various levels; party statutes were adopted; the Central Committee staff and the Secretariat grew and became more complex. The party began to separate itself from administration: Only half the Cuban cabinet belonged to the party's Central Committee by 1976 (Domínguez 1978:313), and it was estimated that in 1980 more than 60 percent of all administrative leaders were not party members (LeoGrande 1980:402).

As the Cuban Communist party developed a strong organizational structure and freed itself of administrative burdens, it became able to exert more influence over work and production. It accomplished this through its role in macro-level decision making, its relationship to Cuban unions, and its increased activity at the point of production. The party's influence over production decisions made at the national level was immense. Indirectly, it affected work and production through its policies on, for example, women's equality, social security, international trade, and science and technology. It also affected work and production more directly as a result of its adoption of the SDPE (El Sistema de Dirección y

Planificación de la Economía), its transfer of control over many production and service units to local government bodies, and its role in macro-level planning, for example. The latter included the formulation of policies on investment, wages and work organization, regional development, and environmental protection, as well as on the nature of the planning process itself: who participated, at which stage, in what ways. The party's wider participation in the macro-level direction of the economy was exemplified by a high-level organizational change: In 1965 the Central Committee had only one general economic department; in the mid-1970s it was joined by departments specifically concerned with agriculture and livestock, construction, communication and transportation, sugar, consumer goods and domestic services, and basic industry (Leo-Grande 1980:410–11). The staffs of these departments were integrally involved in all major activities related to their respective economic spheres.

The party's increased influence over work and production also came as a result of increased specification of its relationship with the unions. This relationship was conceived in the following general terms: The party led the workers' organizations in the sense that union activities occurred within the framework of its broad policy dictates; in their alliance with the party, unions accepted the party's political and ideological guidance; the party, while striving to maintain its preeminence, respected union autonomy and workers' specific interests (Cuban Communist Party 1981b:33); the party exercised its guidance indirectly, by persuasion, reason, moral example, and discussion.

Such general pronouncements were operationalized in specific ways. First, some union offices (it is unclear which ones or how many) were included in the party's nomenclature.[4] Despite the potential for damage to union autonomy inherent in this system, the extent of party authority over union positions cannot be automatically determined simply from their inclusion in the nomenclature. In some situations the party could have exerted aggressive control over union posts; in others, it could have shared control or, alternatively, ratified union leaders selected through independent processes. Second, the party influenced the unions through individual *militantes* (the Cuban term for party members) who were either rank-and-file union members or elected or professional union leaders in posts not covered by the nomenclature.

Militantes were expected to influence the unions to implement party goals without acting as official party representatives. If no party members belonged to the leadership of a particular union section, the party nucleus could ask to dispatch *militantes* to section meetings to express opinions or gather information.[5] The party's influence over the unions through individual *militantes* was potentially bolstered when it established control and revision commissions, enabling it to monitor the activities of *militantes* in nonparty as well as party positions.

Finally, the party increased its control over work through its activities at the point of production. Statutes and other party documents specified that both the party nucleus and individual members devote special attention to issues such as workplace discipline, productivity, equipment maintenance, efficiency, quality, conservation, and plan fulfillment. As Raúl Castro explained in 1973, "When the Party is the one that directs and organizes the country's economic activity, the economic sphere occupies a place of top priority among the tasks of the nuclei."[6] Moreover, both informally (e.g., the "brokering" activities of party members in situations of workplace conflict) and formally (e.g., party participation in management councils), the party widened its worksite influence by expanding its total membership and increasing the size of its working-class component.

Precisely because the party's capacity to affect work and production expanded so dramatically between the revolution's first and subsequent decades, it makes little sense to consider the democratization of production further without asking how Cuban workers could affect the party. Central to this question are party size and social composition, internal party decision-making procedures, and non-members' influence in the organization.

PARTY SIZE AND SOCIAL COMPOSITION

We have grown a lot and we have grown well.[7]
—FIDEL CASTRO

Ruling Communist parties are parties of the minority. Only small proportions of any sector of the population become members. Not only do most manual workers, most office workers, most women, and most young people not belong, but neither do most technicians, most managers, most men, or most older people. Despite their universal exclusivity, ruling Communist parties have varied in both size and social composition, features that together offer a preliminary indication of how much influence direct producers have over them. A party that is larger *and* that has a higher percentage of worker members is more inclusive. Other things equal, its policies are more likely to reflect the preferences of those who produce goods and deliver services. In both variables—party size and worker membership—the Cuban Communist party underwent notable changes between the revolution's first and succeeding decades.

The membership of the United Party of the Socialist Revolution (PURS [1963–65]) and of the Cuban Communist party (PCC [1965-]) increased steadily, though slowly, through the revolution's first decade. Membership doubled between 1963 and 1964, then grew at a slower rate during the "Sino-Guevarist" phase in the latter half of the 1960s (see Table 2). It has been calculated (Domínguez 1978:321) that the ratio of party members to the population increased from roughly 2:1,000 in 1962 to 7:1,000 by early 1969. Yet the link between party size and party functioning was downplayed throughout the 1960s, as illustrated by a 1963 article in *Cuba Socialista*, the party's theoretical journal.

> In order to perform its leading role, it is of no importance whether [the party] has so many more or less members, but only that it will be capable of carrying out the directives from the National Directorate of the Revolution, of applying these creatively to specific conditions, of maintaining a close relationship with the working masses, and of leading them onward. (Fagen 1972*b*:211)

By 1969, however, it had become apparent that a vanguard party as small as Cuba's was not capable either of implementing directives or of maintaining a close relationship with working people. The party's relatively few members were simply spread too thin to be effective at either task. So deliberately, but quietly at first, membership was expanded. It increased nearly fourfold between 1969 and 1975 (see Table 2), the date of the 1st Party Congress. Party growth between the 1st and the 2d Party Congress surpassed the expectations of many observers (Casal and Pérez-Stable 1981:84; LeoGrande 1980:397, 400, 406). Whereas party

Table 2
Membership of United Party of the Socialist Revolution and Cuban Communist Party, 1963–1986

Year	Number of Members	Membership as Percentage of Total Population
1963	16,000	0.2
1964	32,500	0.4
1965	50,000	0.5
1966	50,000	0.5
1968	100,000[a]	—
1969	55,000–70,000	0.6–0.9
1970	78,000–101,000	0.9–1.2
1971	101,000–134,200	1.2–1.6[b]
1972	122,000–153,000	1.4–1.8[b]
1973	153,000–170,000	1.7–1.9[c]
1974	186,900–187,000	1.9–2.1[c]
1975	202,800–211,600	2.2–2.4
1979	250,000	2.6[d]
1980	434,100	4.5[d]
1981	443,100	—
1984	454,500	—
1986	492,500	4.8

Sources: Domínguez 1978:321; Enzensberger 1976:126; Bray and Harding 1974:681; Mesa-Lago 1978:71; Fidel Castro 1976:233; Casal and Pérez-Stable 1981:84; Cuban Communist Party 1981a:77; Suárez 1971:10; Hamberg 1983:37; González 1981:412; LeoGrande 1979b:467; Azicri 1988:78–79.

Note: Membership figures are rounded to the nearest hundred. It is not always clear whether sources counted members and candidates or members only.

[a]This figure, from Enzensberger 1976, is not documented and seems far out of line.
[b]Calculated using total population figures for 1970.
[c]Calculated using total population figures for 1975.
[d]Calculated using total population figures for 1980.

ranks had grown by less than 200,000 in the entire ten years before the 1st Congress, by the 2d Congress, held only five years later, more than 220,000 *new* members had been added to party rolls. By the end of 1980, 4.5 percent of the Cuban population (a ratio of 1:22) had joined the party (LeoGrande 1978:13). Following the 2d Party Congress the rate of party growth slowed, with membership estimates indicating that approximately 60,000 to 90,000 new members joined between 1980 and the middle of the decade.[8]

From the perspective of the democratization of production, a larger membership meant the party could increase its day-to-day contact with workers and thus potentially become more responsive to their opinions and preferences. This workplace "coverage," as it has been called, was minimal in the 1960s (LeoGrande 1980:399–400). At that time many work centers, including key ones, had no party nucleus; nuclei that did exist were often so small and disorganized that meaningful interaction with most workers at the center was impossible. The qualitative change that became possible in the 1970s, in terms of increased worker access to the party and vice versa, may be deduced from quantitative data.[9] The number of party nuclei increased from around two thousand in 1963 to more than twenty-six thousand in 1980. Whereas work centers with nuclei were estimated to be only 16 percent of the total work centers in the mid-1960s, by 1975 the percentage had risen to nearly half, and at the 2d Party Congress, Castro announced that over the previous three years, 3,195 nuclei had been established at new work centers or at those formerly without them. The average nucleus size also increased, from roughly seven in the early 1960s to sixteen by 1980.[10] Yet party coverage varied by worksite, reflecting, among other things, the emphasis on strengthening the party in areas considered crucial to the country's development. Thus, the following situation, described to me by a worker who had been at least five years in a retail clothing outlet, was probably not uncommon in low-priority work centers: "There was one *militante* here when I first came. But she died. No one replaced her, so we don't have one anymore."[11] Interviews conducted in a box factory about the same time (Harnecker 1980:18) revealed that only 3 percent of the 640 workers were party members. Whereas at a bus terminal 7 percent of the 550 workers belonged to the party in the late 1970s, at a construction center of about the same size 53 percent were party members (*Trabajadores* 12 May 79:2; 31 May 77:5).

A larger party may well broaden the opportunities for interaction between members and ordinary workers, but it does not necessarily heighten the degree of workers' influence over the party. For one thing, expanding party ranks might be filled with people not directly involved in producing goods and services, potentially moving the party further away from, rather than closer to, a worker orientation. Therefore, even if a vanguard party adopts a "semi-mass" character, information on the percentage of party members who are actual workers is of vital importance.

During the period when the party was the smallest in Cuba, indications are that its worker composition was also reduced. Judged on the basis of current activity, probably little more than one-third of party members were workers before 1970. This figure is not surprising inasmuch as recruitment was carried on mostly in the central ministries in the late 1960s (Domínguez 1978: 216,321). The principal reason, however, for the difficulty in keeping a high percentage of members actively engaged in production was the common party practice of drafting such people for administrative and political posts.

Although this practice had not entirely disappeared by the 1980s, around the time the party began to expand, it also began to make a conscious effort to increase the percentage of its membership engaged in producing goods or delivering services. To ensure a more acceptable social composition, the 1st Party Congress in 1975 suggested that officials be more careful about transferring workers to administrative positions; it also recommended that the Communist Youth League (UJC) strive to increase the number of workers (versus students) in its ranks (Partido Comunista de Cuba 1978:28). The Congress proposed a countrywide review of the party's social composition, and social composition goals were determined for the various levels of party structure. A member of the UJC explained one mechanism for reaching the goal established for her work center. In the past, she said, when a UJC member reached the prescribed age, transfer from the Communist Youth League into the party was "almost automatic," but now such transfers were predicated on the need to improve the party's social composition. At her workplace, for example, two of the four UJC members who qualified to become regular party members were asked to postpone their entrance for one or perhaps two years.[12] The issue of social composition received more attention than any other internal party matter both during and after the 1st Party Congress and, according to William LeoGrande (1980:400, 406,409), was surrounded by some controversy at the Central Committee's 8th Plenary Session held in 1979.

My interviewees, with two exceptions, supported the party's emphasis on recruiting worker-members, usually citing an economic rationale: Workers were pivotal to the country's development, and a party solidly grounded in the working class was best able to prepare and mobilize producers to perform this central economic task. In a more political vein, a factory administrator added that the "worker composition of the party is important and it is becoming more important all the time. You have to have a proletariat party to avoid problems, like the socialist contradictions that are so evident in Poland."[13] At the 1st Party Congress workers from sectors considered vital to the country's economic and political health (sugar and other basic industries, agriculture, construction, transportation, and education) were targeted for recruitment. The 2d Party Congress in 1980 documented notable advances in these sectors and also in public health.[14] Some workers interpreted the party's post-1970 recruitment policy as a worker-versus-intellectual issue. Previously, the party had comprised mostly intellectuals, they said, but its potential for growth in intellectual work centers was now limited. One teacher ruefully explained that in his immediate family, as a consequence of the the party's current worker emphasis, he and his mother, who taught Marxism-Leninism courses, were not party members, whereas his father, a mechanic, was. He added that it was harder for people like himself to get into the party and that only rarely were individuals at his work center proposed for membership anymore.[15] Another worker, also not a *militante*, expressed related sentiments.

> It gives me a slight feeling of injustice when I see people who are obvious party material like Alfonso, who aren't in the party because of being intellectual workers. But basically I do agree with the party's position on worker composition. I just hope the day will arrive when all qualified workers can become *militantes*.[16]

Between 1972 and the mid-1980s, the Cuban Communist party showed an improvement in worker composition (see Table 3). Interpreting the percentages shown in the table is not, however, a straightforward task. For one thing, categories are not always reported consistently across sources. For another, people disagree over who should be classified as "workers." Depending on how this determination is made, between 1974 and the mid-1980s the party's worker composition increased by 9.9 percent (considering categories 4 and 8) or by 17.2 percent (considering categories 4, 5, and 8). The most important issue here is whether to classify technical and professional personnel (category 5) as workers. Officially they are so regarded; consequently, the effort to improve worker composition plainly called for drawing more of this group into the party. There were legitimate reasons for classifying Cuban

Table 3
Social Composition of the Cuban Communist Party, 1970 to Mid-1980s (In percentages)

Member Category	1972	1973	1974	June 1975
1. Industrial workers	12			
2. Agricultural workers	28			
3. Various fields of material production		55		
4. Workers in industrial production, agriculture, construction, services			36.5	35.9
5. Technical and professional workers			9.2	9.2
6. Administrators			33.5	33.4
7. Political leaders			9.1	8.7
8. Clerical workers			4.0	4.1
9. Small farmers			1.9	1.8
10. Other			5.8	6.9

Sources: Domínguez 1978:320; Partido Comunista de Cuba 1978:19, 23; Cuban Communist Party 1981a:78,289; Casal and Pérez-Stable 1981:87; Azicri 1988:80.

technicians and professionals (*técnicos*) as workers (*obreros*). First, the gap in earnings between *técnicos* and service and production workers was narrower than in many other places. Information offered during some of my interviews illustrates this: A top specialist in children's orthodontics earned 375 pesos a month; a driver for a ministry earned 220; a cashier earned about 130.[17] Second, because Cuban socialist culture and ideology continuously focused attention on the ordinary worker, the difference in status between workers and technicians and professionals was hardly comparable to the wider gaps prevailing elsewhere. Finally, a long-standing priority of the revolution had been to give more people the opportunity for training that enabled them to cross the divide between *obrero* and *técnico*. From the perspective of these arguments, the aim of rooting the party more solidly in the working class would be badly distorted if technical and professional personnel were not classified as workers.

On the other hand, Cubans I spoke with did perceive a distinction between ordinary workers and professional and technical personnel. Economic scarcity, coupled with a political and ideological system that stressed equality, served to magnify differences in income, status, and privilege wherever these differences occurred and to sensitize people to their existence. Undoubtedly, some professional and technical personnel in Cuba would have been more exactly classified as "political" and "administrative leaders" than as workers. Increasing their membership in the party was unlikely to

December 1975	1979	December 1980	Mid-1980s
36.3	44.9	47–48	44.5
	13.5	14–15	16.5
	26.2		20.7
	4.8		3.0
	4.8		5.9
	1.3		2.6
	4.8		7.4

contribute to the construction of a political organization closely identified with, and representative of, the mass of Cuban workers.

The party's progress appears in a different light when worker membership is contrasted to the overall composition of the Cuban labor force. The party itself took this approach at its 1st Congress when it published a table comparing the composition of the labor force with the representation of corresponding occupational groupings in the party. While the publication of the table suggested the party considered this a valid comparison, it also demonstrated that, from this perspective, workers (industrial, service, construction, agricultural, and clerical) were underrepresented in the party by 30 percent and that professional and technical workers were underrepresented by 3 percent. Administrative and political leaders, in contrast, were overrepresented by 34 percent. This situation improved notably by 1980. Workers were still underrepresented in the party compared to their percentage in the labor force, but the difference was reduced to 15 percent. On the other hand, administrative and political leaders were still overrepresented in party ranks, but their overrepresentation was reduced to 13 percent.[18]

INTERNAL PARTY PROCEDURE

Although a larger Communist party with a higher percentage of direct producers was a potentially positive development for the democratization of decision making in Cuba , party size and social composition are only crude indicators of workers' power. To gauge the effectiveness of the new- and worker-members of the party in furthering the interests of rank-and-file producers, we must also consider how the party's internal operating procedures changed and how these changes affected the participation of party members in decision making. This kind of evaluation of any Communist party is not a simple matter, for most relevant data are simply not obtainable. Some information is available, however, on three pertinent topics: the method of selecting party leaders, the social composition of party leadership, and the general character of party decision-making processes.

During at least the first decade of the revolution nearly all party leaders were appointed and could be removed at the behest of superiors. Although the claim seems overdrawn, K. S. Karol (1970:458) contends that every party officer from the Central Committee down to the base was appointed by Castro himself or a by a few close collaborators.[19] Because elections for party posts were held only rarely during these years, party leaders were immediately responsible (and therefore primarily responsive) to those above them in the party hierarchy. Beginning in the early 1970s, however, all party leadership posts—including regular officers at all levels and delegates to party congresses—were elective. These party electoral procedures have been found wanting by many observers. Jorge Domínguez (1978:331–32) dismisses them as "unrepresentative as usual," "rigged," and "mere formalities." According to Edward González (1976:5), "as in the Soviet Union, elections serve only to ratify and formalize the *de facto* political powers enjoyed by elites." Such critiques leave the impression that methods for selecting party leaders after the mid-1970s differed little from those of the preceding decade. These later party electoral procedures were indeed imperfect in many ways, but nevertheless they signaled an important departure from earlier ones. With more input from lower- and middle-party ranks into the selection of leaders at every level, patterns of accountability between ordinary members and their officers changed.

After the mid-1970s, the procedure for electing officers was similar in at least one way to the electoral process in other Cuban organizations. Elections for base-level officers were direct; elections for higher offices were not (see Figure 1). Although the formal

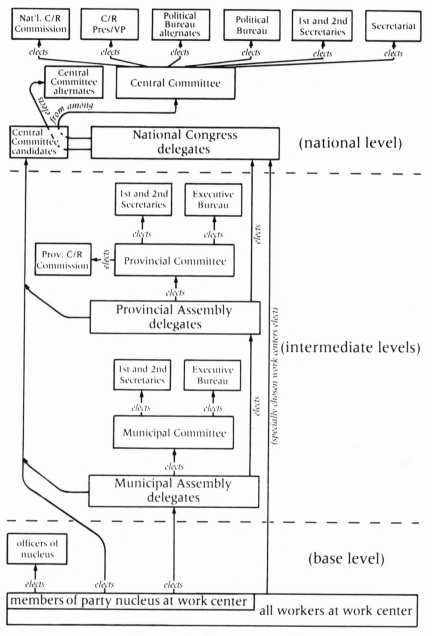

Figure 1. Communist Party Electoral Procedure

mechanisms for electing party officers were carefully spelled out, there is scant information available on how these mechanisms actually functioned. At the base level, the party nucleus, usually organized at the work center, elected three types of party leaders: officers of the party nucleus, delegates to the municipal assemblies, and precandidates for posts on the Central Committee. Party Statutes did not specify nomination procedures for any of these offices, nor is it clear whether these posts were contested. Voting for the nucleus leadership was open, though delegates to municipal assemblies seemed to be chosen by secret ballot (Cuban Communist Party 1981*b*:16).

At the next-higher level, the municipal assemblies, delegates elected three kinds of party leaders analogous to those elected at the base level: members and alternates of the municipal committees, delegates to the provincial assemblies, and precandidates for posts on the Central Committee. Nominees for municipal committees were proposed by their current counterparts, and the number of nominees had to exceed the number of officers to be elected.[20] This procedure suggested a change from 1974, when nominees for leadership posts were proposed, and could be vetoed, by the next-higher level of the party organization (Domínguez 1978:334–35). In his main address to the 1st Party Congress, Fidel Castro (1976:237) reported that the number of municipal (and provincial) committee officers had increased, partly because modifications of the election rules stipulated that any candidate receiving more than half the votes cast was elected.

At the provincial level the same general electoral pattern prevailed.[21] Delegates to the national Party Congress were individually elected by provincial assemblies in secret ballot, exactly as the provincial assembly delegates were themselves elected by the delegates to the municipal assemblies.[22] In contrast with some other party leadership bodies, the size of the national Party Congress decreased dramatically between its first and second meetings, the number of delegates dropping by over one-half from 3,126 to 1,780, though the number of party members during this period more than doubled.[23] Congressional delegates in 1975 and 1980 came from two separate sources: Some were elected by provincial assemblies (as noted above); others were elected directly by party and nonparty members in assemblies held at selected work centers throughout Cuba. The centers accorded this honor were chosen for their economic importance and their past performance. Among those centers selected in 1980 were a dairy and a bus line, as well as factories that manufactured cane-harvesting combines, plastics, and fertilizers (*Trabajadores* 23 Aug 80:1, 9 Sept 80:3, 11 Sept 80: 3, 30 Sept 80:3). The number of congressional delegates elected in this fashion is not certain, though they reportedly accounted for 12 percent of the delegation from Oriente province in 1975 and 18 percent of the delegation from La Habana province in 1980 (Domínguez 1978:331; *Trabajadores* 30 Aug 80:1).

Congressional delegates from these two sources elected the party's Central Committee and its alternates from among candidates proposed by lower levels of the party structure (see Figure 1).[24] Balloting for the Central Committee (and lower-level committees as well) was secret, and a majority was needed for election, thereby precluding the selection of especially unpopular people. Electing top party leaders (the Political Bureau and its alternates, the first and second party secretaries, the Secretariat, and the National Control and Revision Commission) was an important focus of Central Committee activity: Of the twenty-two issues the Central Committee is known to have considered between December 1975 and May 1979, eight concerned such elections (LeoGrande 1980:408). The Central Committee set membership levels for the Political Bureau, the Secretariat, and the National Control and Revision Commission and devised standards for representation and for the conduct of elections of delegates to the national Party Congress and to municipal and provincial party assemblies. The Central Committee could also empower leadership committees at base and intermediate levels to accept, in "exceptional cases," members who had not been elected by their corresponding assemblies.[25]

It is instructive to review changes in the social composition of party leadership that occurred as the procedures for selecting leaders were altered. Worker representation in the party leadership is necessary, though not sufficient, to ensure that the points of view of people in Cuba's factories, farms, offices, and service facilities receive consideration in the party decision-making process. Furthermore, growth in the worker component of the party leadership would suggest, though it would not conclusively prove, that the procedural changes discussed above allowed worker-*militantes* to increase their influence over the selection of party officers.

Information on the social composition of party leadership, es-

pecially at lower levels, is sparse. Party policy stressed the desir-
ability of choosing leaders who were from working-class back-
grounds and those currently engaged in producing goods and
delivering services (Partido Comunista de Cuba 1978:62); the elections preceding the 1st Party Congress revealed a tripling of the
number of party leaders classified as workers on the basis of current activity. In a factory where Marta Harnecker (1980:22) conducted interviews in this period, the party secretary (who was a
manager) offered his interpretation of the party's policy on leadership composition: "The Party official must be an ordinary worker,
and at least a third of the leadership in the factory must be workers
directly connected with production. And you will see that in many
places an ordinary worker is the secretary-general for the leadership and the manager an ordinary Party member." Nationwide figures indicate that in 1975 a little more than one-half (51 percent)
of the base-level party leaders were workers.[26] It must therefore be
assumed that the remaining nuclei leadership posts went to administrators, who were thus overrepresented in base-level leadership positions in comparison with their overall party membership.
Unfortunately, it is not known how this percentage compared with
earlier ones or how, or if, it changed after that. My guess, based on
the interviews I conducted, is that the percentage would have differed only slightly in 1982 and 1983.

Comparative data on the social composition of municipal and
provincial committees for the period between the 1st and 2d Party
Congresses indicated substantial improvement in worker representation judged by current activity. The percentage of workers on
municipal committees almost doubled (from 29 to 53 percent) and
on the provincial committees nearly tripled (from 13 to 33 percent).[27] These increases were even more significant in view of the
fact that intermediate-party branches were then assuming new responsibilities, as economic and political decision making was decentralized under the SDPE and OPP (People's Power), which together placed many production and service delivery units under
subnational control.

Before reviewing changes in the social composition of the
Central Committee, it is worthwhile to examine changes in the
social composition of the group that elected it and other national
leadership bodies. In 1975, when 35 percent of the delegates to the
1st Party Congress were workers, Fidel Castro (1976:237) ad-

mitted to a desire that "the Congress not be a meeting of big shots. We didn't conceive of it as a Congress of Party and State leaders, and this is reflected in the composition of the delegates." He would have been even more pleased had he foreseen that the number of worker-delegates at the 2d Party Congress would increase by nearly 10 percent (*Trabajadores* 20 Dec 80:1). Changes in the composition of the Central Committee itself, which was elected by these delegates, have been discussed elsewhere (Domínguez 1976: 39–65; 1982:19–20; LeoGrande 1978:1–31; 1980:397–419). Most of the discussion on this subject, however, says little about worker representation, focusing instead on military-civilian, "*Fidelista-Raulista*," "old Communist-new Communist," and bureaucrat-politico divisions within the Committee. Although details on worker inclusion on the Central Committee are scant, Castro, at both party Congresses, made a point of calling the delegates' attention to this issue. At the close of the 2d Party Congress he exclaimed: The "most important, the most revolutionary thing about this Congress was the composition of our Central Committee. The leadership of our Party was given a strong dose of worker cadres."[28]

According to the available data on changes in worker-members of the Central Committee, in 1980 workers had two kinds of representatives on the Committee: people currently involved in the production of goods and the delivery of services, and union leaders. People in the first category, who comprised 4 percent of the members of the Central Committee (*Trabajadores* 22 Dec 80:1, 23 Dec 80:1), were all outstanding workers who had received nationwide honors in their respective economic sectors. Yet, in terms of the legitimacy of a Central Committee member's claim to represent workers' viewpoints, it is more reasonable, so long as union leaders themselves are selected democratically, to have Committee positions occupied by union officers rather than by extraordinary individuals distinguished by personal labor merits. It is therefore significant that Central Committee elections at the 2d Party Congress increased from 5 to 12 the percentage of full Committee members who were union leaders (LeoGrande 1978:15; *Trabajadores* 22 Dec 80:1, 23 Dec 80:1). The resultant Committee included two national officers of the CTC (Central de Trabajadores de Cuba), six provincial CTC secretaries-general, the secretaries-general of nine sectoral unions, one second secretary of a sectoral union, and the secretary-general of an international union (*Traba-*

jadores 22 Dec 80:1). Those skeptical of the degree to which Cuban unions represented the rank-and-file will not find the presence of union leadership on the Central Committee indicative of worker influence in party decision making. Yet, given the expanding role of the unions during this period and the increasing importance of the party in making decisions about work and production, it would have been a poor sign indeed had union leaders not been more visible in upper-level party decision-making bodies than they had been previously.

The dearth of available data from any of the time periods of interest makes changes in the general character of party decision-making processes very difficult to assess. René Dumont, a specialist in economic and agricultural planning, is one of a handful of people to have commented on internal party operations in Cuba in the 1960s. Dumont does not paint a complimentary picture. In the early ruling Cuban party he discerned many features of European communist parties which he deplored. The party, Dumont claimed, was hierarchically organized; power and authority were held at the highest levels. Communication was a top-down affair: Castro controlled the Central Committee, the Central Committee controlled the party, and the party controlled the workers. No free discussion existed within the organization. Participation at lower-party levels was limited to approval of actions already taken.[29] Enzensberger (1976:127–28), who lived in Cuba in the late 1960s, also stressed the heavy concentration of party power in Castro's hands. Even the Central Committee played a "purely decorative role": It had "nothing to say," was merely a "facade," and reached "no decisions whatsoever." Domínguez (1978:329, 335), agreeing with Dumont and Enzensberger, cites examples of how higher-party ranks monitored their subordinates and intervened in their affairs in the early 1960s, creating a fearful and paralyzed party leadership.[30] In short, observers have described internal party process in this early period as highly centralized, personalistic, closed, and arbitrary.

Many accounts of party decision-making process in the 1970s and early 1980s leave the impression that little, if anything, changed. The party remained oligarchic and tightly controlled by Castro; it was intolerant of dissent within its ranks; it was decidedly undemocratic and non-participatory in its decision-making procedures.[31] I do not argue that such assessments are wrong. Instead, focusing on these three principal contentions, I will inject evidence and interpretation, both Cuban and non-Cuban, into the discussion of party process that highlight the differences, rather than the similarities, between the post-1970 period and that just described. My intent, in view of the scant data available, is to at least raise the possibility that party decision-making processes have not been completely static in Cuba and to discourage acceptance of any final judgments about how democratic these processes were.

The argument that the party continued to be oligarchic and tightly controlled by Castro requires several comments. First, though power and autonomy continued to be vested in the party's top echelons, as they are in most modern organizations, an important change after the 1960s was the leadership's expansion. The party elite in Cuba became less exclusive. Most leadership bodies, including the Central Committee, the Political Bureau, the Secretariat, and municipal and provincial committees, increased in size and thus drew more people into top-level deliberations than in the past.[32] The Central Committee, for instance, grew from 25 members in 1962 to 148 in 1980.[33] According to LeoGrande, as the Central Committee grew it also became a more important decision-making forum that was mandated to meet at least once a year and that, in fact, met twice that often after the 1st Party Congress.[34] Before its 8th Plenary Session in 1979, the Central Committee probably did no more than "provide *pro forma* ratification of prior decisions by the Political Bureau and Secretariat"; after that session, however, the Committee issued an important public document evaluating the revolution, and though the level of debate within the Central Committee was unknown, it seemed to LeoGrande (1980:408–9) "to be emerging, for the first time, as the principal locus of intra-elite communication and coordination."[35] The Central Committee did more, however, than increase its decision-making authority. It began, according to Antonio José Herrera and Hernan Rosenkranz (1979:39), to make an effort to "redistribute the tasks more evenly through the ranks." Decentralization meant that mid- and lower-level leadership bodies became more visible and more active in party life. A widely disseminated 1977 Political Bureau resolution, for example, called upon grass-roots structures to broaden the scope of their activities, and the provincial party apparatus grew stronger as well (*Trabajadores* 14 Jul 79:1; LeoGrande 1978:17).

Second, the party began to stress collective decision making. It has been argued that the revolution's errors in judgment during its "idealistic" phase in the late 1960s were attributable to the "lack of collective leadership which systematically analyzed problems" (Casal 1976:24). According to the 1980 Party Statutes, however, all its constituent bodies were "duty-bound" to apply principles of collective leadership (Cuban Communist Party 1981b:15). In closing his main report to the 2d Party Congress, Castro noted that "at the highest levels of the Party the principles of collective leadership have been solidly applied. The most disparate international topics of a state and Party nature have been analyzed collectively. No important questions were decided in any other way" (Cuban Communist Party 1981a:84).

Finally, though directives were formulated and decisions were taken at high organizational levels, and though inferiors were bound by the decisions taken at higher levels (Cuban Communist Party 1981b:15), formal mechanisms were created for holding superiors accountable and for changing decisions from below, as substantiated by party documents. In fact, a good portion of the Party's Statutes were devoted to detailing how this should be accomplished through periodic reports and work reviews. The Statutes also stated that any party member had the right to "take any decision with which he is in disagreement to a higher Party level," and to "raise issues before, ask questions of and make requests and proposals to any Party level, including the Central Committee, and to receive a specific and timely answer" (Cuban Communist Party 1981b:11–12). Again, none of what has been reported above can be read as definitive evidence that the party operated less oligarchically after the 1970s or that Castro's power within it had diminished. Mostly, this is because it is impossible to tell whether party decision making in practice approached the ideal set forth in its statutes, and because virtually nothing is known about the character of deliberations inside various party bodies. Nonetheless, in my view, a thorough assessment of changes in party practice cannot be made before considering such information.

A second argument, put forward by those skeptical of meaningful party change, concerns lack of opportunity for either free discussion or organized dissent within party ranks. The freedom to speak out against or to organize opposition to a policy or an action is central to democratization, so such assessments should be considered seriously. There is no doubt that factionalism was prohibited; the Party Statutes stipulated that members counter, report, and expose factionalism if ever they discovered it. By prohibiting factions, the Cuban party was abiding by a fundamental principle of Leninist party organization,[36] but it was also heeding the words of José Martí, the indigenous hero of Cuba's independence struggle:

> [The party's task] is to unite [us] in discipline that is at once firm and democratic. Unity of thought in no way implies the servitude of opinion. It is without a doubt indispensable to the success of all political programs. . . . If our new and strong power is to be found in our unexpected union, we would voluntarily let go of power were we to give up our unity of thought. (*Trabajadores* 9 Dec 80:2)

Following Martí, the prohibition against organized factions was not regarded as incompatible with intra-party dissent. Major party documents often proclaimed the validity of open debate as a prelude to arriving at decisions, and party leaders frequently applauded free discussion within the organization.[37] More cogently, the Statutes called it the duty, even the right, of every member to "express his opinion."[38] The party had high ideals for open discussion, but these were surely not always realized in practice. For example, two workers (nonparty members) told me that, from their own experience, lower-ranking party members felt it was not worthwhile to speak up freely, in part because their comments would have no impact on decision making.[39]

The 1st Party Congress stressed that a knowledgeable membership was a prerequisite for free discussion and informed decision making:

> Free discussion, in which every member has the right to defend his or her point of view, regardless of his or her position in the party, has to be genuine. That is, it has to be based on the fact that everyone who will be involved in making the decision has the opportunity, and plenty of time, to become familiar with the topic. Free discussion is not guaranteed by giving people a chance to speak. All members must to be able to become familiar with the subject and to prepare themselves adequately, so that they can freely express their opinions. (Partido Comunista de Cuba 1978:41–42)

Consequently, the party strongly encouraged members to study basic party documents and agreements, some of which established party policy and others of which summarized important information on Cuba's economic, political, social, and cultural status and prospects.[40] Still, much remained to be done in this area. As one worker told me:

> Party members at the worksite can't really explain many of the positions and policies that are backed by the party and that affect workers because they don't understand them themselves. They don't get information. When issues are discussed, they can't follow what is going on, but they agree to whatever is proposed. Then, after the decision is finally made and implemented, they begin to understand its full meaning, and then some of them may not even like it very much.[41]

Two other workers I talked with (nonparty members) expressed similar opinions, but they blamed *militantes'* incomprehension of complex issues on their low educational level. Not surprisingly, these two were also the only ones I interviewed who lacked enthusiasm for the party's policy of increasing its worker component. They argued it would lower the party's intellectual level and narrow its perspective.[42]

In the party's view, free discussion rested not only on well-informed members but also on the implementation of criticism/self-criticism. A basic tenet of Marxist-Leninist group process, criticism/self-criticism has been adopted by a variety of other organizations in an effort to democratize their decision-making processes. Although the party leadership in Cuba frequently and publicly demonstrated its willingness to adhere to this tenet, the most memorable occasion being after the failure of the 10-million-ton sugar harvest, 2d Party Congress documents indicated a need for improvement.

> We should recognize that criticism and self-criticism are not yet practiced as extensively as they should be in the daily activities of the grass-roots organizations and leadership branches of the Party, even though they are absolutely necessary for tackling and correcting the weaknesses and shortcomings that arise in the individual and collective activities of our cadres, members and candidates—especially in the grass-roots organizations and leadership branches—but some encouraging

results have been noted since the Secretariat of the Central Committee adopted an agreement in this regard. The Party branches and organizations should continue to give special attention to rigorously carrying out this norm for Party activities. (Cuban Communist Party 1981a:79)

As this passage suggests, into the 1980s the Cuban party continued to view this principle as a cornerstone of free discussion within its ranks, even while success in its application remained difficult to achieve.[43]

The third line of argument adopted by those who see no changes in the internal party decision-making process centers on the character of prominent party events claimed to epitomize its participatory and democratic character. In particular, party congresses have been judged little more than forums for legitimizing decisions already made by party elites, for socializing members to accept this nondemocratic reality, and for mobilizing them to work hard within these limitations. The Political Bureau and the Secretariat, according to one assessment, "guided" and "supervised" preparations for the 1st Party Congress and had "veto power" over everything that could be submitted to it, thus rendering the Congress relatively unimportant in the party decision-making process.[44] Nor has voting at congresses and at other party meetings been viewed as genuine participation, a position lent credence by the regularity with which party votes were virtually unanimous.[45]

But do such interpretations of major party events like the party congresses capture their full significance as party decision-making mechanisms? In my view they do not, because they pay scant notice of the interesting and lengthy middle stage of congressional preparations, the period between the time initial plans for a congress are formulated (generally the responsibility of special commissions of high-ranking Communists) and the time of the actual meeting (where the vast majority of actions are usually approved unanimously). One of many important decisions made at the 1st Party Congress in 1975 was the approval of the party's first set of statutes. A careful look at the middle stage of congressional procedure, with respect to the formulation of these statutes, will contribute to a more informed assessment of the value of party congresses as participatory events.[46]

The first step in formulating the statutes was the issuance of a set of provisional statutes by a high-level party commission.[47] Seminars were organized to clarify them, and special materials were provided on articles that were unclear or the focus of frequent questions. Next, the provisional statutes were submitted to all party nuclei and leadership branches for study and discussion; they were also put into practice by some party branches about a year before the Congress met. On the basis of this practical test, as well as on the discussions and seminars, a second draft of the statutes (Anteproyecto de Estatutos) was prepared.[48]

Discussions on the second draft of the statutes were extensive. They occurred in 99 percent of the nuclei and in intermediate-level leadership bodies, with 86 percent of all *militantes* participating. The discussions produced a total of 1,365 suggestions for changes[49] in all but two of the seventy-one articles comprising the statutes at this stage. Closer examination reveals, however, that on average only one of every thirty-one nuclei forwarded even a single suggestion, whereas one change was suggested by every three municipal committees and seven by each provincial committee.[50] Of more interest is what happened to the 1,365 suggestions. The decision on each suggestion was left to the top-level commissions that planned the Congress and drafted the statutes. Not all suggestions ultimately found their way into the final document. A small number, reportedly calling for considerable substantive alterations in the statutes (their content is not known), were among those not incorporated, but it is significant that they were at least proposed. The majority of those omitted dealt with details felt to be covered more appropriately in party by-laws. According to Isidoro Malmierca, the 1,365 suggestions led to modification of two-thirds of the seventy statute articles, with sixteen of these undergoing major revisions.

A short article dealing with voluntary and involuntary deactivation received so many proposals for change (493) that Malmierca joked that the article's number—27—was its only feature still recognizable in the end. The intense interest sparked by article 27 indicated that party members wanted assurance that involuntary deactivation could be distinguished from disciplinary procedures, which might also result in termination of party membership. *Militantes* also seemed concerned that voluntary deactivation be a clear option.[51] Proposals called for making the application of the deactivation option more explicit, specifying the reasons for deactivation, subjecting a nucleus's decision to deactivate a member to a vote and to ratification by a higher-level body, devising a process for reinstatement of a deactivated member, and giving a deactivated member a certificate showing what party work had been completed. Most of the proposals relating to article 27 found their way into the final draft of the statutes. Voluntary deactivation was clarified; by-laws were to be drawn up listing possible reasons for deactivation; it was stated specifically that deactivation was not a sanction; deactivation had to be approved by a two-thirds vote of the nucleus and ratified by a higher-level party organ. The various proposals for altering article 27, and their fate, revealed that the middle stage of Congress preparations could be significant in the party decision-making process. The proposals put forward at this stage, which were substantive rather than frivolous, were largely incorporated into the final draft of the statutes.

The middle-stage discussions led to a third draft of the statutes (Proyecto de Estatutos), the version presented to a commission of 249 Congress delegates. They called for clarification of certain points and took four votes on additional proposed changes. Only then were the statutes submitted to the full Congress, which approved them, not unexpectedly, by unanimous vote. This review of the complete congressional procedure on just one decision made at the Congress, puts this final unanimous vote (and others like it) in perspective. Despite the doubts raised by unanimous votes, viewed in context, they were less important indicators of the overall quality and level of member participation in decision making through party congresses than many commentators have suggested.

NON-MEMBER INFLUENCE IN THE PARTY

So far I have concentrated on changes in workers' potential to influence the party through their status as *militantes*. Yet, because the majority of Cuban workers were not party members, no matter how high the proportion of worker-members nor how open party decision-making procedures, this alone yields an incomplete picture of how direct producers might affect party functioning. To round out the analysis of the party's ability to serve as an avenue for democratization, we must also consider whether and how workers who were *not* party members were able to influence the party's decisions and actions.

The first relevant consideration is how party members were chosen. The Cuban selection procedure was apparently unique among socialist countries. Although non-members did not have the final word in selecting *militantes*, their participation in the process helped ensure that party members would have the confidence and the support of Cuban working people. Following a short period during which new party members were appointed, sometimes secretly, by current members, Castro publicly supported workers' involvement in the selection process as the PURS was being formed. At that time political cadres held work-center assemblies where nominations for candidates for party membership were made (Domínguez 1978:211–12, 365; LeoGrande 1978:8–9; 1979b:463; 1981:612). The procedures for involving workers in the selection of party members soon became regularized and were eventually codified in the party's first statutes.

The first step in joining the Cuban Communist party was to be elected by one's fellow workers as an exemplary worker. Exemplary workers were a select group. One worker, a party member, estimated that only three of every one hundred workers held this title.[52] Elections in work-center assemblies were held at varying intervals,[53] becoming more frequent in times of rapid party growth. In the first half of 1975, for example, more than three hundred thousand workers participated in assemblies to choose exemplary workers (Fidel Castro 1976:233). Assemblies were also held more often at work centers in economic sectors targeted for party growth. Some workers in these sectors told me that such assemblies were practically an annual event, whereas some workers in low priority sectors said that their work centers no longer proposed potential party members at all.[54]

After nomination as an exemplary worker, a candidate's qualifications were evaluated by the assembly.[55] According to one of Harnecker's (1980:37) interviewees: "If I nominate Olivares, for example, I've got to explain why I am nominating him, and we see how others react. . . . Maybe if they know something that goes against Olivares, they may stand up and say: 'Well look, I understand Olivares is not qualified because of this, that and so on.'" When Harnecker commented that becoming a party member seemed difficult, the interviewees agreed. "It's not easy," they responded. Available information suggests that workers took seriously their role in selecting exemplary workers and that assemblies were active, often charged meetings.[56] "*Everyone* shows up at these meetings!" claimed one informant. "Analyzing potential party members is a delicate and important task," said another.[57] Nominations could be withdrawn or rejected on the basis of facts or opinions that emerged in assembly discussions.[58] Nominees could also decline. Age, inability or unwillingness to continue studying, and family problems were some of the reasons. More common, however, were sentiments like those expressed by my next-door neighbor, a working woman who was caring for her pregnant niece and two young children: "I declined because being a party member is an awful lot of work and responsibility. It's voluntary, you know, whether you want to be evaluated for membership. I was honored, though there is no real advantage to being a member. I just want to have my free time free"![59] A strong supporter of the revolution and definitely not lazy, she merely expressed what many were aware of—that the demands of party membership were taxing. As I discovered, members' readiness to take on party work, in addition to their regular jobs and domestic obligations, was closely tied to the respect that most of them enjoyed among their co-workers.

Selection as an exemplary worker, however, was only the first step in the process of becoming a *militante*. Once in the pool of exemplary workers, a worker had to apply to become a party member. The application was followed by a party investigation of the worker's background, beginning in prerevolutionary days. If the evaluation was favorable, the worker was accepted into the party on a one-year, probationary basis.[60] If the application was unfavorable, not an uncommon event, the worker could reapply for membership after having had a chance to correct whatever deficiencies blocked her or his entry.[61] Harnecker (1980: esp. 13–19) interviewed a number of workers who, after being chosen as exemplary workers, had applied to join the party and had been turned down, some more than once. Most unsuccessful applicants seemed to take their rejection in stride, though one worker told me that while you could reapply as many times as you liked, it was embarrassing to be turned down, so many workers waited a while before reapplying.[62] I was also told that, after the probationary period, but before the party nucleus admitted a candidate to full membership, the candidate was again brought before an assembly of workers for their approval. I do not know if this procedure was standard practice.[63]

There were, however, other avenues to party membership which did not rely so heavily on worker input. Those wishing to join the party could apply directly, often with the encouragement of the local nucleus. Some *militantes* told me they did not particularly like this method. "It's better all the way around," said one, "when the masses propose the members."[64] A more important alternative to the exemplary-worker route to membership was entrance through the UJC which could, however, require some input from the outside. One method of joining the UJC was to be elected a model youth at work or school.[65] Nonetheless, the UJC was criticized for being too exclusive and for having too many students and not enough workers directly linked to production and services (Domínguez 1978:321–22). Beginning in the early 1970s, the organization took steps to rectify both deficiencies, with at least some success. Castro announced at the 2d Party Congress that the number of working-class UJC members almost doubled between 1975 and 1980, though the total was still only seventy-nine thousand (Cuban Communist Party 1981*a*:74; Partido Comunista de Cuba 1978:22).

Despite these efforts, and the fact that some youths were elected to the UJC, people who joined the party via the UJC were subjected to much less intensive scrutiny by the workforce than those who entered via the exemplary-worker route. It is important, therefore, to know what proportion of party members entered through the UJC and if the proportion changed. Reliable data on this topic are hard to find, however, and partly as a result, a mini-debate has occurred among observers of the Cuban Communist party over which route was being favored. Domínguez (1978:315–16) argued that by the mid-1970s the UJC avenue was being emphasized, and several years later LeoGrande (1980:405) agreed. In 1981, however, Lourdes Casal and Marifeli Pérez-Stable (1981:85) claimed a lack of evidence that the exemplary-worker method was losing hold. On the contrary, they contended that Casal's 1977–78 interviews revealed that the method was gaining more attention because of the party's emphasis on improving its worker composition. Both positions contain some truth, which is probably why the sketchy figures available indicated little change in the proportion of new party members coming from the UJC between the 1st and 2d Party Congresses.[66] On the one hand, the party clearly stressed the UJC entry method (Cuban Communist Party 1981*b*:6, 1981*a*:291;

Partido Comunista de Cuba 1978:28–30). Yet improving its social composition seemed to have been an even more pressing priority.[67]

Despite the party's attention to the UJC entry route, workers whom I queried about entrance into the party ordinarily responded by recounting the exemplary-worker process in full detail. Most of them favored this method, even though they knew about alternative avenues to party membership. If as widely held as it seemed to be, this prejudice together with the emphasis on increased worker membership, may help explain why the UJC entry route did not become more predominant. Since the worksite party nucleus was ultimately in charge of admitting new members, the tenacity of the exemplary-worker route probably reflected a preference at grass-roots levels, among members and non-members alike, for the method that gave workers the most influence in the selection of *militantes*.

The indirect influence over the party wielded by rank-and-file workers via their involvement in the selection of party members was complemented in the 1970s and early 1980s by other more direct means, both formal and informal, through which non-members could affect the party's stance, decisions, and actions.

After the party began to assume a more active and visible presence in Cuba, rank-and-file workers (as well as citizens in general) were given a number of formal opportunities to comment on party positions and policies, as well as on problems facing the country.[68] In structured, island-wide series of workplace assemblies, party leaders solicited producers' opinions and comments. Workers' power at these events, however, was advisory only. Yet the topics on which non-members' input was gathered in these forums were usually of the utmost economic and political importance. They were issues around which policies with significant ramifications for work and production would ultimately be formulated.

Examples of formal party efforts to solicit the opinions of non-members occurred during preparations for the 1st and 2d Party congresses.[69] In the period preceding the 1st Party Congress the Programmatic Platform was submitted to non-members in 110,000 meetings covering a four-week period and involving four million citizens (González 1976:4).[70] Despite the large number of meetings and participants, the discussions yielded only 179 different proposals for change in the Programmatic Platform, though the same proposal was sometimes suggested at a number of assemblies.[71] One of the most widely proposed recommendations concerned the need for improvement in housing, which led to changes in several parts of the Platform.[72] Many of the party's Theses, including the Third Thesis, on the equality of women, were also scrutinized by non-members in approximately 700,000 assemblies attended by an estimated 19 million persons, the most inclusive series of such assemblies on record (Fidel Castro 1976:240; and Malmierca 1976: 92). The party put substantial effort into preparing and conducting the assemblies and into tabulating and analyzing the results. Although not all the meetings were organized among workers per se, the figures suggest that many Cuban producers had more than one formal opportunity to comment on the party's Theses.

The most widely discussed 2d Party Congress document was the *Socio-Economic Guidelines for 1981–5*, later to serve as the basis for Cuba's second five-year plan. This lengthy document set forth general goals for the economy as a whole (e.g., industrial, agricultural, wage, and export policies and the perfection of the SDPE), as well as more detailed quantitative and qualitative targets for about thirty economic sectors.[73] The Congress revealed that the guidelines had been discussed by nearly 2,593,000 workers, peasants, and students. In all they proposed 7,515 changes, about 7 percent of which were incorporated into the final draft. Most of the suggestions reportedly dealt with "concrete issues relating to specific economic sectors," rather than with the overall strategy put forward in the guidelines (Partido Comunista de Cuba 1981:179–80).

In talking with Cubans, however, I soon discovered that these formal mechanisms were not the only or the most frequently employed ones through which non-members communicated their ideas and opinions to the party; nor were they necessarily considered the most effective. A more common way in which rank-and-file workers exerted influence over the party was through their informal personal relationships with party members at work. In its statutes the party encouraged these informal exchanges, and, without exception, everyone I interviewed knew exactly which of their fellow workers were party members, partly because of the exemplary-worker method of selecting members but also because party members were usually influential at the worksite. This alone was no guarantee, of course, that an ordinary worker would feel comfortable in approaching a *militante* with a problem or a criticism or that such a worker would consider it worth the trouble to do so. My clear impression, however, was that many Cuban workers felt that party members in their immediate work groups were accessible and that they would definitely consider consulting informally with a *militante*. A few workers seemed to regard approaching *militantes* as almost a right. "This is one of the multiple routes available to workers with problems," a member of the Health Workers' Union insisted.[74]

Comparison of my interviews in 1982 and 1983 with those conducted by Pérez-Stable in 1975 suggests that non-members' accessibility to party members at Cuban worksites had increased. Only two of Pérez-Stable's (1976:43–44) fifty-seven informants acknowledged that they would take worksite problems to party members, but when I posed the same question in the early 1980s, more than half of the workers I interviewed told me they would do so. Similarly, in response to a question asking what workers could do if they had a bad boss, about two-thirds of my respondents said that one alternative open to them was going to the party nucleus. A couple of explanations may help account for the differences between Pérez-Stable's responses and my own. First, when I conducted interviews, the party was much larger than in 1975; nuclei existed in more work centers and a higher proportion of party members in the nuclei were themselves workers. More workers were thus able to become personally acquainted with *militantes* at work and to use such contacts informally to convey their opinions to the party. Second, as the party had also become more influential and more active, non-members who felt compelled to air their opinions were more likely to perceive individual *militantes* as key people with whom to communicate. In other words, what party members said and did at the point of production was seen as more pivotal to the eventual outcome of a situation or resolution of a problem; non-members would therefore view it as more worth their while to approach them.

Nevertheless, workers were reluctant to discuss certain issues with *militantes*. "Going to a particular party member and criticizing his or her actions *as a party member*, to his or her face, is out," said one worker.[75] So touchy a situation could be handled more diplomatically and more effectively by approaching some other party member.[76] Complaining about an ineffective or unqualified party member was an internal party matter and, as another worker put it: "You don't go to the party to criticize their internal affairs or procedures."[77] Nor, I gathered, would it be appropriate for a worker to criticize established party policy in this informal fashion, except under unusual circumstances. Workers discerned a fine line here, however, for many acknowledged they could talk to party members about policies already adopted or supported by the party (e.g., Laws 32 and 36 or the SDPE) and could express opinions on specific difficulties attending the implementation of any such policy (e.g, managerial abuse of Law 32 or unsatisfactory distribution of the stimulation funds).[78]

Moreover, non-members' ability to influence the party through informal channels was decreased by its lack of formal or institutional grounding.[79] The effectiveness of informal channels of communication, therefore, came to depend on idiosyncratic factors likely to vary from one situation or work center to another. For instance, a non-member's individual characteristics, such as their prestige or position in the job hierarchy, might influence a party member's reaction to their suggestions or criticisms. Equally likely, particular characteristics of party members might affect their accessibility and their aggressiveness in pushing a worker's point. What were an individual's motivations in becoming a party member? Might he or she harbor ambitions of moving up in the ranks of the party or in the internal labor market? To what extent did a *militante* understand or empathize with the worker's position?[80] Did she or he have enough confidence and experience to argue successfully on behalf of a non-member? To pose such questions underscores the importance of the method through which party members were chosen in the first place. Strengthening non-member input into the selection process, though it offers no firm guarantee, increases the likelihood that the people eventually chosen as party members would treat their obligation to be receptive to the concerns of non-members both seriously and sensitively.

CONCLUSION: DEMOCRACY WITHIN AND OUTSIDE THE PARTY(IES)

The issue of whether production can be democratized under socialism has often been distilled into a simple set of questions concerning the single, vanguard party: Is such a party necessary, though clearly it is not sufficient, to defend social ownership, viewed by many as fundamental to enduring and thoroughgoing democratization of production? Or, alternatively, does such a party pose the most serious internal threat to democratization at work?

The foregoing examination of change in the Cuban Communist party suggests that posing a different set of questions might prove more fruitful. It may not be as important to ask whether one party or multiple parties will best foster economic democracy, as it is to investigate how much influence working people exert over the party(ies)—a question that directs attention to a number of the democratization considerations raised in Chapter 1. Nor may it be as important to ask whether one or more parties is most conducive to economic democracy, as it is to address the issue of multiplicity. For the democratization of production to flourish, the party(ies) must operate in a participatory environment where, among other things, unions are strong and active and where viable structures exist at the workplace for involving people in economic decision making. The party(ies) in such an environment, *and* over which workers have considerable influence, provides one additional avenue through which producers can be included in making decisions that affect their working lives. The availability of multiple channels that allow workers to voice their opinions and act on their preferences, one of the most important of which is the democratized party(ies), provides the most reasonable hope for lasting and meaningful control by the many.

Chapter 5

CHANGES IN ENTERPRISE AUTONOMY

From Budgetary Finance to the SDPE

To be democratic a system of production must provide for workers' involvement in decision making both at the worksite and above it. For democratization of both arenas to occur, economic decision making can be neither excessively centralized nor excessively decentralized. In socialist countries, overcentralization has been the more common impediment to the democratization of production. The center so often overshadowed the workplace that little of import remained to be decided at the point of production. Democratization of the workplace thus became a moot point: Economic decision-making forums above the worksite proved meaningless in the absence of any opportunity for producers to participate where they worked; the greater possibilities afforded at the workplace for involving larger numbers of workers in making decisions of very direct and immediate import to them, in smaller and more intimate groups, were lost.

In Cuba attempts were made from the mid-1970s into the 1980s to decentralize economic decision making with the implementation of El Sistema de Dirección y Planificación de la Economía (SDPE). This period was preceded, however, by one of budgetary finance, in which Cuban enterprises had very little decision-making autonomy.

THE GROWTH OF BUDGETARY FINANCE

The "Great Debate" of the early 1960s in Cuba between advocates of a budgetary-finance method of economic organization and supporters of a cost-accounting or self-financing method has been well publicized (Guevara et al. 1974; Edelstein 1985:180–81; Zim-

balist 1985:215–17). Che Guevara, the best-known proponent of
the former position, instituted budgetary finance in the industrial
sector before 1966, and, there was an attempt to organize the entire economy in the same manner.

Although supporters of the two positions agreed on some issues, such as the necessity for national economic planning, budgetary finance imposed stricter limits on the decision-making
powers of individual enterprises than did cost accounting. Under
budgetary finance, the basic production unit ceased to be the single
enterprise. Instead, "consolidated enterprises" were formed in each
economic sector, grouping numerous (sometimes all) and often
widely dispersed firms (e.g., sugar, textiles, mining). By the mid-
1960s the entire industrial sector in Cuba consisted of only fifty-six
consolidados and the agricultural sector of no more than eighty.[1] All
production units within each *consolidado*, sometimes numbering in
the hundreds, had a common management and were directly subordinate to a central ministry. Even though economic plans were
often not operative during the 1960s, under budgetary finance
planning targets were established at the center with no participation by production units. All inputs, including labor, investment,
and operating funds, were centrally allocated. Individual enterprises, not considered independent financial units and not expected to balance their budgets or to produce a surplus, could not
establish credit or secure bank loans. Their performance was not
evaluated on a monetary basis; any deficits they incurred were
merely canceled in the national budget. Revenues resulting from
enterprise operations were remitted to the center, rather than being retained for use by the units that had yielded them. As one
high-ranking government official remarked, during this period:
"Decisions made by the work units didn't mean much" because all
matters affecting work and production were determined above the
enterprise.[2] Under these conditions, neither workers nor even enterprise management exercised much control over production or
service delivery.

INSTITUTION AND CONSOLIDATION OF THE SDPE

Cuban efforts to decentralize economic decision making began formally in December 1975, when the SDPE was adopted. Its
implementation began in earnest in 1977. Although the pace at

which the SDPE was instituted was less rapid than anticipated, the subsequent period saw continuing consolidation of the new management and planning system throughout the island (Mesa-Lago 1982:131).

The purpose of the SDPE was a dramatic reordering of the complex relationships among state organs, administrative bodies, individual enterprises, and direct producers. This end was attempted through a variety of methods. First, monetary-commercial relationships were introduced in the economy, meaning an increased reliance on prices, credit, taxes, budgets, interest rates, cost calculations, and profits as devices for regulating and measuring economic performance.[3] At the same time, the independence of individual production and service units vis-à-vis national and subnational political and administrative bodies was increased. Separate spheres of action and responsibility for each were demarcated. Ideally, under the SDPE, Cuban enterprises were to become relatively autonomous from such supraworksite organs.

Despite changes enacted under the SDPE, however, most Cuban sources argued in the early and mid-1980s that many production units were still not sufficiently autonomous (Quesada 1980b; Junta Central de Planificación [JUCEPLAN] 1980b:356; Domínguez 1982:48–49; *Bohemia* 23 Sept 83:56; Mesa-Lago 1988:65). Superordinate bodies sometimes demanded things or took actions that violated the independence of individual enterprises, and the latter occasionally hesitated to take advantage of opportunities for autonomy granted by the SDPE.[4] The antecedents to these problems in Cuba were similar to those that have plagued decentralization reforms in other socialist countries: opposition to the reforms from some supraworksite political and economic authorities and some workers and enterprise managers, difficulties with the reforms themselves (e.g., their complexity and a reluctance to alter price structures), problems endemic to the overall functioning of socialist political and economic systems (e.g., shortages and poor quality), and characteristics of the global political economy.[5]

Clearly, the gains in enterprise autonomy made under the SDPE did not fully satisfy its formulators. Most outside analysts of the new system also argue that it failed to produce a fundamental change in the underlying logic and dynamic of the Cuban economy (Roca 1986; White 1987; Zimbalist 1989). Nonetheless, most Cubans and non-Cubans also recognize that the SDPE made limited progress in realizing some of its decentralization objectives. Probably this progress varied by enterprise and by economic sector: An administrator I interviewed claimed that gains in enterprise autonomy at his steel factory were "enormous," while a planning official reported frequently being asked by other managers, "When will we have autonomous enterprises?"[6] Although the SDPE accomplished only part of what it set out to, it is instructive to examine exactly how it intended to increase enterprise autonomy in three key areas of economic activity: planning, production, and the disbursement of earnings.

Planning. In essays written after adoption of the SDPE, Cuban economist Raúl Martell (1979:92–93) argued that, though individual enterprises should not be totally free to determine all aspects of their plans, neither should the center have the power to dictate plan content down to the "last nail" needed in production.[7] Some planning decisions had to be made at the base where such details were best known.[8] To explain how Martell's general characterization was to have been translated into practice, I begin by examining the different categories of figures that went into making up the yearly technical-economic plan (*plan técnico-económico*) for an individual enterprise. In its final form this annual plan was composed of figures that embodied proposals originating both within and above the enterprise.

Decisions on Cuba's national economic goals, priorities, and strategies were political and were made by the country's top party and government bodies. Within these broad parameters, the Central Planning Board (JUCEPLAN), assumed responsibility for devising a set of *preliminary* figures that considered, among other things, the division of the gross social product between investment and consumption and the role of the export sector. This was accomplished through consultation, review, and information exchange within JUCEPLAN and between JUCEPLAN, on the one hand, and ministries, state committees, and various political bodies, on the other.[9] Out of this process emerged a set of *control figures* which set more concrete targets for each economic sector. Once disaggregated, the control figures were sent to individual production and service delivery units.

The control figures, however, did not constitute the final production plan for the worksite. Instead, enterprises then began the process of reviewing and revising the plan figures sent down to them. On the basis of the control figures, a production unit proposed an array of *directive figures*. Discussions to that end were held in over 94 percent of all Cuban enterprises in 1980.[10] In arriving at their proposed directive figures, production units were instructed to make every effort to maximize efficiency, labor productivity, and quality, to avoid technical bottlenecks, and to ensure that their proposals were both well reasoned and workable. They had also to analyze the demand for their products or services and evaluate their past performance.[11] Discussions of the plan at the enterprise level were not without difficulties. Enterprises were criticized for analyses that lacked sufficient depth and sophistication. Many such criticisms were traced to the complexity of economic planning, the lack of technical expertise within enterprises, the short period enterprises had participated in the planning process, and the fact that they often had inadequate time to complete their planning tasks.

Once the enterprise had compiled its directive figures they were sent back up the administrative ladder for balancing, cross-checking, re-aggregation, and approval. Which supraworksite organ initially received the enterprise's proposed directive figures depended on whether the work unit was a national or a local one (Quesada 1981:32–34). Because of their strategic importance for the economy as a whole, national work units (e.g., refineries, fertilizer plants, and large sugar *centrales*) reported directly to a national administrative body. Local work units, on the other hand, were subordinate to either municipal or to provincial organs of People's Power (OPP), as their economic activity was mainly relevant to a particular area of the country.[12] If some or all of the directive figures proposed by an enterprise were not judged acceptable, superordinate bodies could reject or amend them, but they had to give reasons for so doing. The second review of SDPE implementation, however, revealed that in 1979 this occurred in only slightly less than half the cases. The same review criticized superordinate bodies for submitting directive figures more demanding than those proposed by enterprises without explaining how these more ambitious targets might be met (JUCEPLAN 1980*b*:121, 232). With final approval, however, the directive figures formed the basis of an enterprise's yearly technical-economic plan, and the production unit was obliged to uphold them.

Enterprises engaged in two additional kinds of planning. First, most of them broke down their annual technical-economic plan into a number of operating plans for smaller subdivisions, such as departments, sections, shops, and work centers. This procedure familiarized workers in each subunit with the activities necessary to meet the goals of the overall enterprise plan. It also provided a basis for evaluating a subunit's efficiency, which was linked to material rewards under the SDPE. Enterprises apparently had almost complete independence in developing operating plans for their subunits. Although ultimately limited by the parameters of the technical-economic plan, enterprise-level decisions on these lower-level operating plans directly affected what workers did, how hard they had to work, and what their rewards would be. Presumably the operating plans were devised under the supervision of the *consejos de dirección*, meaning producers' participation was indirect.

Second, enterprises seemed to have had a high degree of independence in formulating plans for secondary production. Under the SDPE they were encouraged, whenever possible, to produce goods and deliver services beyond those formally stipulated in their plans. The rationale was to raise the standard of living and to increase enterprise earnings through imaginative use of leftover materials that might otherwise have gone to waste. Secondary planning was supposed to coincide with development of an enterprise's yearly technical-economic plan, but it was solely the province of individual production units.

Although secondary production was another planning area in which Cuban enterprises were to have expanded their autonomy under the SDPE, its significance can only be determined by having some idea of its importance in the Cuban economy. Secondary production was subject to limitations. For example, it could not interfere with planned production or with promised deliveries, and raw or new materials used could not exceed 30 percent of all the materials the enterprise consumed. Moreover, the chronic shortage of material inputs of all types placed severe constraints on the overall potential for secondary production. On the other hand, according to a JUCEPLAN official, enterprises' planned production varied widely, sometimes dropping as low as 40 percent of their total production. And, perhaps because secondary production became too important in some enterprises, JUCEPLAN, just four months after the legal regulations governing secondary production were promulgated, decreed that workers could earn only 20 percent of their basic salaries in this endeavor.[13]

Production. For a complete analysis of the relationship between enterprises and supraworksite bodies, we must move beyond plan formulation to plan execution or production. It is in this area that the SDPE actually had the most to say about enterprise autonomy.[14] Only with knowledge of what kinds of production decisions were made at the enterprise level can we understand the possibilities for the democratization of micro-level decision making introduced with the SDPE.

The SDPE's prime rule governing production was that an enterprise realize enough income to cover its expenses. In reality, an enterprise was expected, not merely to break even, but to earn more than it spent, to strive for "constrained profit maximization" (Bornstein 1977:301). In working toward this end, Cuban enterprises were subject to two general types of SDPE stipulations— those governing the management and utilization of resources (material, human, and monetary), and those governing the relationship of enterprises to one another. Examining these two areas of SDPE control helps clarify the degree of autonomy Cuban enterprises had in executing their economic plans.

A newly created Cuban enterprise received both its fixed capital (*medios básicos* [e.g., equipment, machinery, buildings]) and its working capital (*medios de rotación* [e.g., raw materials, replacement parts, fuels]) from the state. Bounded by the societal responsibility to use these material resources as productively and efficiently as possible, the enterprise had some maneuverability in their management. For instance, it could rent fixed capital to or from other enterprises or sell it with previous authorization from the appropriate superior organ. The income thereby generated was divided between the enterprise and the state. Within certain constraints, enterprises were also free to sell excess working-capital inventories. To facilitate the exchange process, the state set up special markets where enterprises could buy and sell such resources (JUCEPLAN 1980*b*:23). The first such market was held in 1979, and, together with that held in 1980, realized sales totaling 40 million pesos.[15] Enterprises could also dispose of defective items they produced themselves. It is important to remember, however, that Cuba continually faced shortages of many such fixed and working capital assets. Thus, although there was undoubtedly a large market for the extra equipment, raw materials, and so on that any enterprise might want to dispose of, there were probably fewer production units that would care to sell or rent them, even though those that did might expect a nice price. In actual practice, therefore, enterprises were likely to have had less autonomy vis-à-vis their material resources than SDPE stipulations allowed them.

In managing and utilizing labor, Cuban enterprises had to comply with a variety of centrally specified laws and regulations, detailing both their obligations to employees and their societal responsibilities to make efficient use of human resources.[16] Moreover, enterprise autonomy in wage and salary disbursement was subject to important central constraints under the SDPE. In order to ensure that an enterprise's projected increase in productivity was larger than the average salary increase, the National Bank examined the quarterly breakdown of the enterprise plan. Then, when the enterprise made its last salary withdrawal for the quarter, the bank compared the amount the enterprise had planned to pay in wages with its actual production levels. If warranted by these levels, the enterprise could withdraw more than it had planned from its salary fund. It had to get prior approval from a superior organ, however, if it wanted to withdraw more in wages than its production levels permitted. It was then required to present that organ and the National Bank with a detailed explanation of its plans to rectify the situation and its estimates of the time it needed to pay back the excess it requested for wages. Moreover, the bank could send a representative to verify the enterprise's explanations and to approve its plans for making amends. If the representative found that the excess salary claim had been caused by factors beyond the enterprise's control, its superior organ made up the difference. If, on the other hand, the claim were judged unjustified, the enterprise had to make good the overdraft within a year by withdrawing less from its salary fund than it was entitled to in subsequent quarters.[17]

Although the SDPE dictated enterprise subordination to the center in such respects, in others it gave production units more latitude in managing human resources. The greatest gain in this area for individual enterprises was the authority to contract directly for labor and to sign individual employment agreements with workers, which enterprises began to do on a trial basis in 1979.[18] Whereasas workers previously were allocated to enterprises by regional branches of the Ministry of Labor, now they could approach employers directly or seek work through the municipal employment office run by the OPP (People's Power). For their part, employers could initiate their own searches for workers, soliciting help from the unions and the Cuban Women's Federation (FMC), if they so desired. Individual employment contracts stipulated the worker's obligation to perform his or her assigned job satisfactorily as well as the enterprise's obligation to pay the worker a specified salary, to guarantee certain working conditions, and to fulfill any other responsibilities contained in the collective work commitments or in the enterprise's own statutes. A contract could be terminated for various reasons, among them the employee's willingness to end it, within a period not exceeding four months after notice was given. By the beginning of 1981 more than 855,000 Cuban workers had signed employment contracts, and, although difficulties with the new system were noted in the press, the anticipated problem of higher turnover rates apparently did not materialize. In fact, just the opposite was reported.[19]

In the area of monetary resources, within certain centrally determined limits, the SDPE also increased firm autonomy. Monetary assets, which were part of an enterprise's working capital, came initially from the state.[20] Thereafter, Cuban enterprises were expected to aim for financial self-sufficiency. Some of them, however, were unable to operate in the black, either temporarily or permanently, because of international prices or the government's commitment to keep prices low on certain commodities. In post-SDPE Cuba, therefore, the state clearly intended to subsidize certain firms for indefinite periods.[21] The overall intent of the SDPE, however, was to minimize the extent to which Cuban production and service delivery units were dependent on state subsidies.

Although financial self-sufficiency was the goal of many enterprises, throughout much of the period under consideration, most depended on the center for fixed capital investment funding. Once approved, funds were assigned to a special bank account, and each production unit was responsible for using them efficiently and for carrying out its investment projects on schedule. An enterprise could also divert some of its own resources into investment and repair projects ("small and medium-sized" ones, according to one JUCEPLAN official),[22] so long as this did not impair its ability to meet production targets. Indeed, the share of enterprise-financed investment rose from 1 percent of total investment financing in 1981 to 30 percent in 1985. Nevertheless, in the main, the state still decided the character of these investments (Zimbalist 1990*b*:12–13).

This system of financing investments had problems: Firms

complained they did not receive investment funds when they needed them or in the amounts required; some enterprises drew on operating funds to finance investments, thus reducing their ability to meet other financial obligations; efficiency of investments was difficult to monitor. The challenge of the future was to develop a more decentralized investment scheme that minimized existing problems without sacrificing sound, nationwide economic planning. Possibilities considered at the time included strengthening the role of administrative bodies in financing the investments of enterprises subordinate to them and giving enterprises more leeway to finance investments from their stimulation funds (see below), something proposed in the early days of the SDPE but later abandoned. In 1985 National Bank credits began to be extended for fixed capital investments.[23]

Under the SDPE, firms were free to solicit credit from the National Bank to finance purchases of working capital, though they were prohibited from loaning money to one another. The bank granted loans and established terms, not only on the basis of the acceptability of the enterprise's application, but also in accordance with its own guidelines, which were based on national economic priorities. Interest rates were set centrally at 6 to 12 percent (Quesada 1981:94). The state tried to encourage particular kinds of credit applications by offering lower interest rates. An enterprise that did not meet its repayment schedule incurred penalties. Nevertheless, many enterprises failed to do so, prompting the bank to extend the repayment period on outstanding loans. Data gathered during the second review of the SDPE showed that the credit repayment situation deteriorated for a second time in early 1980 (JUCEPLAN 1980*b*; esp. 210–12). Reminiscent of the situation vis-à-vis the excess resources markets, however, the autonomy gained by enterprises, as a result of financing their own working- and fixed-capital investments, met limits due to economy-wide scarcities and inconsistencies within the SDPE itself (White 1987: 159).

Lastly, with regard to enterprise control over its monetary resources, each Cuban enterprise came to be considered an independent financial unit under the SDPE. Indeed, without this prescription, the SDPE's goal of promoting enterprise solvency could not have been realized. Production units therefore had to assume a great deal more responsibility for their own financial management than they had in the 1960s. Each enterprise developed a financial plan based on the various categories incorporated within its technical-economic plan. The financial plan, specifying the source and the destination of an enterprise's monetary resources,[24] had to be approved by the appropriate superior body. Each enterprise directed its own accounting process, though it was required to supply financial information to and could be audited by its superordinate central state or local government organ. Each enterprise maintained its own bank account and was subject to financial penalties if it did not keep it in good order.[25]

The degree of autonomy Cuban enterprises exercised in their relationships with one another, both as suppliers and as consumers of goods and services, was also affected by the SDPE. Before the SDPE horizontal relations among enterprises were minimal, but afterwards monetary-commercial connections between firms were stressed, and the regulatory role of contracts in such relationships was emphasized. As a result, a new area of decision-making authority opened up for Cuban firms, which began to negotiate such contracts and later modify them, if desired.

Enterprise authority varied, however, according to the contract, of which there were two types: *contratos planificados* and *contratos no planificados*. An enterprise entered into the former in order to fulfill its technical-economic plan. According to a JUCEPLAN official, supraworksite bodies decided on the parties to the *contratos planificados* and specified the quantities of goods to be produced or the services to be delivered. An individual enterprise, however, could set delivery dates, specify the quality of goods or services, and establish product or service specifications. According to the same official, an enterprise had "total autonomy" with regard to its *contratos no planificados*, which were not tied to the fulfillment of its technical-economic plan.[26]

The introduction of inter-enterprise contracts was accompanied by the establishment of a state arbitration system (SAE) to handle contractual disputes. Arbitration panels began to function in late 1980, resolving pre- and post-contractual disputes, deciding on penalties and awards, and even at times modifying or annulling contested agreements.[27] Although increasing numbers of contracts were signed by Cuban enterprises, in its first nine months the SAE heard only 944 cases, a number considered inadequate. Its smallness drew attention to a difficult problem: Since inputs were chronically in short supply, enterprises were extremely reluctant to damage their relationships with suppliers by bringing them before state bodies to respond to contractual complaints. This structurally induced tendency was likely to persist despite the SAE's public pledge to go on the offensive against parties afflicted with "enterprise inertia" and unilaterally to ferret out violations of inter-enterprise contracts.[28]

Disbursement of Earnings. Under the budgetary-finance system, enterprises had virtually no control over the disbursement of their earnings: all the income generated by work units was remitted to the national government. Under the SDPE, although the national government continued to claim the major share of these earnings through circulation taxes, social security contributions, and payments for fixed capital resources, among other levies,[29] work units enjoyed considerable control over a portion of their own earnings.

The SDPE achieved this improvement through the creation of enterprise stimulation funds (*fondos de estimulación*). The idea was implemented in 1979 in an experimental group of 191 enterprises. By 1985, the number of enterprises that formed such funds had grown to 1,167. (Zimbalist and Brundenius 1989:135, 189). Although Jorge Domínguez (1978:420) described the funds as "profit sharing" schemes, a closer look at the methods for forming and distributing them suggests this characterization is misleading.

Stimulation funds were of two types: The prize fund (*fondo de premios*) gave material rewards to workers; the fund for housing construction and socio-cultural projects (*fondo para medidas socio-culturales y construcción de viviendas*) financed housing, day care, canteens, medical and sports facilities, and other projects benefiting the work collective. The administration and the union in each enterprise together decided how to use the latter fund. At a steel factory outside Havana, which first formed its fund in 1981, I was told the money had been used to build dwellings and a neighborhood health clinic. The amount of time worked, base wages paid, and bonuses earned were all considered in the distribution of rewards from the prize fund; the amount of the prizes top managers could receive was limited. Approximately 90 percent of the prize fund was divided among the workforce as a whole, with up to 10 percent reserved for each unit's most outstanding workers; some workers could thus receive a double award. A worker who had a poor attendance record, whose work has been of consistently poor quality, or who had regularly violated other work rules received only a portion of her or his prize, or perhaps none at all; this decision was made jointly by the administration and the union at the enterprise level. Workers familiar with the funds told me that, partly as a consequence, base-level union responsibilities were on the increase. As one worker explained: "Union involvement with the *fondos* gives them a lot of new power. There are guidelines for forming and distributing the funds, sure. But the union has to make certain that they are correctly enforced."[30]

As both kinds of stimulation funds were created from an enterprise's net profits, production units that planned to make a certain profit but did not were forced to reduce the amount of their funds. The rules for fund formulation were complex and underwent several modifications in the period under consideration.[31] The two principal criteria for calculating the funds were productivity and cost per unit of production (*costo por peso de producción*). For each indicator, the stimulation funds received 1 percent of an enterprise's salary fund planned for the preceding year, so long as it *planned* to match that year's productivity and cost per unit *and* succeeded in doing so. In addition, for each 1 percent *improvement* in the two criteria over the preceding year that an enterprise planned *and* attained, its *fondo* received another 0.25 percent of its salary fund. The stimulation funds were also entitled to additional sums if the enterprise performed *better* than planned in either productivity or cost per unit of production. In order to discourage enterprises from making loose plans, they received a smaller percentage for overfulfillment than for attainment of planned goals.[32]

The SDPE, however, limited the size of enterprise stimulation funds by setting a maximum for the two funds of 8.4 percent (8.5 percent in 1985) of an enterprise's planned salary fund for the preceding year—2.8 percent for the fund for housing construction and socio-cultural projects and 5.6 percent for the prize fund.[33] The SDPE also tied the establishment of stimulation funds to performance indicators other than those mentioned above. For example, production units that underfulfilled their quantitative planning targets had to subtract money from their funds in specified proportions; if underfulfillment reached 5 percent they could not form stimulation funds, no matter how large their earnings. Similar deductions from the funds were mandated when production failed to meet quality standards or product specifications or when an enterprise did not fulfill its contractual obligations to other production units. Finally, if the increase in the average salary (after distributions from the prize fund) exceeded the increase in the firm's labor productivity, its prize fund was reduced accordingly.

Obviously, these rules would have prevented enterprises that had no hope of operating profitably from setting up stimulation funds.[34] To preclude the resultant inequities in firm autonomy (not to mention rewards for labor) among branches of the economy and among enterprises, the SDPE established guidelines for fund formation in "unprofitable" enterprises. For them, the criterion was a planned decrease in the state subsidy received the preceding year. Nonprofitable enterprises were also allowed to form funds on the basis of a planned decrease in the state subsidy per unit of production, because for some each increase in production necessitated a larger net subsidy. In either situation, the funds might receive the total decrease in the state subsidy up to the maximum of 8.4 percent of an enterprise's planned salary fund for the preceding year. Although the limitation on the size of both funds together was the same for unprofitable as for profitable firms, the allocation between the prize fund and the fund for housing construction and socio-cultural projects was determined by a firm's superordinate organism, though the latter fund was to receive no less than one-third of the total.[35]

After the first stimulation funds were formed in 1979, a number of difficulties came to light. Among them was one that *Trabajadores* called "the most important problem with the prizes": workers' lack of information about planning, forming, and distributing the prize fund, leading to workplace conflicts when the prizes were awarded.[36] Nevertheless, the *fondo* system grew steadily from 1979 into the mid-1980s. From around 10 million pesos in 1979, the funds expanded to over 71 million pesos in 1985. While only around 4 percent of the workforce received money from the funds in 1979, 32 percent did by 1985, and the average prize per worker rose from 61 pesos the first year to 130 pesos in 1984 and 123 pesos in 1985 (Mesa-Lago 1988:75–76; Zimbalist and Brundenius 1989:135; *Trabajadores*, 6 November 1986:1). The significance of this trend for enterprise autonomy is that Cuban enterprises came to control ever larger amounts of their earnings as the SDPE matured.[37]

CONCLUSION: THE NECESSITY OF CENTRALIZATION AND DECENTRALIZATION FOR ECONOMIC DEMOCRACY

Viewed in terms of planning, production, and the disbursement of earnings, enterprise autonomy unquestionably increased under the SDPE, as compared to the budgetary finance period. This change is significant, for when decision making about production is highly centralized, when there are few important decisions made at the point of production, meaningful democratization of work is not possible. I would, therefore, conclude that the potential for the democratization of production definitely expanded under the SDPE. At the same time, I would also argue that continued increases in enterprise autonomy, beyond what the SDPE had accomplished by the mid-1980s, could enhance it even further.

There remains, however, an important question concerning the issues of centralization, decentralization, and democratization: While the possibilities for the democratization of production are evidently diminished when enterprises are overly dependent on the center, does this mean they will reach their zenith in a highly decentralized system? Many people think not, for two reasons. First, it may only be managers, professionals, and political cadres who gain much control from decentralization. As Rudolf Bahro puts it:

> As far as the dilemma between centralization and decentralization goes, as a theme of "economic reform," it will remain an unproductive model of *inter*-bureaucratic activity, a tug-of-war between the *leaders* and the *middle* ranks of the *managerial* pyramid, as long as there is no autonomy for the social forces at the base that are outside the administration. (Bahro 1978:379)

Second, the democratization of production demands a vital macro arena where future economic goals, longer-term and less obvious concerns, and, above all, the needs of the most vulnerable and least powerful in society can be deliberated democratically. If this is sacrificed in the process of decentralization, control by the many is partial and restrained. Thus, precisely because pre-1985 SDPE attempts to heighten enterprise autonomy were more cautious and limited than Yugoslavia's or even than prerevolutionary Hungary's or China's, they deserve serious scrutiny.[38]

We arrive, then, at the seemingly contradictory conclusion

that both decentralization and centralization, enterprise autonomy and central state direction, are fundamental to democratizing production. Edward Boorstein (1968:132) recognized this from his work in Cuba nearly two decades before the SDPE was implemented: "Along with centralization," he wrote, "there must be decentralization. The problem is how to combine the two: what and how to centralize, what and how to decentralize." Actually, the problem is more complicated than Boorstein suggests, because a tilt in one direction, even while opening new possibilities for democratization in one arena, very often restricts them in the other. Said another way, a delicate and subtle mix of decentralization and centralization, at once difficult to determine and to achieve and that always remains open to renegotiation, is essential for majority control of production.

Chapter 6

THE ROLE OF WORKERS IN FORMULATING WORKPLACE PLANS

The extent to which producers are involved in economic planning lies at the heart of the problem of the democratization of production. Surprisingly little, however, has been written on this aspect of planning in socialist countries. Particularly lacking have been analyses of the topic that focus on the workplace.

Before the early 1970s, the disarray in which economic planning found itself, coupled with the severe limits imposed on enterprise autonomy, meant there was really very little to say about participation in workplace planning in Cuba. After that, however, the situation changed. In notable contrast to the earlier period, workers throughout Cuba began to become involved in the formulation of annual technical-economic plans at their worksites. And, significantly, a survey of more than 300 Cuban workers and peasants revealed their view that the discussion of plans was by far the most important area of workers' participation in decision making (Herrera and Rosenkrantz 1979:48–49).

WORKERS AND WORKPLACE PLANNING BEFORE 1970

In contrast with other postrevolutionary situations where mixed economies have persisted for relatively extended periods, in Cuba most productive property was socialized soon after the 1959 victory. The land and the industrial holdings of supporters of Fulgencio Batista were seized almost immediately, and the first agrarian reform law, promulgated in May 1959, nationalized all rural holdings larger than 995 acres, including many sugar operations. By the end of 1960, after a series of confrontations with the United States, most major foreign properties, as well as many owned by

Cubans, had been seized. Finally, with the second agrarian reform in October 1963, the socialization of all agricultural holdings larger than 169 acres began. Thus, within five years of its ascendancy to power the Cuban government faced the monumental task of administering and coordinating 70 percent of the country's agricultural enterprises, virtually all its industrial, transportation, construction, and financial operations, and 75 percent of its retail trade establishments (Mesa-Lago 1981:15). Under these circumstances, planning was an immediate necessity. Further impetus to begin planning came from the rapid shift of much of Cuba's trade from the United States to socialist countries, which to minimize resultant disruptions to their own economies, wanted to regularize their exchanges with Cuba as quickly as possible.

Even under ideal circumstances so rapid a change from a market-oriented to a planned economy would be difficult, and in Cuba conditions were far from ideal: There were few essential economic data available on which plans could be based; those that did exist were scattered among thousands of production units and the home offices of foreign corporations; virtually no one in Cuba had had any planning experience; many of Cuba's highly skilled technicians and professionals abandoned the country in the first years after the July 26 takeover;[1] such basic equipment as business machines was in short supply; with counterinsurgency remaining a serious threat for a number of years, economic matters were often forced to take second place behind military ones.

The 1960s, therefore, witnessed a great deal of trial, error, and improvisation in economic planning. Technically, national-level economic planning began with the establishment of JUCEPLAN (Junta Central de Planificación) in 1961. A year later, under advice of Czechoslovak planners, JUCEPLAN formulated the country's first annual plan. Edward Boorstein's (1968, chap. 5) first-hand account of the process of devising and implementing this plan is fascinating, though the plan itself was practically useless, for a number of reasons. It was inflexibly patterned on the experience of the more highly developed Czechoslovak economy; it was based on data that were unreliable, indeed often invented; its goals were overly ambitious; it went through at least seven variants. The annual plans for 1963–66, though somewhat more satisfactory, suffered similar defects, and as a result none was ever fully enforced. The country's first mid-range plan, covering the years 1962–65, was similarly unworkable. Further complicating economic plan-ning, one-third of the country's work centers, mostly in agriculture and foreign trade, operated on decentralized, cost-accounting prin-ciples, while the other two-thirds, mostly in industry, were highly centralized and subscribed to the tenets of budgetary finance.

Between 1966 and 1970, Cuba attempted to organize all pro-duction according to the budgetary-finance system. Simultaneously, JUCEPLAN's authority was curtailed, and upper-level political leaders increasingly assumed personal responsibility for the func-tioning of the economy. It is not certain that any annual plans were devised during these years; if they were, they were definitely not fully implemented. Mid-range macroplanning ceased alto-gether. Instead of comprehensive, nationally coordinated economic plans, the country's leaders began to rely on multiple, overly ambi-tious mini-plans governing production in individual economic sec-tors or regions, and on special or extra plans (such as the 1965–70 Sugar Plan) covering particular projects or modifying previously developed plans.[2] The situation was well summed up by Gordon White (1987:154): "During 1966 to 1970, Cuba could not be called a 'centrally-planned' economy."

The foregoing account suggests there were few opportunities or inducements for workers to participate in worksite planning be-fore the early 1970s. Because of inefficiencies, inadequacies, and rapid changes in the planning system, plans were frequently never even formulated in many areas or for many time periods. Those that were developed were often so unrealistic and faulty as to be useless as guides to production in individual work units. Other plans were revised so frequently that enterprises were forced to ignore them, and sometimes plans arrived at worksites too late to be of any use. In 1963, for example, agricultural plans for Las Villas province were not dispatched to individual farms until No-vember (Dumont 1970a:43). Under these chaotic conditions, even though greater workers' participation in base-level planning may have improved the plans, the overall planning effort was so defec-tive that the limited worker discussions about planning that did occur in the 1960s would have been largely futile and frustrating exercises.

In addition, the shift of many production units from cost ac-counting to budgetary finance after the mid-1960s raised a familiar obstacle to workers' participation in enterprise planning. Under this system, few issues of any importance remained to be decided about the plan at the micro level. Direct worker involvement in planning was rendered impossible by the enormity of the units into which the Cuban economy was divided: The whole economy was regarded as a single production unit in terms of inputs and outputs, and, although production was carried out by distinct administrative units, these consolidated "enterprises" in reality encompassed entire economic sectors.

With one exception (Zeitlin 1970:xxxii), accounts of the decade corroborate these bleak expectations concerning workers' participation in planning. Cuban citizens did not even see their first annual or mid-range economic plans prior to publication (Mesa-Lago 1968:41). Workers in a box factory recalled that their participation in planning before 1970 consisted merely of being informed by management (on a blackboard) of how much progress they had made in meeting monthly production goals, presumably well after the plan had been drawn up. René Dumont (1970*a*:50, 80–81), adviser to the Cuban government on agricultural matters during the 1960s, observed that base-level contributions to planning were limited to details of implementation, and that less and less was said about workers' involvement as the years went on. Finally, Adolfo Gilly (1965:39–40, 42, 45), who lived in Cuba for a year in 1962–63, described base-level activity in plan elaboration as formal and limited; workers showed little interest in discussions of production plans; they did not feel the discussions that did occur decided much of importance. In theory, Cuban planning was to have been more democratic, and at least one attempt was made during the 1960s to increase base-level input. But, in fact, workers wielded little influence in this important area of decision making during the revolution's first decade (Bray and Harding 1974:662; Mesa-Lago 1968:40–41).

WORKERS AND WORKPLACE PLANNING AFTER 1970

Beginning slowly after 1970, major changes began to occur making it imperative, if democratization were to expand, that producers have a voice in enterprise planning. To begin with, in contrast to the 1960s, plans started to mean something in Cuba. In the early 1970s the country began to systematize, computerize, and extend economic planning. Data gathering and analysis were vastly improved. Annual plans began to be formulated regularly after 1973 or 1974, and in 1976 they began to be coordinated with five-year plans. As enterprise plans became sufficiently accurate and realistic and began to serve as the actual blueprints for productive activity at the worksite level, their contents became distinctly important to producers. They represented the parameters within which their coming year's labor would be expended: the size of the workforce, the organization and intensity of work, health and safety goals and conditions, and so forth.

Planning was not fully regularized and solidified in Cuba, however, until the institution of the SDPE (El Sistema de Dirección y Planificación de la Economía). Subsequently, Cuba could be counted as having, "mature central planning, with stable institutions and defined functions."[3] The SDPE's stipulation that enterprises retain a portion of their earnings to be distributed to the workforce, on an individual and a collective basis, further increased the significance for producers of the contents of enterprise plans and how they were determined. Recall from the previous chapter that the amount of earnings retained by a firm was maximized when high plan targets were both formulated *and* met. As a consequence, explained one worker:

> If the figures are too unrealistic, too high, then the workers slough off because they know they can't reach them anyway. But when workers have a say in deciding what the figures of the plan should be—and they, after all, have the most realistic notion of this—then you get plans that can be reached and workers will work as hard as they can to fulfill the planning goals, because they know they have a chance to get some extra money.[4]

After the SDPE, workers thus assumed, at least in the short run, a direct and easily discernible material interest in participating in the formulation of the plan for their work centers. Their involvement helped secure their maximum material benefit by ensuring that the work center ultimately received the most ambitious annual plan its workers thought they could realistically fulfill. Nevertheless, in the long term, an enterprise that consistently fulfilled its production goals risked being presented by central planners with production targets higher than workers would be able or willing to fulfill. Although the short-term financial gains accruing to workers through their participation in enterprise planning could thus be undermined in the longer term, that possibility should not necessarily dispel their motivation to participate in annual plan deliberations. Instead, inasmuch as workers' participation was meaningful rather than perfunctory, it helped workers protect their long-term interests by counterbalancing the endemic pressures from the center to assign production targets that workers judged unrealistic.[5]

Regular and widespread workers' participation in formulating enterprise plans began in mid-1974, before the SDPE was implemented, with the well-publicized discussion of the 1975 annual plan in the Aceros Unidos steel plant. Thereafter, the number of workers taking part in similar discussions increased: Sixty-five percent of all union members discussed the 1976 plan; the 1977 plan was discussed in 75 percent of all enterprises, and the 1980 plan, in more than 90 percent. The number of workers participating in planning discussions rose by 15 percent between 1975 and 1980.[6] In that year, the 2d Party Congress declared that workers' participation in drawing up plans was "a basic principle of socialist democracy," a right formally specified by Article 16 of the Cuban Constitution and reiterated in a 1980 decree regulating state enterprises.[7] Every worker I interviewed in 1982 and 1983 affirmed base-level input into planning, and it was reported that participation in discussions of the 1984 plan were the most extensive to date (Zimbalist and Brundenius 1989:139).

Direct producers took part in worksite planning both before and after the final plan was drawn up and at the levels of both the enterprise and its constituent work centers. This procedure meant that they were involved both in the formulation and implementation of planning decisions, that their participation was both direct and indirect, that workers constituted the overwhelming majority in some planning discussions, and that some producers had the opportunity to discuss their work centers' plans in small groups, something the CTC (Central de Trabajadores de Cuba) recognized as preferable (*Trabajadores* 7 Jan 85:1; 5 Feb 85:2). The first plan discussion took place when the control figures (*cifras de control*) for the following year's plan arrived at the worksite. In work center assemblies, producers analyzed the figures, usually by comparing them with analogous figures from past years, and either approved them or proposed modifications.[8] Proposals originating in the assemblies, which in 1980 numbered about twenty-five thousand, were then discussed at the enterprise level. These discussions did not include all workers; only members of the management council, union bureau officers, and worker representatives elected in the earlier work center assemblies attended. More than 113,000 such representatives were chosen in 1980. In that year all but approximately eight thousand of the original plan modifications proposed by workers were dealt with in these enterprise-level meetings. Those not acted on were forwarded to ministries, provincial or municipal governments, or JUCEPLAN for further review.[9]

Workers had their second opportunity to discuss planning figures in work-center assemblies held, ideally, in the first quarter of each year, when the directive figures (*cifras directivas*) for the annual plan were announced. These figures were derived from the control figures, modified above the work center on the basis of workers' and managers' suggestions and shifts in such things as world market prices and interest rates. Workers' contributions to planning in this second round of discussions concerned only implementation of the plan, not what the plan would consist of, as in the prior discussions of the control figures. Once again workers' representatives met afterwards with *buró* officers to discuss implementation of the directive figures.

Worksite technical-economic plans discussed in these forums comprised many substantive categories, or indicators. According to two highly placed officials, planners were attempting to reduce the number of indicators, which varied according to type of enterprise. Whatever indicators were disaggregated to this level, however, were supposed to be discussed by workers.[10] The following list includes all plan indicators workers mentioned discussing, although some of these items may have been topics that came up in discussions of particular indicators, rather than indicators themselves. As the list suggests, planning discussions spanned a wide range of topics aside from the volume of production and service delivery. According to both workers and planning personnel, health and safety standards, worker training, finances, and especially the supply and budgeting of raw materials and other inputs were indicators that prompted the most intensive discussions at the base level. A JUCEPLAN official designated the first five indicators below as examples of ones analyzed in almost every Cuban worksite.[11]

- Volume of goods produced and services delivered
- Productivity

- Salary fund
- Health and safety standards
- Work norms
- Quality of goods produced and services delivered
- Maintenance of equipment and facilities
- Raw material and energy consumption
- Sales goals
- Prices of inputs and outputs
- Production costs
- Size and distribution of labor force
- Supply and budgeting of raw materials and other inputs
- Training of work force
- Discipline
- New construction and investments
- Finances (cost of producing goods and delivering services compared to income and net earnings or losses)

A Cuban survey of one thousand respondents published in the latter half of the 1970s, revealed that across occupational categories most workers reported participation in planning assemblies to be active.[12] I noted one major difference in the reports different workers gave me about their planning assemblies. Workers in centers producing tangible goods often described their planning discussions as "arduous," "difficult," "animated," and even, in one instance, "violent."[13] On the other hand, workers in service delivery units tended to describe their planning discussions as less combative, because plan indicators were less directly linked to the day-to-day character of work or to their wages. A different reason for the comparatively tame planning discussions in service delivery units was put forward by a worker who explained that many production workers had had a history of membership in unions with militant traditions of negotiating with managers and state officials, stretching back into the prerevolutionary era. Most service workers, he noted, lacked such a history, since they had been organized into unions only after 1959.[14]

What happened when workers proposed control figures for certain indicators that differed from those sent down by supra-worksite agencies and possibly supported by worksite management? This was not an uncommon occurrence, and though it was true, as Jorge Domínguez (1978:419) has noted, that the "Central Planning Board and the top party and government officials retain full power to accept or reject suggestions from lower ranks," this statement does not give a complete picture of what actually occurred in such situations. Although workers' participation in planning discussions was technically just advisory, higher authorities did not always, immediately, or categorically reject workers' suggested modifications of control figures. Rather, a discrepancy sparked a process of bargaining and compromise. Often the compromise reached was a contingent one, as, for example, when workers insisted on receiving more raw materials or having facilities improved before agreeing to produce the quantity of goods desired by planners or managers.[15] Workers told me that when supra-worksite planning officials steadfastly supported a figure to which producers had objected they were obligated to defend their stand before the workers in full detail. They were also expected to explain how their figure could be met and to supply any technical aid needed by the worksite to reach the disputed goal. Several workers suggested that, if planners did not take this obligation seriously, producers might "make sure" the indicator wasn't attained so as to reinforce their position vis-à-vis planners or managers in the event of a similar debate in the future.

A JUCEPLAN official claimed, however, that with the increased use of material incentives such as the *fondos de estimulación*, whenever workers began to gain monetarily from fulfilling higher production targets, their disagreements with planners usually arose because workers proposed larger, not smaller, control figures than the planners did. For example, it was not uncommon, he stated, for workers to suggest larger allocations of materials and investments than the state was able to provide. "The budget of the United States wouldn't be enough to cover all the planning requests made by Cuban workers," the official joked.[16] There was, however, another possible reason for such requests: Workers, very likely with management's backing, may have requested extra materials and investments, not in order to fulfill larger current planning targets, but as a reserve against an excessively taut plan they might face in the future.

Despite increased workers' involvement in plan elaboration in the 1970s and 1980s, compared with the 1960s, problems persistently plagued the endeavor.[17] Even though by 1979 work-center and enterprise-level assemblies discussed control figures at nearly every worksite,[18] the process was often far behind schedule. By mid-July 1979, when all assemblies to discuss control figures for the 1980 plan were to have been completed, only 9 percent of them had been held; approximately three weeks after the scheduled completion date for discussions of the control figures for 1981, only 61 percent of the assemblies had been held; several weeks after the date when all the control figures for the 1982 plan were to have been reviewed by workers, only 55 percent of the assemblies had met (*Trabajadores* 10 Jul 79:1; 24 Jun 80:1; 5 May 81:1). Workers' discussions of the directive figures were also delayed.[19] As delays were cumulative, a planning process that was late one year forced delays in subsequent years. The Agricultural Workers' Union, the Construction Workers' Union, the Commercial and Restaurant Workers' Union, and the Health Workers' Union were regularly reported to be behind schedule in their planning discussions.

Often, the blame for these delays lay with supraworksite planning bodies and enterprise management, which were slow in disaggregating planning figures for discussion at the work-center level. In fact, 1986 was the first year when delays in the delivery of planning figures to enterprises reportedly did not occur (Fitzgerald 1989:308; *Trabajadores* 25 Feb 85:2). Schedules were difficult to keep for various reasons. Technical and human resources were inadequate. Frequent and severe fluctuations in world market prices necessitated plan alterations and perhaps the elaboration of more than one plan to cover different contingencies. The quantity and quality of workers' participation in planning suffered as a result. Discussions of control figures could be so long delayed that they became pointless, as upper-level planners already had started to reaggregate the figures into the country's annual plan, which had to be approved by the National OPP (People's Power) Assembly in December of each year. Unions complained that delays in disaggregating control and directive figures cut short their time for preparing workers' assemblies. The level of the discussion and the number of workers who participated declined as a result. Continuing concern with this problem was revealed in resolutions approved at the 15th National CTC Congress in 1984.[20] Partly as a consequence of such difficulties, one commentator complained that there were planning assemblies full of workers who were "there but not there," a situation that was no better than if only a few had shown up in the first place (*Trabajadores* 16 Apr 81:2).

Another problem affecting workers' participation in planning was management's neglect of workers' proposals to modify control figures. Even though 59 percent of enterprises did incorporate such suggestions in 1980—up from 42 percent in 1978—at times, workers' ideas were simply ignored by enterprise management, in some instances for years (JUCEPLAN 1980b:27–28). In reporting to the 14th National CTC Congress, Roberto Veiga (1978:11) called this practice "inadmissible," yet it was still occurring in subsequent years (Pérez-Stable 1985:301; *Trabajadores* 25 May 85:1). The unions shouldered part of the blame for allowing the neglect to continue, as some of them did not adequately record workers' suggestions for plan changes. To remedy the situation, the draft of the Theses for the 15th National CTC Congress called on unions to supervise more carefully the gathering and compilation of workers' suggestions and to push more aggressively for their eventual incorporation into the plan (CTC 1983: art. 1.6.1).

A related difficulty was the failure to provide an adequate explanation when workers' proposals were not included in drawing up the final worksite plan. This failure apparently occurred rather frequently in 1979 and was subsequently addressed in a resolution adopted by the 15th National CTC Congress (JUCEPLAN 1980b: 121; CTC 1984:123). In Cuba's developing economy, one of the most likely explanations for overlooking workers' suggestions was the scarcity of supplies and raw materials. Most workers, undoubtedly aware of this difficulty, were thus particularly annoyed when no explanation for the oversight was forthcoming. The draft Theses of the 15th National CTC Congress underscored the attendant risk.

> Although the limitation of material resources that often prevents the inclusion of suggestions made in assemblies is known, nothing explains why a corresponding explanation is not offered in each instance. Such a situation justifiably generates irritation among the workers because of what they consider to be an underestimation of their opinions and suggestions. This works against the aim of obtaining, every time and in the best manner, their active and conscious participation in planning and in everything that is concerned with economic management. (CTC 1983: art. 1.6.1)

The Cuban unions were central to workers' participation in the planning process at both base and supraworksite levels in a number of ways. First, the process created opportunities for

workers to expand their comprehension of production and economic matters, one of the aspects of democratization as empowerment discussed in Chapter 1. Yet this required of workers a certain
level of general and technical knowledge, as well as an understanding of economic planning, if they were to avail themselves of
these opportunities. The effort the union devoted to these educational tasks could be the subject of a study in itself. To name a few,
union activities in this area included organizing seminars and
courses for members on a variety of topics, preparing written materials, and regularly publishing educational pieces in *Trabajadores*.
Furthermore, prior to worksite planning assemblies, unions offered
training seminars to familiarize their leaders with the most successful methods of soliciting workers' input. In my view, such union
educational endeavors contributed to the significance of the work-
center planning assemblies as yet another forum through which
workers could become involved in decision making about production.

In addition to the unions' ongoing educational programs,
during the early stages of preparing the annual plan, each sectoral
union was responsible for devising requisite guidelines for its own
economic sector. Also, before the base-level planning assemblies
were held, national and provincial union branches met with state
officials to receive control figures for their respective economic sectors together with the government's analysis of the entire planning
document.

Once this preparatory phase was completed and the control
figures were disaggregated, union leaders at the enterprise and
work-center levels, in coordination with management, organized
the base-level assemblies where workers or their representatives
discussed the plans. A JUCEPLAN official told me that the administration was obliged to give base-level union leaders the control
figures well in advance of the assemblies to allow them time to
discuss the figures with workers, or, if necessary, to request help
interpreting the data from upper-union levels.[21] The union's role of
chairing the planning assembly was not limited to that of facilita-
tor. Rather, union officers were supposed to make sure that
workers had every opportunity to air their opinions, that all important points of the plan were covered, and that management's
responses and explanations were clear, consistent, and well understood.[22] The union was also to record all workers' comments re-

garding the plan. It then used these records to argue with enterprise management for the inclusion of workers' suggestions in the proposed directive figures sent to JUCEPLAN and the ministries or, if necessary, to urge for inclusion of workers' suggestions before supraworksite bodies directly. A union's success in advancing workers' perspectives on the plan depended partly on its ability to persuade planners and managers of the validity of producers' opinions through informal channels. A front-page article in *Trabajadores* (8 Nov 79:1), however, reported that one union, citing Article 16 of the Cuban Constitution, took an enterprise to court for failing to discuss control figures with the workers properly. Unfortunately, the outcome of the case is not known.

CONCLUSION: THINKING COMPARATIVELY ABOUT THE DEMOCRATIZATION OF PLANNING

As economic planning assumed greater importance in Cuba in the 1970s and 1980s, so too, compared to the 1960s, did workers' involvement in the process at the workplace level. Nonetheless, this chapter has brought to light a number of shortcomings with the procedures as they operated in the latter period. Some of these were well recognized in Cuba. Others, such as the difficult yet essential project of concomitantly democratizing planning at the supraworksite level, were not discussed at the time, at least not publicly.[23]

Within limits, however, Cuban procedures allowed workers at the micro level to propose, and their unions to argue for, alternatives to the plan figures devised at the center. Observers have commented that, compared to those in other socialist countries, these planning procedures were more democratic (White 1987: 157; Zimbalist 1985:215). My own research in the German Democratic Republic supports this view. The worksite planning assemblies I learned about there sparked minimal interest among workers and little debate, covered a narrower range of topics, and had less of an impact on the final form of the work-center plan (Fuller 1990). The comparatively more activist role that the Cuban unions assumed in planning accounts, in part, for the difference.

Chapter 7

RESOLVING DISPUTES AT CUBAN WORKSITES

A universal characteristic of people's day-to-day social relationships at work is an unequal division of power: At most worksites a few owners or high-level managers or both monopolize power, while the majority of workers possess very little. Although this lopsided distribution of power at work is typically seen as natural and inevitable, it has always been challenged by the ideology of the Cuban revolution. Yet, has Cuba put its ideology of workplace egalitarianism into practice?

It is helpful in answering this question to focus on those times when overt disputes between workers and managers erupt over issues of discipline and workers' rights, for it is on these occasions that the nature and division of workplace power is usually most transparent. What mechanisms were designed in Cuba to resolve such workplace disputes and how did they operate? Did they reinforce existing power inequalities or did they encourage control by the many? To what extent were they biased towards management-preferred outcomes? Or, conversely, how much power did Cuban workers have to discipline themselves and to interpret and enforce the rules governing their working conditions? The answers to these questions varied widely from one postrevolutionary period to the next, and so, once again, change will emerge at the forefront of the discussion.

A TRIPARTITE SOLUTION: THE EARLY GRIEVANCE COMMISSIONS

The first six years of the revolution were unsettled ones in terms of workplace dispute resolution. From 1959 to 1962 there were four different pieces of legislation outlining methods for resolving conflicts between workers and managers or employers.[1] The first three systems established by these laws failed to function satisfactorily, if indeed they were used at all at many worksites. The rapidity of legislative changes simply rendered one system after the other obsolete soon after it was set up.

Rather than reforming prerevolutionary arbitration systems, the structures and the principles on which they had been based were rapidly nullified in this early succession of attempts to establish workplace arbitration mechanisms. By March 1960 the prerevolutionary bipartite (worker-employer) principle governing the resolution of labor conflicts had been superseded by a new arrangement: The Ministry of Labor was brought into the process as an active participant, not just a neutral moderator. Other important changes were the elimination of the judiciary from the primary arbitration level and the minimization of its role at the appeals level.[2] Clearly, the July 26 leaders felt that Fulgencio Batista's models for resolving workplace conflicts would not be appropriate in the new society they envisioned.

The fourth in this early series of arbitration systems was established in 1962 by the Law of the Administration of Labor Justice. It remained in place for over two years, making it the first relatively permanent postrevolutionary system for settling workplace conflicts. It established tripartite (one delegate each for workers and management and a chair representing the Ministry of Labor) grievance commissions (*comisiones de reclamación*) at worksites with more than twenty-five employees.[3] Although direct producers were in the minority on the commissions, the revolutionary leadership emphasized their importance in conflict resolution. "The direct participation by workers in solving labor conflicts," read a precursor to the 1962 law, "makes their solution easier, not only because of their practical knowledge of the matters in question, but also because they are in daily contact with the activities of the work center," (Cuban Economic Research Project [CERP] 1963:131). The incorporation of a provision allowing oral presentation of cases made it easier and less costly for workers, many of whom were illiterate at this time, to make effective use of workplace grievance mechanisms.[4]

The grievance commissions had primary jurisdiction over conflicts arising from violations of workers' rights, such as sick leave, transfers, social security, and compensation claims. They were not allowed, however, to hear cases concerning certain wage disputes or "the qualification, registry, distribution, selection and promotion of manpower."[5] The commissions also heard disciplinary cases—dismissals and appeals brought by absentees who had incurred punishments ranging from public warnings to transfers. They decided all cases by majority vote after evidentiary hearings. Appeals of commission decisions were heard at two levels by five-person bodies appointed by and representing the CTC (Central de Trabajadores de Cuba), the state administration, and the Ministry of Labor.[6] Assessments of the functioning of the commissions vary. Maurice Zeitlin (1970:191) says they "succeeded to a great extent in gaining the workers' approval," but they were also criticized for supporting workers too often or, contrariwise, for siding with management and for excluding private enterprise (Hernández and Mesa-Lago 1971:220, 247; CERP 1963:47, 134–36).

WORKERS' CONTROL OVER WORKSITE CONFLICT RESOLUTION: THE *CONSEJOS DEL TRABAJO*

In 1965 the grievance commissions were eliminated by a new law establishing work councils (*consejos del trabajo*), which have played a meaningful, though varying, role in resolving worker-manager disputes ever since. The most significant change was the discontinuation of administration and Ministry of Labor representation on worksite grievance bodies. Throughout the rest of the 1960s and 1970s, only workers would judge disciplinary cases and alleged violations of labor legislation at Cuban workplaces. Thus, in terms of their relative proportions, Cuban workers were in the optimal position in the *consejo* forum.[7]

Under the 1965 law, five council members were elected at each worksite by secret ballot. In the following decade the number of councils increased, though the original number formed is unknown. In 1971 about sixty thousand workers served on more than eleven thousand work councils; by 1978, nearly eighty-eight thousand sat on almost eighteen thousand councils (*Granma Weekly Review* 1 Aug 71:2; *Trabajadores* 14 Oct 78:3). The main qualification for council membership was a good work record.[8] Council members were elected for three years; many were regularly elected to consecutive terms. The position could be a delicate one, not to everyone's liking. A teacher explained that council members in his work center served as long as they cared to: "Nobody really *wants* the job. But," he added, "everyone recognizes that it's better than having the boss do it."[9] Beginning at least in the early 1970s, *consejo* members took a thirty-day course (Harnecker 1980:42) at the National School of Labor Judges run by the Ministry of Labor on labor law and on the work councils' role. The training was deemed essential to enable council members to make judgments independently of management or political cadres.[10]

Workers' participation on the *consejos* represented an example of involvement in the implementation and evaluation, as opposed to the formulation, stages of decision making. The work councils were empowered to resolve conflicts between workers and administrators over regulations concerning both discipline and workers' rights. Absenteeism, the outstanding disciplinary problem in the 1960s and 1970s, evidently took up and much of the councils' time. Other disciplinary issues handled by the worksite grievance bodies included tardiness, failure to meet work quotas or time schedules, disobedience, negligence, lack of respect for superiors and fellow workers, damage to equipment or property, fraud, and robbery.[11] In 1969, of all the work council cases that were appealed, 89 percent dealt with disciplinary offenses. In 1972–73, of all the cases before the *consejos*, 83 percent involved indiscipline, and although the percentage decreased during the 1970s, it is clear from the union newspaper that until the 1980s cases involving such things as absenteeism, workers' violations of health and safety legislation (considered as indiscipline), and appropriation of work-center property for personal use continued to occupy much council attention.

The second major kind of case the councils heard concerned alleged violations of workers' rights. Included were disputes over issues such as wages, working conditions, transfers, temporary or permanent layoffs, vacations, and demotions. The councils also took over from the grievance commissions the processing of disability, retirement, and death pensions and the verification of workers' claims to these benefits. Between 1965 and the late 1970s, cases arising from violations of workers' rights probably constituted an increasing portion of council work: In 1969 only 11 percent of council cases going to appeal dealt with workers' rights, whereas in 1970 the figure had risen to an estimated 25 percent

(Hernández and Mesa-Lago 1971:223; Pérez-Stable 1975:73); three years later at least 78 percent of the cases moving to the final appeal level from one province concerned violations of workers' rights (*Trabajadores* 22 Mar 77:2). The percentage of such cases rose, in part, because the councils began to deal with matters such as wage disputes, evaluations, and promotions over which the grievance commissions had had no jurisdiction. And, as Marifeli Pérez-Stable suggests (1975:73), after 1970 the stronger emphasis on tying remuneration to output probably heightened the potential for wage and salary disputes between workers and managers.

Once the *consejo* concluded an open hearing , it issued its finding in accordance with relevant legislation. In disciplinary cases a council could decide to uphold, change, or even nullify administration sanctions.[12] Sanctions for indiscipline varied over the years, ranging initially from warnings to postponement of vacations to discharge.[13] During the Sino-Guevarist period of the late 1960s, the councils were urged to refrain from imposing punishments of a strictly material nature and, in cases of indiscipline, were advised against employing punitive sanctions.[14] Along with the shift away from moral incentives in the 1970s, however, union leaders began to complain that the sanctions available to the councils were too limited (Bray and Harding 1974:669). Throughout the 1970s, the grievance bodies handed down judgments imposing a wide range of punishments for indiscipline, from warnings and permanent or temporary transfers with attendant wage adjustments to outright dismissals.[15] If a council determined that workers' rights had been violated, it could order workers reinstated in their jobs, grant wage adjustments, transfer workers to other worksites or other jobs, and return withheld wages. The councils were also expected to notify judicial or administrative authorities when, in the course of deciding a case, they discovered, or suspected, that management had acted improperly or illegally.[16]

If either party were unsatisfied with a council's decision, it could be appealed to two higher bodies, the Regional Appeal Council and the National Review Council. Neither of these, however, was composed entirely of workers. The Regional Appeal Council had three members, one each from the Ministry of Labor, management, and the union. The National Review Council had two members each from the Ministry and management and one from the CTC. Thus any case taken above the worksite level was

no longer resolved solely by workers. The single union representative on either appeal body could hardly have prevailed against the
combined opposition of Ministry and management representatives.
Moreover, as the unions were more closely identified with worksite and supraworksite managers before 1970 than they were afterwards, the balance of power on the two appeals commissions was
even more skewed than apparent by their composition.[17]

Democratization was further constrained by the broad powers
over the entire arbitration system held by the Ministry of Labor.
The Ministry, for example, had to approve transfers, could dismiss
or replace any member of a work council, and could take over a
case at any level of the hearing process and issue a verdict that
could not be appealed. It could also overturn the decision of any
labor justice body, leaving neither party with recourse to appeal
(Hernández and Mesa-Lago 1971:221; Bonachea and Valdés
1972b:370–71; Zimbalist 1975:47). I have no information on how
often the Ministry exercised these wide-ranging powers over *consejos* and appellate bodies, but its authorization to do so placed
potential limits on workers' power to enforce legislation protecting
their rights and to curb managerial abuses in disciplinary matters.

LATE 1970S CHANGES IN WORKPLACE
DISPUTE RESOLUTION

Despite numerous changes throughout Cuba in the early and
mid-1970s, the basic method of resolving workplace disputes continued to function from 1965 until 1978. In 1977, however, the
National Assembly of People's Power (OPP) approved legislation
significantly altering the system of work councils and appellate
bodies. Law 8 transferred authority over the *consejos* from the Ministry of Labor to the unions, though the union organizations did
not inherit the Ministry's earlier power to override verdicts or to
dismiss council members.[18] Thus, for the first time since 1959, the
unions, rather than a governmental organ, were empowered to
oversee the administration of labor justice. The CTC regarded this
as evidence the unions were satisfactorily fulfilling the expanded
responsibilities being assigned them (Veiga 1978:26; *Trabajadores*
24 Aug 78:2). Law 8 specified four particular activities in conjunction with union supervision of the *consejos*: oversight of council
work, organization of elections (and recalls) of council members,

member training, and union participation in council proceedings at worksites.[19]

Overseeing council work included answering questions posed by council members, making sure councils were operating at all worksites,[20] and seeing that management provided meeting rooms and necessary supplies for the councils. The unions also evaluated the councils in on-site visits during which they reviewed their past performance and developed plans for the future.[21] In addition, each council had to forward copies of its minutes and findings and present an activities report three times annually to its union section.[22] Council members could also be summoned to meetings of section or bureau officers to report on specific topics (*Trabajadores* 24 Aug 78:2).

The procedure for selecting council members, over which the unions assumed responsibility, differed little from the prior one: Five members were elected by majority vote in workplace assemblies.[23] Qualifications for council membership specified by the law were a good work record, a satisfactory educational level, upstanding conduct outside the workplace, and active incorporation into the revolution.[24] Although, in many cases, both union leaders and administrators would have met these qualifications, the law specifically prohibited their election to council posts. When I asked workers what kind of individual made a good council member, I was regularly told they had to be dedicated and energetic because the job was a big responsibility; they also had to be serious and objective, not people who would "treat their friends better than their enemies."[25]

To train council members, unions set up educational programs focusing on labor legislation and workers' rights, among them radio, television, and correspondence courses as well as self-study packets. In addition, seminars, conferences, and courses, sometimes lasting as long as six months, were sponsored by the CTC and the sectoral unions. By mid-1978, of all council members, 40 percent had received instruction in labor legislation; by 1985 the figure had risen to 65 percent (*Trabajadores* 14 Oct 78:3, Management's occasional reluctance to facilitate workers' attendance at training sessions, however, created tension between workers and their bosses. In response, the 14th National CTC Congress resolved to compel management's cooperation by including ongoing education and training of council members in the collective work agreements, documents which specified the rights and obligations of workers and managers at Cuban worksites (*Trabajadores* 2 Dec 78:5).

Although workers whom I interviewed talked the most about the fourth task the unions assumed after 1977—involvement in the resolution of actual cases heard by the work councils—Law 8 devoted little attention to it.[26] The procedures for initiating, hearing, and deciding cases included provisions designed to encourage workers' use of the grievance system: Work councils continued to be composed solely of workers; lawyers were not required at any stage; proceedings could be initiated verbally; strict time limits were set for each stage of the process; all council hearings were public; a notice of the time and place of a hearing had to be posted at least three days in advance; workers could present evidence or bring witnesses to support their cases; they could seek redress individually or in groups; they could represent themselves, hire lawyers, or persuade others to present their cases.

Nevertheless, when a worker and a boss were at loggerheads—the defining feature of most work council cases since it was commonly felt that no dispute should be taken to the *consejo* before informal efforts had been made to resolve it—these safeguards were not always sufficient to ensure that workers utilized the hearing procedures.[27] Cuban workers insisted that the organized, active, and informed presence of union leaders and members to support and advise them at each stage of the conflict resolution process was also necessary. "The union has got to be the one to watch that the *consejo's* actions are fair to the worker," one man told me.[28] Another worker said the union must serve as the "worker's advocate from the beginning of the conflict until it is finally resolved."[29] In short, workers expected their union to function as a lawyer of sorts. They expected to be able to go to the local union before formal council proceedings began for help preparing their cases and for advice about defending themselves against administration allegations. Workers also hoped to get the union to argue on their behalf at the hearings (though a union officer could refuse to do so) and to make sure the proceedings were conducted according to the law. I was also told that the union was responsible for seeing that council findings favorable to workers were enforced.

This kind of union support was what workers with whom I spoke hoped to receive if they ever became embroiled in a dispute serious enough to be taken before the *consejo del trabajo*. Worker-management conflicts this serious, however, were not everyday occurrences; a few workers I interviewed had never even heard of any that made it to the council where they worked. The majority had never been personally involved in any dispute of such magnitude. Yet the following two quite different stories, related to me by a cashier and a worker in an assembly plant, illustrate the value of union assistance in the resolution of conflicts serious enough to be taken to the councils.

> When I think that both myself and another clerk were sent by the administrator to work somewhere else for three months, just because of personality differences and a few pieces of badly marked merchandise! I cried when that happened to us, I don't mind saying. But in the end both of us were reinstated at our old jobs, and it was the administrator who got booted down to an inferior one. What made the difference was our union. The union stuck with us from the beginning, arguing our case with the administrator's boss, before the *consejo*, all the way up through our appeal. The union did it. They even packed the courtroom with our *compañeros* and union officials![30]

> I was the secretary for labor and social matters in my *sección*. I was trying to resolve absentee cases that came before the *consejo*, and I began to notice that it was the same workers who were brought before the *consejo* month after month for absenteeism. But I knew they were not the only violators in the factory. Many others were actually administrators. And so I took up the matter with the administration. I said, "Listen, why don't you haul some of these administrators before the *consejo del trabajo* for absenteeism?" The administration was reluctant. I said, "I can prove that of the twenty-four administrators' time cards in this work center, eighteen show unjustified absences!" But still the administration balked at bringing a case. I tried other routes. I talked to the union, but the union wouldn't back me up. It was just too hard for the union leaders to force the issue because it meant going against *jefes* [bosses]. The situation was never resolved. The *consejo* could never do anything at all.[31]

Besides the transfer of authority over the *consejos* to the unions, a second major change occurred in the Cuban labor arbitration system in 1977. Appeals of council verdicts, formerly handled by tripartite commissions of management, Ministry of Labor, and union representatives, were forwarded to labor chambers (*sa-las de lo laboral*), newly created organs of the regular Cuban judicial system.[32] This specification made the councils the last recourse for settling labor-management disputes before they spilled over into the formal legal arena, an incentive for council members to make extra efforts to persuade disputants to accept their verdicts.[33] If either party disagreed with a council's decision within ten days, however, the case could be appealed to a municipal and then to a provincial tribunal. Or, if a council found in favor of a worker but the administration did not comply with the ruling, the worker could initiate an appeal within six months (*Trabajadores* 4 Jan 79:3). Some of the same inducements built into council procedures to encourage workers to use that system were also incorporated into the procedures of the municipal and provincial labor chambers.[34]

Did the new appellate system increase workers' power over the resolution of labor-management conflicts? To answer this question, information would be needed on the outcome of work council cases going to appeal before and after 1977, and on the extent of workers' influence over the composition of the tribunals. I have no comparative data on the outcome of the appealed work council cases. Tribunal judges were elected by the corresponding OPP assembly, a procedure that indirectly may have, compared to earlier years, expanded workers' influence in resolving labor disputes brought to appeal.[35] However, these assemblies did not make nominations for judgeships; judges were elected from a slate submitted by the Ministry of Justice and compiled on the basis of proposals from the unions, the party, and relevant state agencies.[36] This information, however, is too scanty to permit an assessment of the extent to which appeal benches reflected workers' preferences; I do not know how the unions decided on their nominees or how much weight their recommendations carried in the final compilation of candidate slates.

After 1977, the councils heard cases similar to those that had previously concerned them. Workers' comments and press reports indicated that absenteeism continued to account for a high percentage of the disciplinary cases they handled. According to Roberto Veiga (1980:30–31), absenteeism and tardiness made up 85 percent of such cases.[37] Workers told me that work councils, though loath to uphold the firing of a fellow worker, did occasionally do so, particularly when the worker was guilty of repeated and serious acts of indiscipline. Single but serious infractions of work discipline were most frequently punished by temporary transfers to lower-paying jobs or by postponement of vacations. In the late 1970s, work councils were required to become involved whenever an administrator applied a sanction, regardless of the seriousness of the alleged offense. In very serious disciplinary or criminal cases, an administrator could immediately sanction a worker, but the next day had to appear before the work council, which could uphold, revoke, or modify the sanction (*Trabajadores* 5 Jul 77:1; 19 Dec 78:2). In less serious infractions, the administration was prohibited from applying a sanction at all without first taking the case to the council, which then decided whether the requested sanction were warranted.[38] Administrators in violation of these procedures were subject to imprisonment or fines or both.[39]

After 1977, the councils also continued to review cases involving violations of workers' rights.[40] According to workers' comments and press reports, disputes concerning remuneration were among the most common of these.[41] It is easy to understand why this issue might have sparked controversy in Cuban enterprises. A worker's basic wage or salary was based on a detailed job classification containing numerous pay grades; it was also affected by regulations governing historical wages,[42] bonuses and prizes, difficult or unsafe working conditions, sickness and accidents, and interruptions in production. The determination of a worker's wage for any given period could, therefore, be complicated, and was subject to various interpretations. Additionally, efforts in the 1970s to strengthen the link between pay and output, and the post-SDPE (El Sistema de Dirección y Planificación de la Economía) emphasis on enterprise profitability, made remuneration a primary focus of worker-management disputes.

A second common type of workers' rights case involved transfers.[43] A 1969 regulation permitting workers to change jobs and to move from one worksite to another left plenty of room for worker-administration clashes. According to the regulation, this right had to be balanced by society's need to distribute the labor force in a rational way (*Trabajadores* 7 Nov 78:3). An administrator had to respond to a worker's request for a transfer within sixty days, and a negative decision could be contested before the work council. In that event the council faced the unquestionably difficult task of balancing the administration's case for denial against the worker's desire to be closer to ailing family members, to continue her or his studies, to accept a better paying post, and so on. The increasing use of employment contracts under the SDPE, however, which could be unilaterally terminated by a worker, probably decreased the frequency of such cases.

The post-1977 grievance system, despite the power it gave direct producers in settling labor disputes, was criticized by union officials and workers as well as by management. Criticisms included council members' insufficient knowledge of labor and social welfare legislation, the length of time required to settle cases, inadequate investigation of particular cases, incorrect preparation of pension documents,[44] and workers' tardiness in bringing cases before councils or appeal bodies. In addition, some councils were criticized for being too lenient, others for being too strict. "We have problems with *consejos* of both stripes," a worker told me.[45] Finally, a few workers I interviewed reported hearing that some worksites did not have councils, an impression corroborated by the union press.[46] Solutions to such problems seem straightforward. The union might devote more attention to training and educating both council members and rank-and-file workers. It might activate councils where they were not functioning and form additional councils. And workers themselves might elect (or recall) stricter (or more lenient) council members in workplaces where they were dissatisfied with how their grievance organs functioned.

Other difficulties with the conflict resolution mechanisms, rooted in persistent power differentials between workers and managers, could not be rectified so easily. Reflected in management misuse or abuse of the councils, such problems required sustained and ingenious corrective efforts by workers and unions. Managers, for instance, sometimes simply failed to appear at hearings on workers' complaints or sent an uninformed representative to testify (*Trabajadores* 7 Nov 78:3, 15 May 79:3). They sometimes conveniently missed deadlines for presenting disciplinary cases involving favored workers, thus invalidating sanctions they themselves had "imposed."[47] Some administrators asked for mild sanctions for relatively serious offenses; others brought workers with exemplary records before councils for minor offenses or ones for which the worker had a reasonable explanation. Still others let minor instances of indiscipline accumulate until a worker could be charged with a major offense.[48] Despite possible penalties, managers were even known to bypass the work councils entirely, applying sanctions without notifying grievance bodies in the hope that the *consejos* would prefer to ignore the matter if and when they finally heard about it.[49] The most common complaint, however, was that some managers simply disregarded work council rulings (and occasionally those of appellate bodies), refusing to modify or suspend disciplinary measures they had imposed, or declining to make reparations when they have been found guilty of infringing workers' rights.[50]

In such situations, the union was a decisive factor. Where it was weak or deferential, managers would be more likely to succeed in short-circuiting the work council and, thus, retaining for themselves the power to discipline workers and to interpret legislation on workers' rights. On the other hand, an alert, combative union that enjoyed the confidence of rank-and-file members would make it more difficult for managers to circumvent the laws governing the resolution of workplace conflicts.

THE *CONSEJOS* LOSE AUTHORITY OVER WORKPLACE DISCIPLINE

At the end of February 1980, the Council of State passed a law which most workers I spoke with simply referred to by its number—thirty-two. Law 32 abrogated the work councils' jurisdiction over disciplinary cases. The law gave Cuban managers the power to discipline workers without notifying or involving the work councils at all.[51] The only requirements were that sanctions be imposed within thirty days of the offense, that the offending worker be notified in writing with a copy of the document going to the union, and that the administrator making the charge take into account the gravity and consequences of the act of indiscipline, the circumstances surrounding it, and the worker's past conduct. The first recourse of a worker who felt unjustly disciplined thus became the labor chamber of the municipal tribunal.[52] Disciplinary measures imposed by management remained in force *until* the municipal tribunal (or the provincial tribunal if a second appeal were made) rendered a verdict, whereas previously sanctions could be enforced only *if* approved by a *consejo* or *after* a worker had received an unfavorable ruling from the municipal (or the provincial) tribunal. The work councils operated as before in cases of alleged violations of workers' rights.[53] The unions did not abandon their involvement with the councils, although their number dropped by over five thousand between 1978 and 1986 (*Trabajadores* 9 Jun 86:4).

Law 32 obviously marked a major departure from the trend toward democratization in the resolution of workplace disputes. Among Cuba's political leaders the genesis of the law could be traced to a growing sense that workplace indiscipline was rising to unacceptable levels in the latter half of the 1970s.[54] Fidel Castro himself commented on this when speaking at the 1979 National Assembly of People's Power (OPP). In October of that year commissions, which included local OPP and union representatives, began a study of labor discipline. Their plan was to visit 20 percent of Cuba's workplaces to gather data from workers, administrators, union officers, work councils, and municipal and provincial tribunals. In December, after half the scheduled work centers had been visited, their preliminary report was presented to the 1979 National OPP Assembly. Their final report, with recommendations for corrective action, was to have been presented to the National OPP Assembly in 1980, but by then Law 32 had been adopted.[55]

When I asked workers why Law 32 had been promulgated, a number of them stressed delays in settling cases. The councils, they told me, simply could not handle all the cases referred to them. Said one, "The *consejos* had a hand in everything. They had way too much to do!"[56] Another remarked, "The *consejos* were causing divorces, I swear! Members had to meet for hours and hours."[57] Such perceptions were borne out by the evidence. During the 1970s the number of cases brought before the councils increased steadily: For every ten thousand Cuban workers the councils heard 161 cases in 1972, 270 in 1974, 280 in 1976, and 306 in 1978. The union press reported long delays in settling cases, ranging from one and one-half to three and even to four years (*Trabajadores* 25 Jan 77:4, 8 Jul 77:4, 7 Nov 78:3, 17 Mar 79:3, 5 Jun 79:3, 13 Oct 79:5).

The councils' heavy caseload and the attendant delays were, however, only a secondary cause of the passage of Law 32. Heavier use of the councils was itself the combined result of two developments in the 1970s—union revitalization and institution of the SDPE. Stronger more aggressive unions both encouraged workers to challenge administrators who they felt had treated them unjustly and discouraged managers from invoking disciplinary measures without proper recourse to the work councils. At the same time, despite the congruence of worker-management interests it promoted in some areas, the SDPE's emphasis on profitability and efficiency sharpened managers' interest in enforcing workplace discipline. The SDPE also increased conflict over workers' rights, insofar as managers responded to the pressures of their new operating environment by ignoring (or bending) laws governing remuneration, health and safety, rest periods, and so on. And even as the reactivated unions and the SDPE were laying new burdens on the council system, Cuba's economic difficulties as a small, developing country heavily dependent on one export crop in a period of spiraling world inflation were increasing the pressure on the councils to handle cases more swiftly, more efficiently, and even more strictly than they were prepared, or perhaps inclined, to do. The *consejos*, caught in the middle, were thus relieved of their authority over workplace discipline by Law 32.

The tension between *obrerista* (unionist) and *eficientista* (rationalist) tendencies was resolved in this instance in favor of the latter.[58] The danger that a minority of rationalizers would continue to acquire more power at the Cuban workplace cannot be dismissed lightly. After all, with Law 32 an impressive and long-standing trend granting workers increasing control over workplace discipline was reversed by a single decree. The removal of that authority from the hands of fellow workers was likely to make it more complicated, more intimidating, more time-consuming, and less profitable for a worker to counter an unjust disciplinary measure.[59] A close look at union and worker reactions to the institution of *"treinta y dos"* is thus imperative.

Although Cuban unions quickly approved the new law, it aroused more intense debate in the workers' organizations than had any other labor-management issue in the first half of the 1980s. A member of the CTC Secretariat called Law 32 one of the most commonly violated by administrators. Managers were frequently charged with overzealous application of the most severe sanctions allowed: At one point the union announced that only 47 percent of management's dismissals of workers, the maximum sanction possible, were upheld on appeal. In one factory, a full 40 percent of the workers had been disciplined under Law 32. In nearly 40 percent of the cases reviewed in one survey, managers had ignored extenuating circumstances when applying Law 32.[60] Indeed, two workers I interviewed felt this was precisely what had occurred in their situations.

> It hurt me a lot when 32 was used against me. Someone in our office had been ill and basically I was doing two people's jobs, and as a consequence I miscounted some money. Even though I only drew a warning, I don't think it's right at all.[61]

> I sure wasn't happy when they used 32 against me. I knew someone was mismarking a lot of merchandise but I didn't want to rat on them. But when it was discovered, the *jefe* said I was to blame too, because I knew about it. So 32 was applied, though I wasn't sanctioned severely. But I have a good work record, so I ask you, was that really fair?[62]

The unions were especially disturbed that Law 32 and a second law concerning managerial discipline were applied unequally. Law 36, as the latter was called, was promulgated at the same time as Law 32 and detailed a long list of infractions of managerial discipline. But its application was left up to other administrators and appeals were handled at the ministerial level, not at the work centers.[63] Although one worker's guess that the application of Law 32 had been "forty times higher than that of Law 36" was exaggerated, a CTC survey in early 1981 revealed the correct figure to be twenty-five, still excessive when compared with the administrator-to-worker ratio in the labor force. By 1983–84, another survey, this time not conducted by the unions, revealed disciplinary infractions registered for 1 out of every 6 workers but only 1 out of every 111 administrators in the city and province of Havana.[64]

Responding to the imbalance, union leaders called repeatedly, and to some avail, for more union vigilance against abuses of Law 32 and for more rigorous use of Law 36 against administrators guilty of applying disciplinary sanctions incorrectly or of violating workers' rights (Pérez-Stable 1985:302; *Trabajadores* 5 Jan 88:9, 30 Dec 86:9). In addition, at the 15th National CTC Congress the need for legal mechanisms to rehabilitate the records of workers sanctioned under Law 32 was expressed (Veiga 1984:30). Moreover, during work-center discussions of the draft of the Theses for this Congress, union members argued that administrators whose disciplinary sanctions were overturned on appeal should compensate wronged workers from their own salaries. When the idea emerged again at the Congress, however, many participants opposed it on the ground that it would make managers reluctant ever to apply Law 32. Compensation thus continued to be made from enterprise funds: Between 1980 and 1983 enterprises paid over two hundred thousand pesos to workers wrongly sanctioned under Law 32 (*Trabajadores* 15 Jun 85:5). Nonetheless, the 16th National CTC Congress made clear its continued dissatisfaction with the procedure used to resolve conflicts over discipline. Workers did not participate enough, resolved the Congress, and the system should be changed so that they were more involved (CTC 1990:28).

Workers whom I interviewed invariably brought up Law 32, usually remarking on the need for it. Recognizing a connection between the quantity and quality of goods and services and workers' performance on the job, many welcomed a more effective system than provided by the *consejos* for dealing with absenteeism, damage or theft of work-center property, neglect of health and safety regulations, and so on. "There really were some workers who weren't working before and the administration couldn't do a thing about it," admitted one worker.[65] "Everyone else had a law protecting them," said another half seriously. "Couldn't we just have one little law for the administrators?"[66] Despite such statements, however, workers' support for Law 32 was not unqualified. Most of them understood the potential for abuse arising from the new powers it granted management.

> Law 32 will be a good law if it is applied properly. It gives more power to administrators; before they did not have enough. The law itself is just. The problem could come with its application. There is a danger that with this increased power bosses could use the law to get at workers they don't like or to invent charges against workers. But we had a lot of problems with discipline before. Workers with consciousness support the law. Workers without consciousness don't support Law 32, but then they didn't support the work councils dealing with discipline either.[67]

Workers' wariness of Law 32, together with the unions' persistent efforts to curb its abuses, have moderated somewhat the law's negative effects on the balance of power between workers and managers. Hopefully, they can as well keep open the possibility that Cuban producers may once again assume the primary responsibility for discipline at their worksites.

CONCLUSION: THE IMPORTANCE OF UNIONS FOR DEMOCRATIZING CONFLICT RESOLUTION

According to Paul Bernstein (1976, esp. chap. 8), a "minimally necessary" component of workplace democratization is a dispute resolution mechanism independent of management and preferably composed of peers. Such bodies, however, are empirically quite rare. Thus the grievance mechanisms developed in post-revolutionary Cuba—especially the *consejos del trabajo*—are of particular interest to anyone concerned with expanding workers' control over production.

No matter how egalitarian the *form* of decision-making structures, however, managers, having more education, confidence, time, status, money, and so forth than the majority of workers, will almost certainly be able to prejudice the functioning of these structures in their favor. Power will remain skewed, despite democratic appearances. Workers can attempt to overcome their relative disadvantages in various ways, but one of the most important must be through collective organization and action. This grants them a better chance to translate the formal right to make workplace decisions into the power to insure they are made in accordance with their preferences.[68]

Interestingly, in Cuba attempts have been made since the *consejos* were first formed, to prevent them from merging with the unions. Union officers, for instance, have been prohibited from serving on the *consejos* and the unions' obligatory role in council proceedings was limited. These efforts to insure separation between the grievance bodies and the unions are somewhat unique in either socialist or capitalist settings and are related to the historical peculiarities of the development of socialism in Cuba, the topic of Chapter 9.[69] At the same time, however, they have reinforced multiplicity. A woman working in the agricultural sector underscored this point: "There are many routes a worker can go through with her or his ideas, opinions, or complaints. There's the union, the party, the *consejos del trabajo*, the production assembly. That's democracy."[70]

Nonetheless, the postrevolutionary history of grievance resolution demonstrates that unions have been as vital to this aspect of democratization as they have been to workers' involvement in workplace planning, management councils, and production assemblies. Despite the limits on their formal participation, unions have prompted grievance-resolution mechanisms to correct, rather than simply reflect, power inequalities at the workplace. To begin with, the union's presence has provided workers who felt that management violated their rights with the security and the encouragement necessary to initiate proceedings against their *jefes*. The unions have done the same for workers who felt unjustly disciplined, often a more delicate situation. Here union backing has helped workers overcome their understandable reluctance to challenge sanctions imposed on them. Unions have also educated their members about workers' rights and about what constituted an act of indiscipline, making them better able to recognize infringements of the former and inappropriate applications of the latter.

Furthermore, unions have helped workers secure favorable resolutions of their disputes by counseling them on the preparation of their cases, by making sure that management and the *consejos* followed correct procedures, and by arguing workers' cases before grievance bodies. They have tried to make managers abide by verdicts of both *consejos* and appeal bodies, correcting their illegal disciplinary actions or compensating wronged workers as ordered. Also, by equalizing the overall balance of power at worksites through their presence and their activities, the unions have increased the independence of the five worker-members of the councils vis-à-vis management. Finally, union backing has been especially valuable whenever workers' cases moved to appeal, where procedures were more complicated and formal and where cases were not heard by a worker's peers.

Scattered data on the use of *consejos* and appeal bodies provide preliminary confirmation of the importance of unions for the democratization of conflict resolution. After 1970, with the expansion of their functions and organizational revitalization, unions became stronger and more active than they had been in the preceding decade. We would therefore expect grievance mechanisms to be more extensively utilized after 1970 than before, and there is some evidence this occurred. Between 1967 and 1969 the number of appeals of council cases declined despite an increase in the labor force of about 119,000. The National Review Board heard approximately half as many cases in 1969 as in 1967, and the Regional Appeal Council, approximately two-thirds.[71] In contrast, though grievance mechanisms themselves did not change between 1972 and 1978, the number of cases heard by the *consejos* more than doubled. Moreover, between 1969 and 1976 the number going to the Regional Appeal Council increased nearly sevenfold, and the number heard by the National Review Council, almost elevenfold. All three figures far outpace the growth in the size of the labor force. As might have been expected, after Law 32 was passed in 1980 the councils heard fewer cases since only those concerning workers' rights now reached them.[72] As there is no evidence that unions became weaker after 1980, however, we should expect no drop in appeals cases, and indeed they appear to have increased dramatically. Considering *only* disciplinary appeals and *only* appeals before municipal tribunals, the number of cases was expected to triple between 1979 (to around ten thousand) and 1986 (to around thirty thousand) (*Trabajadores* 5 Jul 86:1). In short, data available suggest that since the 1960s, the strength of the unions has been positively associated with the potential of grievance-resolution mechanisms to redress power inequalities at the Cuban workplace.

Chapter 8

THE CHANGING WORKSITE RELATIONSHIP AMONG UNIONS, MANAGEMENT, AND THE PARTY

Four interconnected themes are important to an analysis of the worksite relationship among unions, management, and party nuclei: the degree of union autonomy vis-à-vis management and the party, the extent to which union, management, and party interests are considered parallel and harmonious or distinct and contradictory, the differentiation of functions among the three groups, and their relative power in shaping the nature of work and production at Cuban workplaces.

Although these themes are useful guides for exploring changes in the worksite relationship among these three bodies in Cuba, for several reasons the picture that emerges is not free of ambiguity. First, union-management-party relationships have always varied across worksites because of different leadership personalities and styles, different supraworksite linkages, different production processes, and so on. Second, it is impossible to view any of these four themes in terms of absolutes—full autonomy versus full dependence, totally convergent interests versus totally distinct ones, complete differentiation versus complete separation of functions, and so on. Although Cuban union-party-management relationships have often been characterized in such either/or terms, in my view, it is not accurate to analyze what are often subtle and complicated relations in this way.

Finally, the relational ambiguity I investigate in this chapter was particularly pronounced after 1970. Since that date Cuban unions have performed two major functions that are important for the democratization of production but that also have created conflicts in union work. Unions have attempted to serve as defenders and advocates of workers' rights before managers and politicos, while simultaneously collaborating with the same groups in an effort to draw workers into the decision-making process. This uneasy mix of functions often added contradiction and confusion to their workplace relationship with management and the party. The uncertainty and fluidity in the degree to which Cuban unions acted autonomously, were motivated by specific member interests, performed exclusive functions, and exhibited power at the workplace were rooted in the tension inherent in their performance of these two major functions.

Union Autonomy

The Cubans I interviewed who could remember the 1960s uniformly recalled the dormancy of the unions in that decade. Their views are borne out by published accounts that describe the progressive deterioration of the unions, until by 1970 they had almost disappeared.[1] Although the decline varied from union to union and from year to year, in the 1960s the unions were, in general, heavily dependent on worksite management and the party. Their job was principally to transmit directives and decisions from these two groups down to the rank-and-file and to convince workers to carry out the directives and abide by the decisions without question or discussion. In other words, unions served as the mouthpiece of administrators and the party and were expected to take their side in disputes with workers. Lázaro Peña's description reveals the low level of union autonomy at some workplaces early in the decade.

> They [certain union leaders] back up their positions with threats; because, instead of explaining the reasons for certain measures, they limit themselves to stating bureaucratically, and with a truculent air, that . . . [the decisions] must be accepted because the CTC or the Consolidate or such a [sic] Minister, orders it from above. (Cuban Economic Research Project [CERP] 1963:101)

Under these circumstances it is not surprising that union leaders tended to be nonassertive, thus reinforcing union identification with the administration and the party. In Peña's opinion some union leaders:

More or less comply with the task assigned to them by management. They could be converted into administration employees and nothing would change or matter except that the payroll would reflect the true situation more clearly.

There are committee members of union sections who act more like management than worker representatives. (CERP 1963:101)

This characterization is supported by Adolfo Gilly (1965:21–22), who described a few worksite meetings he attended in 1962 and 1963. Workers usually sat on one side of the room, whereas union leaders joined the administrators on the other. At a meeting in a textile factory, though the physical distance separating the two groups was not great, it seemed to Gilly as if an "invisible wall" separated them. In the ensuing discussion between an administrator and a few workers, the union leader remained silent. Jamaican writer Barry Reckord's description of a heated meeting in a box factory leaves the distinct impression that things had changed very little by the end of the decade. The meeting had been called to discuss the case of a man who, refusing to work on a machine lacking a legally required safety device, had had his pay docked by the manager. What stands out in Reckord's report is the backseat role taken by the union representative whose few interventions were characterized by attempts to avoid confrontation and to bolster management's position.[2]

About 1970 both Cuban perceptions of the proper role of unions, and union behavior, began to change. A central feature of the shift was increased emphasis on union autonomy vis-à-vis administrators and the party. Public discussion of a more independent role for the unions marked the preparations for the 13th National CTC Congress in 1973. Several of the Congress's Theses dealt with the question of autonomy, stating explicitly that unions as non-state organizations, were neither dependent on, nor directed or controlled by any ministry or other state body. The Theses also stressed union independence from the party, and they criticized the common union practice of automatically supporting management and the lopsided union emphasis on conveying orders downward. To paraphrase one worker, the unions would henceforth be a kind of radar, detecting workers' problems instead of telling workers what the administrators thought their problems were (Lopez 1972:6).

The 14th National CTC Congress in 1978 and the 2d Party Congress in 1980 reiterated the basic formulations of union autonomy developed at the preceding CTC Congress, and the Cubans I interviewed in 1982 and 1983 underscored them as well. A national CTC official, for example, repeatedly stressed the obligation of unions and union leaders to publicize workers' opinions, particularly those that differed with or were critical of administration policies, and even if the issues seemed minor.[3] Many workers described the ideal union leader as one who carried out this responsibility firmly, independently, and with authority, and who acted as a colleague of management rather than a crony. Changes in union financing methods undoubtedly increased the possibility that union leaders could approach this ideal. In the 1970s, Cuban unions began to be financed from union dues and paid officers began to receive their salaries from this source. In China, by contrast, the enterprise itself was expected to pay a fee to the union, and in Hungarian factories union leaders were reimbursed, at least in part, by enterprise management (Kemény 1986:182; Wilson 1986:240–41).

The pronouncements provided by unions, the party, and workers that progress in the direction of greater worksite autonomy was indeed made after 1970 would be less convincing had they not been accompanied by additional changes in union organization and by the development and systematization of workplace mechanisms enabling unions to ascertain, organize, and make use of members' suggestions and demands. Workplace assemblies held during the 1960s gathered input from the rank-and-file, but they did not meet regularly and they were often organized on an ad hoc, topical basis. Beginning in the early 1970s, however, the unions' potential to act as independent representatives of Cuban workers was bolstered by their regular involvement in three workplace decision-making forums—production and service assemblies, management councils, and planning assemblies—all created or invigorated about that time.[4] In addition, union sections began regularly to convene meetings of their own during the period.

The post-1970 emphasis on union autonomy was not, however, intended to preclude cooperation among unions, administrators, and the party. That is, unions were expected to work with administrators and the party without totally identifying with them.

Abject dependence and complete independence were not viewed as the only two possibilities. Rather, union autonomy was a matter of degree, and opinions over what was optimal differed.

Thus, despite the post-1970 gains, some high-level party, government, and union officials, as well as some workers, continued to be dissatisfied with the amount of union independence and with the prevailing balance between conveying guidelines downward and directing opinions and criticisms upward. In 1980, for instance, Carlos Rafael Rodríguez, a high-ranking government and party official, acknowledged that, "Our unions are much better at transmitting the party's orientations to the working class than they are at gathering from the working class the desires, the criticisms, the suggestions to which the leadership has to be alert." Similarly, Roberto Veiga criticized workplaces where unions and management acted like "one big happy family" (Harnecker 1981:33; Veiga 1978:25). Through the union press and in interviews with me, some workers also complained about the unions' lack of independence and about union leaders who dealt too timidly or too deferentially with administrators to be effective in representing the rank-and-file. In Cuba as elsewhere, workers' interests were likely to be overlooked in such a situation.

This point is well illustrated by the experience of a worker who had asked for a transfer. The management at her work center kept stalling, neither refusing nor approving her request. Eventually, she asked her union for help, which she had not done earlier because its officers were intimidated by the management and had a long history of backing it up on everything. Just as she had expected, the union sidestepped the issue, claiming they could do nothing until management flatly denied her request. Her problem, and other similar ones at the same worksite, was resolved only after the boss had been removed. The union never did get any better.[5] Other complainants spoke of a vicious circle that was established at such workplaces: Workers stopped expressing their concerns to union leaders when they realized the leaders were unlikely to be firm or persistent in presenting them to administrators. Union leaders thereby lost the confidence of rank-and-file workers. And once management realized this, it was less likely to take union demands seriously, further undermining union authority. If unions were to be effective, managers had to view them as having the respect and support of the rank-and-file, and that depended, in part, on the union's reputation for independent action in day-to-day encounters with administrators.

Converging and Conflicting Interests

The assumption that the interests of unions were identical with those of managers and the party was used to justify unions' pre-1970 lack of independence and their eventual near disintegration. Why should unions behave autonomously if their interests were precisely the same as those of the party and management? Indeed, as the supposed harmony admitted no possibility of conflict, why were special organizations needed to defend workers against their own state and party representatives (Zeitlin 1970: xxviii; Bengelsdorf and Locker 1974:7)? And naturally as unions became weaker, as this theory would require, producers were the ones left without influence. At the time, some foresaw the Advanced Workers' Movement as the socialist replacement for unions. Yet, as one worker recalled, its interests were too close to those of administrators to enable it to close the growing gap between those who held workplace decision-making power and those who did not.[6]

As Cuban unions began to function more independently after 1970, the idea of a complete conformity of interests between unions, the administration, and the party began to yield to the reality that conflicts had existed between the three groups from the beginning of the revolution. As the second revolutionary decade unfolded, the argument of Rolando Bonachea and Nelson Valdés (1972*b*:382), that conflict or differences between labor and the state were not allowed in Cuba, became increasingly inaccurate. The Minister of Labor, in a well-publicized 1970 speech, conceded that the belief that workers, peasants, and administrators always shared the same goals was illusory. A year later, he went a step further: "The development of the constant contradictions that must necessarily turn up between the trade union organizations and the administration will strengthen the Revolution every day. . . . We must not fear contradictions. Rather, we must welcome them. They must be viewed as a positive element."[7]

Once again, however, the interests of unions versus management and the party were not seen as completely contradictory.

Consensus on the need to expand society's material base prevailed, yet there was also recognition, acceptance, sometimes even encouragement, of a diversity of social interests, which differed from the view dominant in the 1960s. Answers to important questions like the quantity an enterprise could produce in one year or the proper balance between boosting output and protecting workers' health and safety were expected to vary, and when they did the union's role was to advance its members' positions. Many Cubans borrowed a phrase from Mao Zedong to describe such disagreements—"non-antagonistic contradictions"—implying the existence of conflicts together with the assumption that they could be resolved within the parameters of socialism. One administrator cautioned me that the hardest thing to explain about worksite relations in Cuba would be the existence of overt conflicts between unions and management and the party that were, nevertheless, fundamentally non-antagonistic.[8]

While often describing them as "non-antagonistic," most workers with whom I spoke readily acknowledged the existence of differing, sometimes discordant, interests between unions and managers. Wider recognition of this divergence, and the conflicts that sometimes resulted, was probably linked to the implementation of the SDPE (El Sistema de Dirección y Planificación de la Economía). Decades previously, Lenin had foreseen that tensions between workers and management would arise from the necessity to maximize both output and efficiency. The SDPE was instituted to accomplish these very tasks, in part through the requirement that firms cover their expenditures with their income.

Increasing output and lowering costs thus became, more than ever before, a focal point of enterprise operations. In other words, after the SDPE, individual production units had to operate in accordance with ground rules that were in some ways reminiscent of those governing the operation of capitalist firms. The result was not hard to predict: Conflicts between the interests of workers and managers escalated insofar as managers overlooked or violated laws or customs specifying remuneration, schedules, work quotas, quality standards, and the like. An additional example was the management practice of diverting funds designated for safety equipment to other purposes, which the unions blamed, in part, for the large increase in work-related accidents in the late 1970s (Pérez-Stable 1985:300). Veiga, addressing the 14th National CTC

Congress in 1978, made reference to the potential increase in union-management tensions resulting from the SDPE and reported that, in preliminary discussions of the Theses of the Congress, two proposals to smooth workplace relationships had been made: legal specification of the rights of union bureaus, and formulation of a unified code governing labor relations under the SDPE, a task that was since completed with the promulgation of the Labor Code.[9]

DIFFERENTIATION OF FUNCTIONS

Accounts of pre-1970 union activities in Cuba reveal a lack of clarity about their functions (Silverman 1973:165; Karl 1975:36; Zeitlin 1970:xxvi, xxviii; Bengelsdorf and Locker 1974:7). As a *sección* officer put it in 1983, "One of the biggest differences between the unions [in the 1960s] and now was that before they didn't know what they should be doing."[10] According to Peña (CERP 1963:101), some union leaders in the 1960s wandered aimlessly through offices and plants, pretending to be busy but actually doing nothing. Peña's suggested remedy was more political education for these leaders, but the reasons why some leaders at the time did not know what to do were more complicated than Peña's solution implied. Their predicament stemmed partly from a lack of differentiation between the functions of unions and those of the party, the administration, and other organizations, especially the Advanced Workers' Movement. Given the dependent posture of the unions and the prevailing emphasis on the harmony of interests in society, lines of authority and responsibility were badly blurred. Tasks that were later viewed as legitimately belonging to unions were taken over by other bodies or abandoned entirely.[11] By the end of the 1960s, unions retained few if any areas of exclusive authority, and at most worksites they settled into a subordinate role of backing up party, managerial, and Advanced Workers' projects. Under such circumstances it is no surprise that in the late 1960s there was talk of eliminating unions as relics of Cuba's capitalist past.

The post-1970 emphasis on union autonomy and the recognition that workers had their own particular interests were logically coupled with attempts to distinguish union functions from those of other worksite groups responsible for production. Attention turned from questioning the need for unions, to recognizing their value as distinct entities, to figuring out how their activities could be separated from those of the party and the administration.

This lengthy process began with general union pronouncements regarding separate spheres and distinctive methods of union work (*Granma Weekly Review* 2 Sept 73:7–12). More concretely, the prevalent practice of the same individual occupying slots in the union leadership and/or the party and the administration was discouraged. Where this occurred, a specific area of union activity was considerably more difficult to create and maintain. High-level administrators were thus forbidden to run for union offices, and after 1970 party members were encouraged not to run for local union office, posts they had tended to hold in the late 1960s, despite the unions' disapproval of the practice (*Granma* 26 Aug 66:3). By 1975, only about 8 percent of local union leaders were reported to be UJC (Communist Youth League) members, and only 5 percent were reported to be party members (Domínguez 1978:319; Zimbalist 1985:218). And although local union leaders who were party members rose to 16 percent by 1982, the separate leadership policy was still stressed (Green 1983:62). A number of workers responded to my queries about union, administration, and party roles at their workplaces by supporting the separation of leadership policy. One of them told me that even musical groups were making an effort to disperse authority deriving from these three sources among different individuals.[12] Others emphasized that leadership of, rather than membership in, the three groups should remain distinct, that the same person should not hold "multiple commands," as one worker put it.[13] Most workers stopped short of recommending that administrators or union leaders never be party members, though some of them argued that the number of *militantes* in these groups should be held to a minimum.[14]

Changes since the 1960s, when union, party, and administrative functions were largely undifferentiated, were reflected in the way Cubans distinguished between the proper workplace responsibilities of the three groups, and also how they understood them to overlap. A major objective of all three was to expand production of goods and delivery of services. Here the unions had three main tasks: to organize and systematize workers' input into decision making, to defend workers' rights, to educate and prepare workers to participate effectively in decision making. For its part, management was expected to facilitate the union's performance of these tasks by, for example, participating in production and service assemblies, implementing health and safety legislation, and adjusting schedules to give workers time for educational and union activities. Its primary responsibility, however, was to administer production according to the plan. In this endeavor unions were expected to help management by, for instance, participating in management councils, the determination and execution of the plan, and the supervision and evaluation of management performance. But if something went wrong at the point of production, management shouldered the ultimate responsibility.

Although the party nucleus sent representatives to management councils and other worksite decision-making bodies, its real power stemmed less from any formal authority than from the party's ideological and political influence throughout society. Its major role was neither to protect workers' interests, organize worker input into decision making, educate workers, nor manage. In fact, it was expressly prohibited from becoming involved in this last activity.[15] The party's main task was to oversee, from a broader perspective, the activities of both union and management (regardless of whether the leaders of either were party members) to ensure that the production process ran efficiently and smoothly and in accordance with its social, economic, and political program. The party's methods were discussion and persuasion, not the issuance of orders. It was to orient and guide the unions and management in a general fashion without taking over either's functions. As a union officer told Marifeli Pérez-Stable (1975:70), the unions' acceptance of party guidance did not mean that they were "going every day to the party to ask what has to be done." Party members were expected to make sure that everyone did his or her job, a worker told me. Precisely because they were supposed to be aware of everything that went on throughout the work center, she continued, it was important that party membership accurately mirror the composition of the Cuban population.[16]

Cubans whom I interviewed cited numerous examples that help clarify the worksite roles of unions, management, and party. In one, the administration of a large factory sanctioned some absentees for slowing production. The union, however, called the sanctions unjust, arguing that the real cause of absenteeism at the plant was management's institution of rotating shifts. In this example, the party backed the administration. The party's job was thus to try to explain to the unconvinced why the administration was not only justified in sanctioning the absentees but obligated to do so, despite union objections. As the factory's output was judged essential to Cuba's economy, the plant had to operate twenty-four hours a day, a demanding schedule that could be met fairly only through rotating shifts.[17] In a second example, a supervisor made improper advances to a female employee; when she rejected them, he began to make disparaging remarks about her around the work center. This time the party supported the union when it publicly defended the woman. The party was also instrumental in ensuring that she was protected from reprisals and that the supervisor altered his behavior. In the view of a number of workers, party backing could help unions get action on workers' demands and support for workers' positions when complex, delicate, or confusing problems arose at the worksite.[18]

The final example helps convey a sense of the proper roles of party, union, and administration by describing a situation in which they became badly confused. The problem concerned the allocation of apartments at a work center, a decision which involved the entire collective. There was disagreement among the workers over who should be awarded units, which was not uncommon given Cuba's housing scarcity. Difficulties really began, however, when the union held several meetings to try to resolve the disagreement, during which the administration and the party intervened inappropriately. The party overstepped its authority by taking over the chairship of one meeting and then by delivering a report offering its opinion on who was right and who was wrong. Hence, the party merely added fuel to the fire, instead of assuming its proper function of helping workers clarify and analyze the disputed issues and find an amicable solution. Management, for its part, introduced further complications at one of the union meetings by revealing information about people's work records, when it should have remained uninvolved in the disagreement which was not its concern. The union meetings, I was told, were "wild and ugly." The dispute was not settled until municipal and provincial branches of the CTC intervened and an outside party leader was asked to serve as arbitrator, an action members of the work center party nucleus should have taken much earlier. The affair had gotten so out of hand, my informant explained, because people were too busy doing someone else's job to do their own, thus turning what could have remained a disagreement within the union into a "crisis" at the workplace.[19]

RELATIVE POWER

Lacking independence and clear-cut functions, and assuming that no important conflicts could arise among workers, managers, and the party, the unions survived the first decade of the revolution, albeit with relatively little power at the workplace. At first their relative powerlessness was partly overshadowed by the exuberant egalitarianism that pervaded postrevolutionary society. Without structural underpinnings, however, the ideological trappings of equality became tattered by the end of the decade. At many production units, the relationships among managers, political cadres, and unions revealed themselves as little more than a benevolent form of socialist paternalism: Workers had only to trust those in charge, and their interests would be realized in the end. Yet their lack of power at the point of production was best reflected in the sorry condition of the unions. As one worker recalled, "A big gap developed between the administration and the workers. The administration was too all-powerful. The workers had no control over anything." A UJC member interviewed in 1969 was less circumspect: "The worker hates the power situation in the factory. The manager uses power all the time; enjoys beating people down. That's authoritarianism."[20]

The balance of power at the workplace began to change after 1970. As the unions gained autonomy, assumed primary responsibility for a number of tasks, and began to expect that they would at times come into conflict with management and the party, workplace responsibility for production began to take on a more tripartite character. The shift was typified by the use of the word "counterpart" (*contrapartida*) to describe the union's relationship to workplace administration. The term appeared in a 1971 speech by the Minister of Labor, and took on a more combative connotation as the decade progressed (*Granma Weekly Review* 24 Oct 71:4, 5). In the early 1980s it was used to refer to the unions' role as overseer of management, work relevant mainly to the evaluative stage of decision making. In fulfilling this counterpart role the unions were required to monitor administrators' performance, inform them of deficiencies or errors, and help them make improvements. Yet a simple union response to management after the fact was not considered enough. Unions were to avoid assuming only this negative orientation and exercise a more positive posture, confronting managers authoritatively even before they acted inappropriately. Management behaviors commonly cited by the union press as calling for counterpart action included irresponsibility, laziness, cronyism, bureaucratism, dishonesty, and poor performance in producing goods and delivering services. A woman worker related an example of how important the union's counterpart role could be in protecting direct producers from the effects of these kinds of management transgressions. By law, available jobs at work centers had to be opened to internal applicants, even those who required further training, before outsiders were considered. It was up to the union in its role as management counterpart, she explained, to ensure adherence to this law. The union had to oversee hiring procedures to prevent irregularities that she claimed had been commonplace "before," when bosses hired their relatives or even people off the street without giving workers at the center an opportunity to apply. This kind of problem would not afflict her workplace anymore, she contended, because the union would not let it.[21]

It was not easy for Cuban unions to exercise their counterpart role, however. Some union leaders, for example, lacked the requisite knowledge and information. Yet to be an effective counterpart, according to one worker, a union official really had to know "as much as the enterprise director" (*Trabajadores* 19 Jun 79:1). Otherwise, she or he would accept whatever a manager said and would be unable to defend a strong position in the face of management error or intransigence. Specifically, uninformed union leaders needed to improve their knowledge not only of labor legislation but also of management and planning topics. According to Veiga, they had to know enough about the operation of the economy to recognize managerial deficiencies *and* to understand their causes (*Trabajadores* 14 Jun 79:2). In the absence of union leaders and members who were sufficiently knowledgeable in these areas, the call for unions to serve as management counterparts could have little practical impact on the balance of power at the workplace.

Lack of knowledge and information, however, was not the only thing interfering with the unions' capability to act as management counterparts. Workers complained that some managers thwarted union attempts to serve in that capacity, either because they did not understand—or chose to ignore—the unions' assumption of this workplace role. This was bound to occur occasionally at every work center. But what about workplaces where it became endemic? What about the case of a manager who in the unions' evaluation performed poorly, yet who consistently refused to recognize the union's right to intervene where supposedly it had authority? Posed another way, what power did Cuban unions have to get rid of a bad boss? What workers' organizations could and could not do in this situation is a good indication of their power at the point of production.

Neither workers nor unions have had formal authority to select or remove managers at any time since 1959. Top administrators, at least, have always been chosen and removed by the production unit's superordinate state body. Yet workers have long had some informal influence over the firing of a manager.[22] In the 1960s, however, this was limited by the weakness of the unions. Workers at the time lacked a strong organizational base from which to challenge ineffective or unjust managers. As one man recalled, "A worker could always confront a manager at an assembly, but the person had to do it individually, without union support. The assembly might even have backed the worker, but that's not enough. You need a structure—like a strong union provides—to be effective."[23]

Although in the 1970s and 1980s the formal authority to fire a bad manager continued to be held by the state, because union power at the worksite had increased, workers had more influence over removal of superiors than in the past. Workers I interviewed were confident they could play a decisive role in such a dismissal. In fact three examples, two in one workplace, were brought to my attention, and a union official reported that the, "workers' opinion that a boss should be removed carries a lot of weight with those who actually have the power to fire him or her."[24] Workers mentioned a number of avenues they might pursue if they were intent on removing a manager, but the variety of responses to my questions on this subject suggested that no one procedure was followed in such situations. The method used probably varied by the type of workplace, the position of the administrator, and the nature of the complaint. Some workers said that the issue of dismissal would first be brought up at a union meeting or a production assembly. A union official also argued this was the most appropriate first step, because it placed the problem in the open where it could be dealt with collectively.[25] My impression, however, was that many workers would not prefer this as a first step. If so, they could approach the base-level union leadership personally or could submit a complaint in writing. If they were not satisfied with the response, they could go to the next-higher union level. Workers also said they could take complaints directly to the party nucleus, most of them finding it inconceivable that the party would stand aside in so serious a matter. Once their case had been presented, workers said, an investigation, usually conducted by the union or the party, would determine whether the allegations were factual. If the inquiry corroborated workers' complaints, the case would be taken to the manager's superiors, possibly by the party or by a higher union body. No one seemed to doubt that, if the charges were serious enough and were confirmed, "the workers with the union [could] move the manager out!"[26]

CONCLUSION: CHANGING UNIONS AND DEMOCRATIZATION

In his closing address to the 14th National CTC Congress in 1978, Fidel Castro proclaimed:

> There is no imagining the revolution without the role played by the unions. Regardless of what the administrators are able to do, the key, the decisive factor, is the worker . . . and it is the union movement that joins together all our workers. It is for this reason that the movement is of such importance. Without it the Party, the State would not be able to face up to their enormous task.

The next year a front-page editorial in *Trabajadores* opened with the words: "The unions are alive and active organisms in our society. They are not just ornamental organizations, as the enemies of socialism have claimed."[27] Are such pronouncements simply polished examples of official rhetoric or perhaps of wishful thinking? Or are they reasonably accurate descriptions of the status of unions and their role in society in the 1970s and 1980s? Having studied their functions, their organizational vitality, and their worksite relationship with both management and the party, I have concluded that Cuban unions in the 1970s and early 1980s were stronger and more influential than they had been in the decade following the victory over Fulgencio Batista. And largely as a consequence, the democratization of production advanced.

Chapter 9

Accounting for Changes in the Control of Production in Postrevolutionary Cuba

Comparing how Cuban production was controlled and organized in the 1960s with how it was controlled and organized in later periods has enabled us to better understand what the democratization of production might actually entail. It also begs a major question: *How* and *why* did the change toward greater democratization of production relations occur in postrevolutionary Cuba?

An immediate, if oversimplified, response might be that the changes resulted from decisions taken by Cuba's top-level political leadership. But why did Cuba's leaders make these particular *kinds* of changes, which expanded the democratization of production, and why did they make them *when* they did? My approach to answering these questions is in contrast to several other, more common, explanations of events in postrevolutionary Cuba, which stress Fidel Castro's personality, Cuba's relationship with the Soviet Union, and Cuba's international economic linkages.[1] Instead, I will address these questions through an interpretation of the internal dynamics of Cuba's political history in the 1950s, but particularly in the 1960s. The latter decade was distinguished by a paradoxical combination of hypercentralization and mass participation, and both help explain the democratization of the 1970s, though in different ways. Widespread dissatisfaction with hypercentralization in the 1960s was the immediate impetus for change. At the same time, enthusiastic mass involvement in the consolidation of socialism during the same decade helped determine the direction change would take.

In examining this political history it is clear that, although the leaders of the Cuban revolution figure prominently in the explanation for changes in production relations, these leaders did not operate in a vacuum. What they did and when they did it were contingent on the real-life circumstances in which they found themselves. Yet these circumstances did not strictly determine their actions. Rather, they rendered some of their options impractical and unacceptable while suggesting others as both possible and attractive.

THE ORIGIN OF THE 1970 CRISIS: HYPERCENTRALIZATION IN THE 1960S

Major changes in the control of production in postrevolutionary Cuba followed an economic and political crisis in 1970. The antecedents of this crisis, which came to a head with the failure to harvest 10 million tons of sugar, lay in the high degree of centralization of political and economic decision making in the 1960s. Throughout most of that decade decision making was the province of a small number of individuals who served simultaneously as the nation's top economic, political, administrative, and military officials. Outside this group few organized centers of power existed. This deficiency was faithfully reflected in how production was controlled and organized. Management of the economy was so thoroughly centralized that even most supraworksite economic and planning officials had little input on matters of importance. So few decisions were made at the work center that even managers, and certainly producers, similarly had little authority.[2] The Communist party was too small, organizationally weak, and uninvolved in important deliberations to serve as an avenue for incorporating people into decision making. Similarly, the unions floundered through the decade with few responsibilities or resources, minimum independence, and limited ability to expand workers' power over production. Nor did worksite structures exist that encouraged the dispersion of production authority. Management councils were non-existent. And although planning and production and service assemblies were sometimes convened, and work councils existed after 1965, none of these bodies was especially effective in democratizing worksite production relations, largely because the unions had deteriorated.

As the decade progressed centralization increased. In production this was evidenced by the militarization that occurred, especially between 1968 and 1970, as the country prepared for the 10-million-ton sugar harvest. Militarization was most obvious in agriculture, especially sugar, but it was apparent in other sectors as well.[3] It had a number of facets. First, soldiers began taking on productive tasks: 100,000 of them apparently participated in the 1970 sugar harvest (Ritter 1974:293). Furthermore, military personnel began to assume the principal posts of authority in the administration of the economy: They increased their representation in ministries and on the Political Bureau; they took over party secretariats in the provinces; they directed harvesting; they were placed in charge of many state farms and other enterprises. In addition, much of the language and symbolism surrounding work was military: Production tasks were battles or wars; workers were referred to as soldiers; they lived in camps and were grouped into brigades, companies, battalions, and squads under the direction of command posts. Finally, work organization and methods were militarized. Producers were moved away from home, from job to job, and from location to location; holidays, pay rates, and hours were rescheduled to conform to military practice; some workers were given preparatory courses on military topics; all in all, producers found themselves at the bottom of hierarchical and authoritarian command structures. Their job was to execute orders, and rigid discipline was the dictate of the day. Clearly, production carried out according to such a model was the antithesis of democratic.[4]

Because the hypercentralization of economic and political decision making in the 1960s precipitated the crisis from which more democratic production relations eventually emerged, it is important to understand what prevented a wider dispersion of power during the early years. Why did individual work units have so little autonomy? Why was power over production not diffused at least into the ranks of the party? Why could unions not provide a separate organizational locus through which producers attempted to exert some influence over work?

In the 1960s highly centralized management of the economy, with concomitantly little dispersion of authority to the workplace, was attractive to the revolution's leaders on a number of counts. Che Guevara, for one, felt that Cuba's small size and relatively

advanced communication and transportation systems were conducive to economic centralization; he believed that Cuba's export orientation, which necessitated a close correspondence between internal and international prices, also required it (O'Connor 1970:265–
66). Looking back on the 1960s, Raúl Castro offered a rationale for
centralization which, though not specifically focused on economic
management, is nevertheless relevant.

> Those first years were marked by a period of rapid change, of
> deep rooted revolutionary change.
>   In those initial years it was necessary to confront contin-
> ual and increasingly violent imperialist aggression and internal
> counterrevolutionary activity. In order to operate in such a sit-
> uation and face the tasks of the moment, we needed a state
> apparatus that was both functional and could be quickly mo-
> bilized, and which would operate as a dictatorship on behalf of
> the working people; a state apparatus in which the legislative,
> executive, and administrative powers were concentrated in
> one body that was able to make quick decisions. (Taber 1983:
> 219)

Economic centralization seemed attractive in the 1960s for an
additional reason: It was judged more congruent with the attainment of important revolutionary goals, among them economic
equality. It was feared that decentralization, demanding some reliance on market mechanisms, would produce pressures curtailing
or even halting the drive for equality. Some unprofitable worksites
would have been closed, and the number of workers in others
would have been reduced, slowing efforts to end unemployment.
Similarly, the income differentials that would have developed between work units and economic sectors would have neutralized
attempts to narrow the earnings gap between the highest- and
lowest-paid workers. Many products and services needed by un-
derprivileged Cubans would not have been produced, delivered, or
invested in, in favor of others desired by well-to-do customers. Another revolutionary goal—rapid expansion of the country's material base—also seemed at the time to be best served by centralization. Since a major contributor to Cuba's prerevolutionary
economic stagnation had been its large number of small and inefficient production establishments (O'Connor 1970:170), the logical
course of action appeared to be the consolidation of multiple production units under centralized management.[5]

Even had centralization not been so attractive an option for these reasons, two additional factors would have militated against a decentralized approach to managing the economy during the first decade. First, in the early and mid-1960s few socialist countries had undertaken any decentralization reforms. Discussions had been held, and limited experiments had even been attempted, but no full scale decentralization attempt had been made in any socialist countries which Cuba might have adopted as a model. An exception was Yugoslavia, but Cuba was unlikely to turn there for inspiration, since Yugoslavia had continued to supply arms to Fulgencio Batista even after the United States had imposed an arms embargo against the dictator (Ritter 1974:227).

Second, Cuba suffered from a shortage of managerial and technical personnel. Economic decentralization would have meant dispersing decision-making authority among a larger number of individuals. Qualified people capable of making production, administrative, organizational, and technical decisions would have been needed in the thousands of worksites around the country. Yet many individuals with precisely these qualifications left the island during the early years of the revolution. Between 1959 and 1962, Cuba lost nearly thirty-two thousand people from both the professional and semi-professional and from the managerial and executive categories, a number representing 22 percent of the former occupational group and 10 percent of the latter (Fitzgerald 1985: 143). Furthermore, this figure did not include foreigners who left after the revolution, nearly all of whom had held positions in the same occupational categories (Ritter 1974:93; Fitzgerald 1985: 137). Emigration depleted some groups of particular value to the economy; for example, of the 300 agronomists working in Cuba on the eve of the revolution, 270 fled.[6] In light of the scarcity of managerial and technical expertise, it may well have seemed that the country could ill afford economic decentralization. The few managers and technical personnel who remained could hardly be "wasted" at individual production units when, after some retraining, each could put her or his skills and experience to use directing production at many different units simultaneously.[7]

A second indication of hypercentralization in the 1960s was the weakness of the Communist party. During the decade, economic and political decision-making power was not even diffused from the apex of revolutionary leadership out to and down through the party apparatus. To understand why we must examine the relationship of the party to the two Batista governments, to the July 26 Movement which led the struggle against him, and to the leaders of the revolution once they had achieved victory. Knowledge of these three things makes it easy to understand why the development of a strong, active party organization was not initially encouraged by the revolutionary leadership or supported by Cuban workers and peasants.

In contrast to their militant posture in the early and mid-1930s, the Communists, adopting a popular-front strategy, formed a strong and mutually beneficial alliance with the official and unofficial Batista governments from the late 1930s until 1944. During this period the party was legalized; it was allowed to organize within the working class; its membership grew rapidly; eventually it led the organized labor movement. Its political clout reached heights unattained in any other period before the revolution, leaving some progressive imprints on Cuban political life. Part of the price paid for the party's successes, however, was its identification as a traditional, collaborationist, and in many ways conservative force in Cuban politics.[8] Batista's relationship with the Communists soured to some extent during his second term, which began in 1952. The party neither enthusiastically supported nor actively opposed the dictator, who pursued a policy of "uneven repression" toward the Communists (Sims 1985:52). Although outlawing the party, Batista allowed the Communists to retain a foothold in the CTC (Central da Trabajadores de Cuba) and appointed some of them to governmental positions. Coupled with the party's earlier history of overt friendship with Batista, it is not surprising that the future leaders of Cuba, whom Batista went on to imprison during his second regime, should look askance, even by this early date, at the Communist organization.

An additional reason for the party's poor fortunes during the first decade of the revolution was its reluctance to support Castro and the July 26 Movement in their struggle against Batista. The Communists repudiated Castro's 1953 attack on the Moncada Barracks as the act of a putschist bourgeois opposition;[9] they labeled reactionary his now famous "History Will Absolve Me" speech at his trial for the attack; they condemned the landing of the *Granma*, denounced armed struggle as misguided and adventurist, prevented at least one armed demonstration from occurring (Suárez

1967:27), refused to support the April 1958 general strike called by Castro, and called for "clean democratic elections" to oust Batista in June 1958. In the face of mounting repression directed against them, the Communists reached some sort of understanding with Castro in the summer of 1958, though the party was divided over the wisdom of this move. Yet as late as December the Communists were still proposing that a coalition government, including moderate elements who had had minimal association with the July 26 Movement, replace Batista![10] This record surely gave those who actively participated in the fight against the dictator ample reason to look with disfavor on any efforts to increase the power of the Communists in postrevolutionary Cuban politics.

The post-victory relationship between Cuba's soon-to-be proclaimed socialist leadership and the Communist party stands in sharp contrast to the relationship between the party and political leaders during analogous historical periods in most of Eastern Europe. In these countries, the two were so close as to be virtually indistinguishable. But in Cuba the relationship between the Communists and Castro supporters remained unsettled after Batista's defeat. Their tense relationship, lasting throughout the 1960s, is an important element in the explanation for why the party did not become a viable center of political power in Cuba until the following decade.

Even though the party was legalized almost immediately after the victory, Communists resumed their activities in the labor movement, and Castro himself was better described early on as a non-Communist than as an anti-Communist, the friction between the party and the July 26 Movement was obvious from the beginning of the postrevolutionary period.[11] Evidence of the strain was apparent in repeated instances of public and private sparring early in the decade. At one point Castro vehemently declared that Communists were "counterrevolutionary and extremists" and that "communism with its totalitarian conceptions sacrifices human rights. . . . Our revolution is not red but olive green" (Enzensberger 1976:115–16; Zeitlin and Scheer 1963:108). *Revolución*, the July 26 newspaper, denounced the party as deviationist and accused its secretary-general of trying to divide the movement (Thomas 1971: 441). According to Herbert Matthews (1969:178), Raúl Castro once fumed privately that "if the Reds got in the way of the revolution 'he would slit their throats.'" For its part the party, now called the PSP (Partido Socialista Popular), criticized the first post-revolutionary cabinet for not acting in a revolutionary manner. It suggested that some of Castro's actions were left-extremist and excessive and criticized him for unleashing a campaign of anti-Communism (Farber 1983:63; Enzensberger 1976:115–16; Thomas 1971:442). Rooted in their strained history, such comments were prompted by tactical, political, and theoretical disagreements over nearly all major substantive issues facing the fledgling revolution: planning, incentives, the missile crisis, agrarian reform, nationalization, the no-strike pledge, the literacy campaign, the law suspending trade union leaders holding office on December 31, 1958, and the role of the urban petty and national bourgeoisie in the revolutionary process.[12]

Although there was gradual improvement in the relationship between the Communists and Cuba's political leadership as time went on, the first attempt to form a single revolutionary party was shortly halted by a purge of prerevolutionary Communists. This 1962 purge, which intensified mutual distrust and indefinitely postponed the development of a vanguard Communist party, took place precisely because the new party, Integrated Revolutionary Organizations (ORI), was beginning to create its own power base on the island. Calling the ORI "the backbone of the revolutionary state", its head, Aníbal Escalante, successfully placed prerevolutionary party people in numerous positions in factories, government offices, ministries, mass organizations, and even the Rebel Army. Escalante began to issue orders on his own, and personnel in authoritative positions had to seek approval from the ORI before carrying out their tasks. In Boris Goldenberg's (1965:265) summation, "The ORI secretariat had become a second government."[13] Castro's assessment of this turn of events indicates how unacceptable he found such a "second government," in the guise of a strong and independent party controlled by prerevolutionary Communists.

> The provincial secretaries have behaved like Gauleiters. Nepotism and terrorism are spreading. We have founded ORI but excluded the revolutionary masses. What does that mean, Integrated Revolutionary Organizations? The only ones who have organized themselves here were the people of the PSP. It's the same in every province: who became the party secretary of ORI? The former provincial secretary of the PSP. It is

the same thing in every local chapter: who became the local
secretary of ORI? The former local secretary of the PSP! . . . If
we look at the results we are forced to conclude: that is a pile
of shit.[14]

Following this purge the party was reorganized, but its relationship with the country's political leadership remained shaky. In
1964 some old Communists were accused of informing on July 26
supporters before the victory and of afterwards participating in a
cover up. Then in 1968, a second purge of the so-called microfac-
tion, again led by Escalante, occurred. There is no evidence that in
1968 the party had made as much progress in establishing an autonomous center of political power as it had earlier. The fear, however, was that a group of party members, through private attempts
to convince other socialist countries that the Cuban government's
internal and external policies were misguided, were again headed
in that direction.

This second purge came only three years after the official
founding of the new postrevolutionary Cuban Communist party,
and this newly restructured party remained weak, small, and
poorly organized as the 1960s closed. More than a decade of postrevolutionary history had to pass before wounds had healed sufficiently for Cuba's new political leaders to feel that the advantages
of a strong Communist party outweighed the political threat its
earlier existence would clearly have entailed.

A significant cause and consequence of the hypercentralization of political and economic decision making in the 1960s was
the deterioration of the unions. During this period unions were not
effective vehicles for decentralizing political and economic power
to rural and urban workers, the largest segment of the Cuban population. The reason the unions did not counter growing centralization in the 1960s, can be traced back to the prerevolutionary relationship between the leaders of organized labor and Batista on the
one hand, and the July 26 forces on the other.

Recall that since the late 1940s the Cuban labor movement
had been under the control of the notorious Eusebio Mujal, who
presided over an era of union economism, reformism, corruption,
and bureaucratization. Under Mujal, the CTC was fashioned into
Batista's most faithful and, in the end, almost his only political
ally—in the judgment of a former U.S. Ambassador into one of the

dictator's "main props" (Smith 1962:101). In its untiring efforts to bolster Batista's tottering regime, the CTC suppressed strikes and occasionally suspended union elections, mobilized workers for pro-government demonstrations, opposed both the August 1957 and April 1958 general strikes, delegated some labor leaders to assist the armed forces in suppressing them, and threatened workers participating in anti-Batista actions with the loss of their jobs and CTC "protection." Mujal also threw anti-Batista labor leaders out of the CTC and even applauded government repression of July 26 supporters within the union. Not surprisingly, Mujal and many of his chief lieutenants quickly followed the dictator into exile in January 1959.[15]

In light of this history, it is easy to imagine the apprehension with which the victorious July 26 Movement viewed organized labor on the morning of the revolution, a mistrust not belied by its actions. Twenty days into office, the new government promulgated a law dismissing labor leaders holding major posts as of December 31, 1958. The government was thus rid of top-level *mujalistas* in one thorough and undelayed swoop. The replacement of mid- and low-level *mujalista* officers was not so easy, however, given the length of Mujal's reign and the fact that the July 26 Movement could spare few people for union posts. Indeed, many intermediate-level union leaders, even some who had narrowly escaped being tried as *batistianos*, were retained in their positions (Thomas 1971:471). Completely erasing *mujalista* (and pro-Batista) sympathies in the labor movement proved a tortuous task, one that took some unforeseen turns before being completed some two years later.

The first union elections, held in the heady months following victory, demonstrated labor's clear support for the July 26 Movement. Below the surface, however, a political contest of major proportions over control of the unions was brewing. For a time it divided the labor movement internally, threatening to add organized workers to the growing list of those opposed to the course being pursued by the revolution's leaders. Briefly, the Communists tried to capitalize on the power vacuum created by the demise of *mujalismo* in order to rebuild their influence among organized workers. But many of the July 26 labor leaders objected to a strong Communist presence in the unions, whether because of personal ambitions, ideological differences, or because the Communists had not actively supported the struggle against Batista. Anti-Communism gained momentum throughout 1959, as some July 26 labor leaders sought the support of former *mujalistas*. They tempered these new alliances, which were undoubtedly distasteful to many of the rank-and-file, by pressing economic demands and supporting strikes, two activities that moved them still further from the ideological and tactical positions gaining ascendance among the country's political leaders.[16]

Many events in 1959 and 1960 bear witness to a growing strain between organized labor and the national leadership of the July 26 Movement. For example, between January and July strikes, or threats of them, occurred regularly. In February 1959, when labor unrest erupted in the sugar sector, Castro declared that it was precipitated in part by "counterrevolutionary" union leaders. In May 1959, in the midst of national discussions over the first agrarian reform, almost two-thirds of the newly elected leaders of Cuba's thirty-three labor federations pledged to support private property and anti-Communism. That fall, the union leadership in Camagüey supported the mass resignation of Rebel Army officers in the province. The delegates to the 10th National CTC Congress in November 1959 were so badly split over their choice of confederation leaders that Castro had to intervene personally. For a time even he was unable to address the crowd over the shouts from competing sides, and the Congress ended without a definitive victory for Castro's supporters. Finally, as late as December 1960, a sixth of the membership of the Electrical Workers' Union, shouting *"Cuba sí Rusia no,"* protested both the policies of the recently nationalized electric company and the imminent removal of the union's reformist leadership.[17]

Events during the first two years after the victory could only have reinforced the preexisting inclination of Cuba's political leaders to be wary of organizationally strong, autonomous unions, for it was not then sure whether the leadership of such unions would have supported them. By 1961–62, however, the right wing of organized labor (some July 26 labor leaders, former *mujalistas*, and reformists) had failed to muster the support necessary to gain control of the unions. After that time the leadership of the workers' organizations was firmly in the hands of Communists and of former *mujalistas* and July 26 unionists converted in the earlier leadership struggles. Union support for the revolution's leadership was thus certain. Nevertheless, the unions, instead of gaining power, continued to deteriorate throughout the 1960s. How can this be explained?

First, remember that Cuba's political leaders had had no choice but to support Communist unionists in order to eradicate *mujalismo* from the unions. This is not to imply that there was not fundamental agreement between Communist laborites and the nation's political leaders over the role of the unions at that juncture in Cuban history. There clearly was. Yet, as we have just seen, tensions clouded the relationship between Communists and the country's political leaders at the time. The latter would thus certainly have retained misgivings about the growth of strong unions, since the Communists were sure to have had a great deal of influence over the leadership of these organizations.

To some extent, the unions' continued weakness was also a result of the revolution's zealous efforts to shed old capitalist patterns and to forge new relationships among society's members. The debilitated state of the unions during the mid- and late 1960s was also partly attributable to the dearth of models of powerful unions operating in other socialist countries which Cubans could emulate. In addition, the sorry state of the unions was a result of benign neglect; here the enormity of the agenda facing the country during the first postrevolutionary decade must be appreciated. Reconstructing legal, government, and economic institutions according to different principles, educating masses of people, defending the country against external aggression, and learning to relate to a new configuration of allies and trading partners were but some of the projects demanding great expenditures of energy and attention and no doubt siphoning already scarce union talent into other endeavors. Finally, the unions, like nearly every other institution in Cuba, suffered in the late 1960s because the whole nation was focused on one overriding task: producing 10 million tons of sugar in 1970.

CRISIS AND CHANGE

Cuba's failure to reach the 10-million-ton goal in 1970 has been remembered and interpreted in different ways: as preordained by some of her critics and supporters and as the saddest time of the revolution by many Cubans I talked to who had worked hard and had sacrificed much to make it happen. The failed 1970 harvest, however, was something more: It was the culmination of a crisis linked to overcentralization that had been brewing throughout the 1960s. And it marked a major turning point in the Cuban revolution, for it was in that year that the political leadership began to implement a series of changes that spread economic and political decision-making power among larger numbers of citizens, directly and indirectly furthering the democratization of production.

The most immediately visible symptoms of the crisis were economic. The average annual change in Gross Social Product (GSP) and GSP per capita measured only 0.4 percent and −1.3 percent respectively over the years 1966–70, after having increased by 3.7 percent and 1.3 percent in 1962–65.[18] With certain exceptions, both food and total agricultural production declined during the 1960s. Food production per capita, for instance, was 28 percent lower in 1969 than in 1959 (Bonachea and Valdés 1972b:366). Similarly, the production of cement, textiles, tires, and oven ranges declined between 1960 and 1970.[19] Extreme scarcities in both consumer and production goods hastened the growth of black markets and encouraged hoarding, both of which further exacerbated supply problems.

In addition, high absenteeism and low productivity plagued the nation. Absenteeism, an intermittent problem during the 1960s, became particularly troublesome in the latter half of the decade. Available statistics, though scattered and incomplete, give some idea of the problem's severity. In 1968 absenteeism rates in the construction industry reached 17 percent; a 1968–69 study of 200 enterprises revealed that up to 40 percent of the workday was sometimes lost, mostly owing to absenteeism; in mid-1969 absenteeism rates for permanent farm workers never fell below 35 percent in one province; at the peak of the 1970 harvest the absenteeism rate throughout the economy was 29 percent, and that fall it still hovered around 20 percent.[20] In terms of labor productivity, official reports indicate that annual changes from 1963 to 1966 fluctuated between 6.0 percent in 1964, and −2.1 percent in 1966.[21] Although changes in overall rates for the economy are not available for 1967–73, scattered data suggest that productivity was not high in that period. Various sources report, for example, that the number of hours worked per day averaged only four or five between 1966 and 1969;[22] according to Archibald Ritter, between November 1968 and November 1969 the proportion of the workday lost varied from 14 percent to 36 percent in different sectors of the economy; the number of dockworkers apparently increased more than 38 percent between 1967 and 1969, while the tonnage handled fell by over 12 percent; according to the Minister of Labor, productivity was so low during the 1970 sugar harvest that the cost of producing sugar was three times its value on the international market (Ritter 1974:284–85 and Valdés 1972*a*:69). Little wonder that Castro, taking stock in 1970, concluded that "unproductivity is like an abyss threatening to swallow up our human resources and our country's wealth" and that "absenteeism is the thing we must tackle with everything we've got right now" (Ritter 1974:283, 286).

Overcentralization of economic and political decision making in the 1960s may be linked to these economic symptoms of crisis in several ways. First, the lack of mass (or at least more widespread) input into decision-making processes contributed to the adoption of some widely unpopular policies, notable among them the decision to restrict individual consumption levels.[23] The percentage of Cuba's Gross Material Product (GMP) destined for gross capital formation rose from approximately 16 percent in 1962 to a targeted 31 percent in 1968.[24] High investment levels, combined with the purposeful reduction of imports of consumer goods, the export (and underproduction) of products that might eagerly have been consumed at home (e.g., meat, fruits, vegetables, and shoes), and the 1968 elimination of small private retail establishments caused consumption per capita—after rising modestly during the first half of the 1960s—to sink during the remainder of the decade (Mesa-Lago 1971:323). Popular disaffection with these policies has frequently been noted: Consumer goods were so scarce by 1970 that one foreigner living in Cuba expressed surprise that street demonstrations had not occurred.[25] The dearth of purchasable goods lowered the value of workers' earnings, contributing to a decline in work effort that further diminished the supply of consumer goods together with overall economic output.

Second, centralization has been shown to cause numerous operating problems and inefficiencies in socialist countries, and in Cuba such difficulties were greatly aggravated by the extremes to which it was carried in the 1960s. The economy's discouraging performance may therefore be traced in part to economic decision makers, overburdened and isolated at the center by virtue of the structure. They allocated inputs improperly, frequently made wasteful and unsettling revisions in output targets, failed to deal satisfactorily with quality and distribution issues, and sometimes even made blunders as serious as setting planting targets above harvesting capacity. Overcentralization also severely limited the ability and the inclination of firm-level personnel to report operating difficulties to the center or to remedy them on their own initiative.[26] Finally, the overlap of economic and political authority led both to make economically unrealistic decisions and to adopt solutions that could never resolve the growing stream of problems plaguing the economy. Under these circumstances, workers' willingness to sacrifice in the present was eroded as they repeatedly saw their efforts neutralized and their better future denied as a result of errors spawned by a decision-making system that left no room for input from the base. And to the extent that their disenchantment was translated into reduced effort at work, Cuba's economic problems simply grew worse.

Third, the absence of systematic input from the base made it too easy for the upper echelons of the decision-making hierarchy to adopt and then doggedly pursue *combinations* of policies that produced or exacerbated symptoms of deepening economic crisis. For example, pay equity was heavily stressed, especially during the late 1960s. Moves were undertaken to narrow income differentials, both by raising the wages of the lowest paid workers and by severing the monetary connection between effort and output. Overtime pay was renounced, extra pay for overfulfillment of quotas was limited, work norms were disregarded, and an expanded program of moral incentives was instituted. Yet, even as a more egalitarian remunerative structure was being built, inequalities in decision-making power, owing to overcentralization, were everywhere becoming more apparent. So obvious a contradiction cannot have gone unnoticed and was likely to have contributed to the undercurrent of disquiet, cynicism, and declining morale among Cuban producers.[27]

Likewise, the economic crisis was exacerbated by a combination of policies that simultaneously restricted consumer goods production, severed the connection between output and effort, narrowed wage differentials, and provided many products and services free or at minimal cost. (In the late 1960s, electricity, telephone service, buses, sports events, school uniforms, lunches at work, some rents, and water were added to the already long list of things provided cheaply or at no cost. Retirement and illness benefits also began to be offered at full wages.) Since prices were controlled, the result was that many Cubans found themselves with "dresser drawers full of excess cash" (Edelstein 1985:183). It has been estimated that many could have purchased a month's rations by working only two or three weeks, that by 1970 purchasing power exceeded the supply of goods by 87 percent, and that people could live a full year without working, which is precisely what an appreciable number apparently tried to do (Ritter 1974:253; Bonachea and Valdés 1972b:369; Zimbalist 1985:217). By Ritter's account, by 1971 more than one hundred thousand people had simply stopped working, more or less permanently.[28] The vicious cycle of growing absenteeism, falling productivity, more acute shortages, and lowered morale continued its upward spiral.

The impending crisis, however, was revealed not only through its economic symptoms. These also had related political dimensions, two of which are particularly significant. First, the spreading inclination of some producers to minimize their work efforts was placing the unity of the working class—a matter of special importance to the strength and stability of the revolution—under increasing strain. Some producers responded to the government's unworkable policies by restricting their work efforts or by staying home altogether, thus putting heavy pressure on the rest to work even harder. Yet it was distressing for the latter group, who constituted the majority, to see how the neglect of material incentives and the emphasis on remunerative equality permitted slackers to live as well as they themselves were. This undermined morale, weakened the incentive system, and further decreased output, but it also created intra-class hostilities. Despite the structural inducements for slacking, workers were blaming one another for the situation, and this was apparently getting out of hand in some places. "Go to any factory and ask the workers what should be done about the lazy ones, the ones who don't work," remarked Castro in 1970. "If you don't watch out, they'll go so far as to demand they be shot."[29]

Second, though expressed largely in economic terms, over economic issues, and in the economic realm, workers' dissatisfac-

tions were symptomatic of political crisis. Owing to the overt inter-
face between polity and economy in Cuba, workers could easily
trace the source of their economic discontent to the country's political processes, institutions, and leaders. In other words, a fissure
was opening between the politics and the politicians of the revolution and the mass of working people. It is not easy, however, to
judge how serious a political threat workers' actions posed at that
time. My sense is that the threat was not an imminent one. Slow-
downs, tardiness, stay-at-homes, even an uncoordinated but large-
scale "strike," as Jorge Domínguez (1978:275) characterized workers' responses at the time, are one thing. Mass demonstrations,
widespread sabotage, the development of an organized opposition
to the government are something else. The political crisis never
reached such intensity in Cuba, though many observers have suggested that, had the difficulties not been rectified, the revolution
would have experienced some very tumultuous times.[30]

Such an eventuality was averted because the potential implications of popular disappointment and discontent were taken quite
seriously by Cuba's political leadership. The government responded by instituting changes that attenuated the hypercentralization of economic and political decision making characteristic of
the 1960s. The innovations included, but were not limited to,
changes furthering the democratization of production.[31] Thus, in a
narrow sense it is accurate to say that economic democratization
began to increase when it did because of initiatives taken by political leaders. Yet this top-down explanation for the timing of change
in Cuba does not tell the whole story. Despite the genuine concern
of Cuba's political leaders for the plight of the workers in the
1960s, the changes after 1970 did not originate in the largess, be-
nevolence, or democratic inclinations of the powerful. Rather they
came only as the result of pressure from below. They were
prompted in large measure by Cuban workers, even though
workers' precipitating actions were not of an organized or dramatic
kind.

WHY DEMOCRATIZATION? THE INSTITUTION
AND CONSOLIDATION OF CUBAN SOCIALISM

Yet, why did the changes that began to be implemented at
this juncture assume their particular character? Why, in other

words, was increased democratization on the agenda in 1970? After all, history is replete with examples of militarization and intensification of repression as antidotes for economic catastrophe and disquiet among producers. Barring, or in conjunction with this, a further narrowing of the already small circle of people who made major decisions might have been attempted in Cuba. Why were the unions not abolished? By all accounts they were almost defunct anyway. Why were the few remaining avenues for participation in decision making at the workplace not closed? Why were renewed attempts to restrict the authority of individual production units not made? Why did the party not remain small, based largely in upper occupational strata, and tangential to major decision-making processes? In short, why did the Cuban leadership, in response to the crisis of the late 1960s, not tighten its own control over production and clamp down on the workforce?

As a matter of fact, for a time in the late 1960s and early 1970s there were some indications that Cuba's political leaders might be turning in this direction.[32] In late 1969, for example, a new law was passed which decreed updated labor histories be kept on each worker, a detailed one at his or her place of employment and another, less complete, on a labor card to be carried on the worker's person. The more extensive resumé, the *expediente*, contained information on the worker's past employment, productivity, merits and demerits (decided by workers' assemblies), as well as political viewpoint, and it was to be revised every six months by worksite management. The labor card contained summary information about the individual's work history. It had to be produced in order to get paid or if a worker changed jobs.[33] At the end of 1970 a grass-roots campaign against absenteeism was also begun. It started with assemblies where the issue was discussed, and it incorporated a variety of locally instituted measures such as public listing of absentees, their payment in certain specified locations, and denial of some material goods and social and work benefits to offenders. The campaign culminated in workplace discussions of the draft of an anti-loafing law, in which more than three million people participated. The final version of the law, promulgated in April 1971, specified that workers with unjustified absences of more than fifteen workdays be given penalties ranging from observation by fellow workers to up to two years' confinement in reeducation or supervised worksites for repeat offenders.[34] Finally, a campaign begun in 1971 encouraged managers to be more demanding of workers, and the following year new legislation concerned with crimes against the economy was passed.

At almost the same time that actions such as these were being taken, mass meetings were organized across the island to analyze what had gone wrong in the 1960s. They were held in conjunction with public calls for the revitalization and democratization of the unions, the institution of collective managerial bodies, and heightened decentralization of the economy. All these contemporaneous events suggest possible disagreement amongst the country's top leaders about how to respond to the urgent situation facing them. Maurice Zeitlin, who visited Cuba in 1969, found evidence of this, and late the same year Castro alluded to the existence of coercive currents within high government circles, though he claimed not to concur with this position (Zeitlin 1970:xxxvi, xlii, xliii; Valdés 1972a:52). Although virtually nothing is known about the schism, it was resolved with no major changes in top-level leadership. And, in the main, it was not accompanied by repression, militarization, or increased centralization; rather, it initiated the reconstruction of the country's political and economic decision-making processes along lines that increased the democratization of production.

Two general points about the post-1970 changes need to be stressed in conjunction with this investigation of why they assumed the particular character they did. First, by itself, the decentralization that occurred in many different spheres in post-1970 Cuba should not be equated with democratization. Although democratization demands some degree of decentralization, the reverse does not hold. Most other socialist countries also embarked at one time or another on decentralization drives, mainly in an effort to overcome the sluggishness and inefficiency associated with high degrees of political and economic centralization. The intent of these reforms was usually only to expand the parameters of the elite, to secure the cooperation of technical and professional personnel, of mid-level party officials, and sometimes of the leaders of mass organizations and of intellectuals. Yet these reforms did not spell democratization, so long as they left basically intact the formidable barriers between the elite, albeit afterward slightly larger, and the rest of the citizenry.[35] In this respect the post-1970 reform process in Cuba can be distinguished from many that occurred in other socialist countries. In Cuba the post-1970 changes went further. The changes, particularly in the unions and in workplace decision-making structures, affected the relationship among all participants in production, including the mass of workers.

The second point concerns the order in which various changes relevant to the democratization of production occurred. Significantly, Cuba's political leaders decided *first* to reactivate the unions. Union elections were held before the end of 1970, and the 13th National CTC Congress was held three years later. Following this Congress, workers' participation in worksite decision making solidified: Union officers began to attend management councils; annual plans were disaggregated to permit discussion in planning assemblies; monthly production and service assemblies were stressed as appropriate arenas for involving the rank-and-file in management. The most concerted efforts to expand the party and to strengthen its role in decision making, however, did not come until later. Nor did the institution of the SDPE (El Sistema de Dirección y Planificación de la Economía) begin in earnest until the latter half of the 1970s.

The revitalization of unions and the strengthening of workplace decision-making structures before (sometimes well before) changes in the party or in the planning and management system were completed undoubtedly benefited the democratization process. Workers' organizations, emerging from a long dry spell, were given a little lead time to regroup before managerial and technical personnel assumed increased powers and responsibilities under the SDPE and before party cadres fanned out and took on a larger role in making decisions about production. Furthermore, individual workers had time to become familiar with their rights and obligations as members of more active unions, to gain experience in analyzing plans and solving production problems in assembly settings, and, in general, to learn how to exploit their expanded opportunities for participation most advantageously.

Had the party been rejuvenated and the SDPE instituted before unions were strengthened and participatory worksite structures became operative, the democratization of production in post-1970 Cuba might well have been more limited. Had management and party people had the jump start they might have capitalized on the previously existing power imbalance which greatly favored them. They might have consolidated their power over production so firmly that workers would have been unable to take advantage of new opportunities for increased control to the extent they were able to.

It is noteworthy that the sequence of changes in the reform process was different in some socialist countries where the democratization of production proceeded less far. For instance, in Czechoslovakia, enterprise autonomy began to increase as early as 1966, and intellectuals, judging reform of the party to be crucial, prompted major changes in that organization before workers' councils made their 1968 appearance. Czechoslovak unions, however, were not considered central to reform, and partly as a consequence, they were the last organizations to join the movement for democratizing the economy and polity (Fišera 1978:10 and Fejtö 1974:404). Perhaps the democratization of production, as the late 1960s reform effort in general, would have been more vital and been able to survive longer in Czechoslovakia had changes there followed a different order.

Similarly, in China decentralization reforms in the late 1970s occurred with little attention directed toward the revitalization of the unions, which continued to be viewed with "some trepidation" by the country's political leaders. Partly as a result, unions, rather than finding themselves in the position to promote further democratization, became increasingly susceptible to control by enterprise management, which has, in extreme cases, used its post-reform decision-making authority to abolish the workers' organizations (Wilson 1986:233–39, 242).

The decision in the early 1970s to democratize as well as decentralize, to introduce changes in a certain order, indeed to expand democracy in the realm of production, thus did not follow patterns observable in some other socialist countries. To understand why Cuban leaders made the distinctive choices they did, I turn first to the institution of socialism in the country.

The institution of socialism in Cuba culminated in the seizure of state power by the July 26 Movement in January 1959. It attracted far wider popular participation than had similar developments in many Eastern European countries, where socialism was often imposed without the support, even in spite of the activities, of the indigenous population. As Domenico Nuti (1979:252–53) and Wlodzimierz Brus (1975:61) point out, socialism in Eastern Europe had weak internal roots; it was largely transplanted from the outside. In Bulgaria, for example, socialists gained control of the government by staging a bloodless coup in September 1944, after the Soviet Union had declared war on the country and the Red Army had launched an invasion. In the German Democratic Republic (GDR) socialism was instituted on the heels of the Nazi defeat by a small group of German Communists and Social Democrats, in cooperation with the occupying Soviet Union. In Romania, it was the project of a party numbering around one thousand with "poor or non-existent connections" to the country's rural and urban workers (Nelson 1986:107). In Czechoslovakia, socialism was not entirely imposed from the outside, for the Communists won the 1946 national elections by a substantial margin, approximately 40 percent of the votes. One Communist electoral victory, however, does not suggest the Czech and Slovak populations were anywhere near as involved in the institution of socialism in their country as were the Cubans during their six to seven years' opposition to Batista.[36]

The struggle during those years in Cuba was, in contrast with the above examples, completely indigenous. Castro's forces received no appreciable help from outside. Rather, for many years they were encouraged and aided by the diverse activities of Cubans representing a wide spectrum of the country's principal classes, groups, and organizations. The institution of socialism in Cuba can thus best be described as a multi-sector struggle; though it did not count as many active supporters as, for example, the Sandinistas or the National Liberation Front in Vietnam, it nevertheless attracted numerous participants from a very broad social base.[37]

The story of the July 26 Movement's broad social base begins with rural support for the Rebel Army, which could not have survived without the daily aid of its rearguard, the Oriente peasants and squatters who provided it with food, information, recruits, and cover for years, beginning with the Granma's disastrous landing in 1956.[38] Moreover, as the army's strength grew, other local citizens began to work with its administrative arm in operating the expanding *territorio libre*. By the summer of 1958, *territorio libre* encompassed five thousand square miles, in which agrarian reform, twenty-five schools, a newspaper, a radio station, a taxation system, health facilities, production units, and courts were functioning.[39]

Other sectors of the Cuban population contributed to the

Rebel Army's eventual victory through a wide variety of activities. Urban workers, especially in the eastern part of the country, were responsible for the success of paralyzing strikes in 1956, 1957, 1958, and 1959, which were motivated as much by political as economic dissatisfaction. Bank workers struck. Some unionized workers clandestinely organized anti-government committees within the CTC and eventually formed a labor front which signed the unity pact with Castro in 1958, engaged in acts of sabotage, and sent material aid to the front. Some workers, including purged union leaders, joined the July 26 Movement, and the urban resistance, though small and socially diverse, funneled money, arms, medical supplies, and recruits to the guerrillas and perpetrated numerous acts of sabotage, ranging from planting bombs to setting fires to attacking commercial establishments. Five hundred thousand sugar workers, chanting "Down with the criminal government" (Fitzgerald 1985:92), struck in late 1955 and, later on, workers disrupted the 1958 sugar harvest at the behest of the revolution's leaders.

Aside from peasant and worker support, the Rebel Army benefited periodically from defections of small numbers of Batista's forces. An underground existed within the military, and in September 1957 naval officers, with wide popular support, took Cienfuegos and held it for a short while before being defeated at a cost that may have reached hundreds of lives. Individual students joined the Rebel Army as well. Student organizations led an abortive attack on the Presidential Palace in 1957 and had their own guerrilla detachment, which operated mainly in the Escambray mountains.[40] Two hundred Cuban women, dressed in black and chanting *"¡Libertad!"* demonstrated in Santiago de Cuba during a visit of the U.S. Ambassador. Forty were arrested. At the end of 1958 one in twenty members of the Rebel Army were reported to be women, though they were mostly noncombatants. One by one professional and business organizations, including the Cuban Medical Association, the Bar Association, the Lions, the Masons, and associations of dentists, journalists, pharmacists, surveyors, and public accountants, protested the Batista dictatorship, though it was not always clear they accepted the July 26 Movement as an alternative. The Catholic church and other religious organizations also publicly denounced Batista. Individual priests often went much further, relaying clandestine messages to the resistance, serving as chaplains with the guerrillas, allowing their churches to become centers of political activity, and holding local and national offices in the July 26 Movement (Thomas 1971:162, 210, 212). Finally, the majority of the middle and upper classes, though by and large not giving Castro's forces definitive support, did not offer strong resistance during the institution period. Numerous individuals from these classes held leadership posts in the resistance, participated in the urban underground, and provided material support. In this last regard, Castro is reported to have accepted contributions ranging from five million to ten million dollars from Cuban capitalists during the last few months of 1958.[41]

Numerous citizens from varying sectors of society thus became involved in the process of instituting socialism in Cuba. Indeed, broad, multi-sector social support was a central ingredient in Castro's success. It is also noteworthy that for many Cubans who participated, the institution of socialism was more than a vicarious affair. They were not merely passive supporters of those challenging the status quo. Instead, they accepted risks by participating and were willing to make emotional, intellectual, physical, and material sacrifices to do so. And throughout the 1950s, with each step that brought victory over Batista closer, strong connections were being forged, mutual trust was being established, and reciprocal commitments were being made and honored between the leaders of the resistance and the many Cubans who actively supported them. The resulting domestic political climate, within which the consolidation of socialism began in the 1960s, was thus very different from that which existed when the consolidation process began in much of Eastern Europe. In Cuba the institution process had created a reservoir of mutual goodwill and respect which both leaders and citizens would draw upon and replenish in the difficult decade of consolidation still to come.[42]

Early in the consolidation process Cuba's new political leaders, often responding to demands from below, began to reinforce the social support that had grown up during the institution struggles of the 1950s, and they started to attract such support where it had not previously existed.[43] This was accomplished through an array of new programs and policies. Within around twelve months, thanks to an economic redistribution of massive proportions, 15 percent of the national income was transferred from owners to workers.[44] This was in part accomplished through the agrarian reform. This reform expropriated large private hold-ings, converting some into co-ops and collective farms often em-ploying their prerevolutionary workforces, and distributed land to more than 100,000 individuals who had previously been squat-ters, tenants, or sharecroppers. In addition, public housing was constructed in town and country, and rent reductions of between 30 and 50 percent were decreed. Telephone, gas, and electricity rates were cut, and prices of some items, including medicines, were reduced by 15 to 20 percent. New agricultural credits were offered, installment payment periods were doubled with no increase in in-terest rates, and the minimum wage was raised. The total wage bill registered at least a 50 percent increase between 1958 and 1962, and under- and unemployment fell by 9 percent in the first two years of the 1960s, partly due to the creation of public works jobs.

In addition to economic redistribution measures, the new government took other steps of unquestioned popularity. It dis-solved Batista's police and embarked on ambitious education and medical programs. Technical aid was offered to farmers. Potable water was provided to communities that had never had it. The revolution won the favor of many Cubans of African descent by desegregating all public places as well as other establishments, fa-cilities, and professions. Women benefited through the opening of new job opportunities, child-care centers, and playgrounds. Private clubs and recreational and sports facilities were opened to the pub-lic or turned into workers' centers. For example, the exclusive beach of the Havana Biltmore Yacht Club began to charge fifty cents for admission; a membership had previously cost three thou-sand dollars. New parks were built. According to Zeitlin (1970: 196–202), nationalization significantly altered social relations at the workplace, producing positive changes in people's attitudes to-ward their jobs. Many workers were rapidly promoted into posi-tions left open by members of the middle and upper classes who fled. Finally, protection against arbitrary discharge was extended to agricultural workers; all post-1952 firings precipitated by political or union activities were nullified, and layoffs for economic reasons were prohibited.[45]

Knowledge of policies such as these helps us grasp something of the overall political climate during the consolidation of socialism in the 1960s. Yet it suggests only the outlines of the relationship between leaders and led being forged at the time and of how this relationship might be connected to democratization in the 1970s. The relationship cannot be reduced to an appreciative mass response to social and economic policies adopted by a sensitive, benevolent, or adept elite. Such an interpretation is too simple. Redistributive and social welfare policies may have been necessary for its development, but they were not sufficient. Certainly the policies just reviewed gave a widening circle of Cubans a material stake in the revolution, thus reinforcing their loyalty to and trust in the political leaders who implemented them. But, if my analysis is correct, this alone cannot account for the depth, the durability, or certain unique features of the relationship between leaders and masses existing at the time the 1970 crisis had to be dealt with.

Rather, the key to understanding why the potential for democratization existed at this historical juncture lies in another aspect of this relationship. Not only was a large proportion of the Cuban population predisposed to support the revolution's leaders because of the post-victory policies they pursued, but the leaders themselves had increasing reason to respect and trust those they led. Their confidence in the citizenry came as many Cubans from all walks of life gave time, energy, imagination, and sometimes even their lives in order to build a new social system during the 1960s. Even more than the earlier institution process, the consolidation of socialism was in large measure successful because it rested on significant levels of active popular participation. And this factor held great significance for the direction change took in the post-1970 period.[46]

Once again, this relationship between leaders and led in Cuba stands in contrast to the analogous relationship that emerged during the consolidation of socialism in much of Eastern Europe. There, rather than finding political leaders encouraging or calling for mass participation, we more often find them hostile to it. In Hungary, for instance, the immediate post-war years saw the emergence of a variety of grass-roots committees that might have formed the nucleus of a popular and participatory Hungarian state. Hundreds of thousands of citizens were active in these factory, production, land-reform, village, and county committees; some groups even established their own police forces. The Hungarian Communist party, however, did not join forces with the popular movement. It did not seek its aid or support as a means of consolidating socialism in the country. On the contrary, on assuming political control, the party collaborated in the successful suppression of the grass-roots movement.[47] Similarly, in Soviet-occupied Germany, the Communist party worked to disband around five hundred grass-roots, anti-fascist organizations (the Antifa committees) which had appeared to support the reconstruction. And in Czechoslovakia, as the Communist party assumed power in 1948, it abolished possibly twelve thousand work councils, which had been formed after liberation and which had both safeguarded property and assumed managerial functions (Porket 1986:88).

Important examples of mass participation in the consolidation of socialism in Cuba in the 1960s can be seen in the National Revolutionary Militias, voluntary labor, and the literacy campaign.[48] Each attracted a large number of Cuban citizens, whose participation demanded high levels of mental, physical, and emotional activity and commitment, sometimes for extended periods. In late 1960, André Gunder Frank explained how he experienced this popular involvement.

> As I try to talk with these people, they run off to this meeting or that, at all hours of the day and night, explaining that they are the *responsable* of the local youth group, or of the *Alfabetización* Committee of the 26th of July Movement, or of some political education committee, or of another one of the thousand other voluntary community service and educational organizations which work, not to run dances and picnics, but to advance the revolution and its work. (Frank 1985:416)

Although militias were deemed unnecessary at first, increased counterrevolutionary activity, including an aerial bombing raid that killed forty Cubans, precipitated a call for their formation in October 1959. As Domínguez has pointed out, the militias were thus the first political organizations to be created in postrevolutionary Cuba.[49] Estimates of the number of people in the militias in the early 1960s range from 150,000 to 1 million. Castro reported that more than a thousand companies existed in mid-1960, although they were not supplied with arms until the fall. Women and men, old and young, workers, peasants, and the unemployed, blacks, mulattos, and whites signed up for eight-hour-a-week stints in the volunteer forces.[50] Militia members gave up their free time before and after work and on weekends for training, which Zeitlin describes as "grueling and thorough" and which evidently included academic as well as military instruction.[51] The substantial commit-ment these volunteers made is seen in the following: Militias spearheaded the attack against the U.S. sponsored invasion at Playa Girón in 1961 and suffered the heaviest casualties in the en-suing seventy-two-hour battle; more than ten thousand *milicianos* served in the campaign against the Escambray counterrevolution about the same time; members all over the country were targeted by counterrevolutionary assassins; *milicianos* guarded workplaces, crops, and government buildings twenty-four hours a day, a dan-gerous job because of frequent acts of sabotage (fires, bombings, property destruction) by counterrevolutionaries. The existence and the successes of the National Revolutionary Militia are testimony to the growth of reciprocal trust between Cuban masses and the revolutionary leaders. Through the militias a large segment of the population demonstrated their willingness to respond resolutely to a call for action in support of their leaders and the policies they were pursuing. In turn, the leaders exhibited enough confidence in the Cuban people to arm them, even though in so doing they were creating "a certain source of countervailing power."[52]

The second illustration of mass participation during the con-solidation period was voluntary labor. Throughout the 1960s many tasks in agriculture and elsewhere in the economy were suc-cessfully performed only because thousands responded to requests to put aside their ordinary duties and become volunteer workers. Volunteer labor began in late 1959 when some citizens volun-teered to clean and paint the Havana waterfront (*Revolución* 10 Oct 59:1). Programs continued on a small scale the rest of the year, expanded from 1960 to 1962, and mushroomed in the latter half of the decade, accounting for an estimated 8 to 10 percent of all labor by 1968 (Fitzgerald 1985:121). Carmelo Mesa-Lago (1972:388) estimates that volunteer labor (measured in person-years) increased from about 15,000 in 1962 to about 70,000 in 1967. (The actual number of individuals volunteering would be much larger.) For the sugar harvest alone, the number of volunteer laborers has been estimated at 86,000 in 1966, 93,000 in 1967, 142,000 in 1968, and 1.2 million in 1970.[53]

Volunteer workers fell into three categories. Some were workers on leave from their regular jobs who received their usual wages, with co-workers who remained behind attempting to make up for their absence through intensified effort or unpaid overtime.

It would thus be accurate to consider these people vol workers as well, though they have seldom been so recognizea. A second kind of volunteer labor was performed in overtime or on weekends, holidays, and vacations. The third category comprised unemployed persons, often women, who were recruited by the Cuban Women's Federation (FMC) or the Committees for the Defense of the Revolution (CDR). Room and board and social security benefits were often received by volunteer laborers in the last two groups. Volunteer labor has often been criticized as being economically inefficient and as exacerbating the economic symptoms of the crisis that developed in the late 1960s. At the same time, however, voluntary labor affected the *political* direction the solution to that crisis would eventually take. The willingness of hundreds of thousands of Cubans to give up free time to perform difficult tasks, often for extended periods, away from families, friends, workmates, and the comforts of home, and usually without monetary compensation, was additional evidence of the population's commitment to the revolution. It further reinforced the leaders' confidence in participatory, mass-based solutions to the problems confronting them.

A final example of mass involvement in the consolidation of Cuban socialism is the literacy campaign—the most successful of its time and an important model for other countries in the developing world. The new government focused the country's attention on the problem of illiteracy almost at once. In 1960, when Castro asked for one thousand recruits to go to the countryside where three-quarters of those who were illiterate resided, five thousand responded.[54] Although approximately 100,000 adults were taught to read and write in 1959 and 1960, the campaign against illiteracy did not get fully underway until 1961. During that year literacy teachers were trained, organizational structures were established, materials were written and printed, and a census was completed to determine the number of illiterates and where they resided. Finally, literacy instruction was begun on a wide scale. Altogether, over 1.1 million Cubans, 894,000 as students and more than 270,000 as teachers, *directly* participated in this "passionate, turbulent, sometimes desperate" campaign (Kozol 1978:84).

The literacy teachers were of four kinds. First were the approximately 100,000 student *brigadistas*, mostly high-school and primary age pupils who went to remote areas of the countryside for six to nine months.[55] Usually they lived with their students' families, often under very primitive conditions. Their days were hard and long for, in addition to teaching, they often helped with agricultural chores. Work as a *brigadista* could also be dangerous. As in Nicaragua two decades later, some teachers and students were attacked and murdered by counterrevolutionaries opposed to the idea of teaching peasants to read and write. As the job was demanding and goals were high, in September 1961 a call was made for reinforcements. The generous response enabled the campaign to send a special workers' brigade numbering about fourteen thousand to the countryside to aid the student *brigadistas*. The third main arm of the literacy campaign consisted of more than 120,000 *alfabetizadores populares*, adults who held classes an average of two hours daily, outside work hours, mostly in urban and semi-urban areas. Finally, technical and instructional expertise for the thousands of literacy workers in these three categories was provided by professional teachers. In this way about thirty-five thousand of Cuba's thirty-six thousand teachers assisted in the campaign (Huberman and Sweezy 1969:25). According to Dudley Seers et al. (1964:201), professional teachers and adults active as *alfabetizadores populares* represented one-fifth of the eligible adult population in Cuba.

Aside from those directly participating in the literacy campaign as teachers and students, many more Cubans engaged in behind-the-scenes activities, which often required no less a commitment. These indirect participants, whose contributions to the success of the campaign are not always recognized, included bus drivers who transported *brigadistas* back and forth across the island; workers who took over the jobs of those who joined the workers' brigades; workers who made uniforms and other equipment for the *brigadistas* and who built additional schools; mass-organization members and other citizens who made and collected material donations ranging from food to pencils; medical personnel and Ministry of Education employees who contributed organizational and technical expertise; and parents of the student *brigadistas* who took food and other essentials to their daughters and sons and to the families they lived with in the countryside. The only estimate I have seen of the number of Cubans *indirectly* involved in the campaign in these ways is very large: 2.25 million (Rojas 1986:18).

In summary, through the literacy campaign and subsequent educational programs a large number of Cubans in the 1960s participated in endeavors that had significant political as well as educational implications.[56] For example, city dwellers and peasants, historically divided, began to recognize the degree to which their economic, social, and political interests were linked. Moreover, the pedagogical process and the educational materials used increased political awareness among teachers, students, and behind-the-scenes participants. Of prime importance, however, is that the 1960s educational efforts influenced the development of the bond being forged between revolutionary leaders and citizens. The large-scale participation, widespread enthusiasm, and active commitment demonstrated by Cubans who worked in educational campaigns, together with the organizational, leadership, and technical skills they acquired in the process, helped ensure democratization a prominent place among the options available to the country's political leaders as they formulated their response to the crisis of 1970.

CONCLUSION: POST-1970 DEMOCRATIZATION AND BEYOND

*It is evident that many things will be simply
"impossible" when considered from the standpoint of
a governing party hopelessly stuck in its opposition
to the masses, a party that cannot demand anything
from them.*
—RUDOLF BAHRO

The political history of the institution, but particularly the consolidation, of socialism in the 1950s and 1960s holds the key to understanding the character of changes in the control of production in post-1970 Cuba. In particular the explanation hinges on the type of relationship that developed between the leaders of the revolution and the Cuban citizenry. The Rebel Army and the July 26 Movement benefited from multi-sector participation in their struggles to overturn the Batista dictatorship. Such broad-based involvement during institution helped foster an internal political climate characterized by reciprocal enthusiasm, support, and solidarity between masses and leaders once victory was achieved. The relationship was further strengthened during consolidation in the

1960s by the government's adoption of some extremely popular policies, but more importantly by the varied, lively, and widespread participation of the population in the arduous process of building a new society. Despite strains between leaders and masses arising from the paternalistic aspects of mass involvement, and from the government's failure to link it to permanent institutions and formal procedures (Griffiths and Griffiths 1979:12; Munck 1984:320; Huberman and Sweezy 1969:204–5), in the main, mass-based and mass-dependent action reinforced the mutual confidence and support between the two groups which had only begun to develop during the earlier struggle against Batista.

It would be wrong, however, to consider post-1970 democratization in Cuba as the mere extension, maturation, or amplification of the type of 1960s mass participation evident in the militias, in voluntary labor, and in the literacy program. Rather, the nature of the relationship between leaders and led forged in the 1960s helps to explain the character of the post-1970 changes in a different way. The relationship that developed was one characterized by a high degree of mutual trust and support and one repeatedly manifest in concrete ways. As people demonstrated their enthusiasm for and commitment to the revolution's leadership through the activities they were asked to take on, as they acquired new skills in the process, their leaders in turn gained ever more confidence in solutions that relied heavily on broad-based participation. They were aware, and said so publicly on a number of occasions, that at certain critical junctures the consolidation course they had charted could not have been successfully followed had not the citizenry demonstrated active and enthusiastic involvement. Few countries in Eastern Europe shared this kind of political history with Cuba. In other words, the politics of the institution and consolidation of socialism in Cuba help to explain how the increased democratization of production became a significant element in the leadership's response to the crisis of the late 1960s, even though such a course would have appeared inconceivable, unworkable, and illusive in other places with very different political histories.

Beginning in the late 1970s and in many places ending abruptly with the revolutions of 1989–90, much of the socialist world was engulfed by reform efforts more radical and comprehensive than those undertaken earlier in their histories. Cuba was not immune to this reform wave, embarking in 1986 on what it termed a process of rectification.[57] The process, which Cuba is still in the midst of at this time (September 1990) and which Castro has promised will be lengthy, prompted changes in many areas of society, including work and production.

While rectification was intended to address some very long-standing problems, a principal impetus behind the campaign was the SDPE.[58] Castro and other political leaders have publicly detailed what they considered SDPE shortcomings on many occasions. Its emphasis on earnings and profitability, together with deficiencies in how these were operationalized, led to abuses and distortions. Some administrators, for example, began acting like capitalists, thinking primarily of the good of the firm, not society as a whole. Certain enterprises made profits by charging inflated prices, neglecting to count some expenditures as costs, focusing on secondary versus planned production, or producing the most profitable, as opposed to the most widely needed or desired, articles. Some inefficient enterprises, including ones whose output was relatively unimportant, became highly profitable, while some efficient firms producing goods and services of great social value could not make a profit. Even where it was unreasonable or undesirable for an enterprise to be thinking in profit terms, it was criticized for not doing so.

Material incentives were revealed to be problematic on many counts. The SDPE's emphasis on them encouraged materialistic, utilitarian attitudes amongst some workers.[59] *Fondo* calculations were so complex that workers had difficulty understanding how the awards were linked to effort. Receiving money from the *fondos*, claimed *Trabajadores* (2 Dec 87:12), was more like winning the lottery. Material incentives were sometimes abused, and unacceptable wage inequalities began to surface. Workers sometimes received multiple awards for the same accomplishment, for instance. The *fondos de premios*, as well as the funds for socio-cultural projects and housing construction led to notable inequities between types of firms. Sugar production complexes (*centrales*), for example, few of which were very profitable, had been unable to do much with their small socio-cultural and housing funds, except spend them on parties. At the same time, enterprises connected to these complexes, such as those supplying their raw materials or equipment, were often profitable. Hence, workers in these firms had their "own" nurseries, their "own" sports centers, and other amenities impossible for most *centrales* to provide.[60]

In the leadership's estimation, however, the problem with the

SDPE went beyond the particular defects that came to fore as it matured. In addition, the SDPE had seductively engendered the mistaken belief that the economic mechanisms it had put into place would by themselves, automatically, promote socialist development. This detracted energy and attention from the politics, the political work, and the political problems of constructing socialism. Cubans were in danger of forgetting that these were the principal means through which their past goals had been and their future goals could be accomplished. In such a view, economic methods of constructing socialism were but auxiliary. Hence, for all the discussion of the economic causes and consequences of rectification, a major theme of the campaign, mass participation, will sound familiar: "A cardinal aspect of the process of rectification, because of its social and political content, is the organized participation of the workers and people in general in the solution of social problems. This has been a characteristic feature of the revolution since its beginning."[61] The extent to which these calls for mass participation have been linked to democratization, a connection more evident in the 1970s and early 1980s than it was in the 1960s, will become clearer as we turn to the changes most relevant to the democratization of production instituted under *rectificación*.

To begin with, given *rectificación*'s emphasis on politics and political work, the party's involvement in work and production was stressed. The party was expected to become more active in these matters at both the worksite and supraworksite levels. One method through with the party attempted this was by redoubling its efforts to train, select, and evaluate personnel to fill key posts.[62] Another was by assuming headship of work-center commissions formed to oversee hiring and firing (Fitzgerald 1989:306).

Because the party's role under rectification has been enhanced, indications of changes in workers' influence in and over the organization deserve continued attention. Party membership increased between 1980 and 1986, albeit at a slower rate than in the late 1970s, but until new figures are released at the 4th Party Congress scheduled for 1991, it is not possible to tell whether the rectification campaign speeded party growth significantly.[63] There were also a few interesting alterations in internal party procedure which coincided with the rectification years. Local party leadership began to be elected in secret rather than open elections (*Cuba Update*, summer 1990:24); reports of 1987 party elections emphasized how nominations for members of the municipal and provincial committees and the municipal and provincial assemblies were circulated at lower levels before voting occurred, that votes were not always unanimous, and that some nominees were defeated.[64] In addition, the party adopted what Max Azicri (1988:247) terms an "affirmative action policy," designed to bring more women and Cubans of African descent into its leadership ranks. The latter goal is notable given past reluctance, in the party and in other organizations, to draw special attention to racial distinctions in membership and leadership. So far some progress has been made: In 1986 the Central Committee was 14 percent female, and Cubans of African descent comprised 20 percent of its members, a large improvement.[65] On the Executive Bureaus of the provincial committees, women improved their representation by 4 percent and Cubans of African descent by 3 percent between 1985 and 1987.

It would be congruent with the emphasis rectification placed on mass participation that the party come to rely more heavily on the exemplary-worker route of party entry, and, indeed, I have been told in personal conversations that this has happened. Moreover, since rectification the party has frequently created formal opportunities to gather input from workers who are not members. Party meetings with workers and the general population occurred in 1986, including one series called to discuss the party program. Also, assemblies with non-members were held in anticipation of the 4th Party Congress, and the themes discussed included the structure and internal functioning of the party itself. When initial assemblies did not prove to be critical enough or to evoke enough participation, the party postponed upcoming ones, altered the process, then reconvened them a month later (Benjamin 1990b: 24–25; Evenson 1990:26).

A second development with implications for the democratization of production was the formation of brigades.[66] The appearance of brigades actually pre-dated rectification, the first ones being organized in agriculture in 1981 and in industry and construction in 1983. Thereafter, their numbers grew slowly until approximately 1984–85. Numbering only in the hundreds before that time, over 1200 brigades incorporating more than 117,000 workers were reported in 1985, and their total jumped to over two thousand in 1986 (*Trabajadores* 5 Feb 85:4; 5 Apr 86:5; 12 Jun 85:1; Zimbalist 1989:87; Fitzgerald 1989:308).

When functioning as intended, the brigades assumed responsibility for organizing and distributing their own work tasks. They were also expected to operate in the black, sometimes a tricky proposition when the firms of which they were a part did not, or could not do so, or when shortages interrupted operations. The brigades in industry could be responsible for part of a larger job or product, or for an entire one. In agriculture, brigades were also ordinarily responsible for the use and protection of a particular plot of land.

The incomes of brigade members were linked to output more closely than were those of many other workers both through *primas* for plan fulfillment and cost savings and through distributions from the *fondos de premios*. The total sum of these was calculated on the basis of unit performance, though they were awarded individually.[67] Brigades might group workers performing the same or different jobs. The brigade had a leader, though reports differed as to whether she or he was elected and could be fired by brigade members or appointed and approved by higher administrators. The leader chaired the brigade council, whose members could include heads of smaller work groups within the brigade, union representatives, exemplary workers, technical staff, and a party representative. When a work center was reorganized into brigades, production and service assemblies were also to be reconstituted at this level. The eventual plan was to reorganize the basic party and union groups at the brigade level as well. Brigades operated on the basis of their own plan, which members were involved in formulating.

Third, from 1985 onwards public statements began to allude to upcoming changes in the process through which workers, whether in brigades or not, participated in worksite planning (White 1987:156; Zimbalist 1989:85). In 1989 these changes were finally implemented, and although it is too early for any analysis of them to have been made, they could increase producers' importance in the planning process. The union had apparently voiced increasing criticism of the old procedures in the preceding two years. The substance of these criticisms was not new: Disaggregated figures arrived at work centers too late; some plan figures never arrived at all; planning assemblies were rushed, and partly as a result their quality was poor; workers' input was not taken seriously enough.[68]

The new process attempted to overcome these problems through one change in particular: It shifted the initial step in the planning procedure to the point of production. The process of devising the enterprise plan thereafter began at the enterprise rather than the supraworksite level. The convocation of work-center planning assemblies no longer awaited the arrival of planning figures formulated outside the enterprise. Instead, planning assemblies were called together on the completion of a report by enterprise management and local union leaders, which concerned such things as prior plan execution, raw materials received in the past and expected in the upcoming year, the state of the physical plant, the possibilities for reducing costs, and so forth. In the ensuing discussions, workers made proposals and suggestions about the plan that the administration and the union later translated into figures and forwarded to the appropriate superior body.[69]

Fourth, the effect of rectification on the amount of firm autonomy allowed under the SDPE was mixed. In two important ways rectification decreased enterprise independence from the center.[70] First, following some initial indications of a different nature, as the rectification campaign progressed continued decentralization of investment was halted. In July 1988 Castro called it "absurd" to leave investment decisions in the hands of enterprises in a developing country with scarce resources. It was the state's responsibility to make such decisions, he continued, and its criteria for making them should not be purely economic (*Trabajadores* 11 Jul 88:2).

The fate of the *fondos*, the most significant indicator of firms' control over their earnings under the SDPE, also suggests a decrease in independence with rectification. The *fondos* came under attack early in the rectification process. Funds planned for 1986 were 12 percent smaller than those planned for 1985, and their distribution was more tightly regulated. The formation of funds for 1987 was put on hold pending the completion of new regulatory guidelines, which eventually disallowed their formation in commercial enterprises. Then, in 1989, it was announced that no funds would be formed after that year. The 16th National CTC Congress in 1990, however, urged the re-establishment of the prize fund on a new and simplified basis (*Trabajadores* 6 Nov 86:1, 3 Jun 87:9, 28 Dec 88:1, 28 Feb 89:2; CTC 1990:26).

At the same time these measures limiting firm autonomy

were taken, however, others with the opposite effect were implemented.[71] New planning guidelines, for instance, reduced the overall number of directive indicators from 206 to 147 (from 28 to 18 per enterprise); the number of commodities or commodity groups subject to central planning fell from 2,300 to 800; the number of occupations subject to central direction was expected to fall from 1,100 to 90; planning was simplified for some 500 non-crucial firms (*Trabajadores* 28 May 88:12; Zimbalist 1990b:27–28; León 1987:126–27).

In addition, horizontal contractual relationships between firms received increased emphasis after rectification. Thus, the state arbitration system, which heard fewer than one thousand cases during its first nine months in 1980 and 1981, heard nearly forty-one thousand in 1988.[72] Secondary unplanned production also continued to be encouraged.[73] Decentralization could also receive a boost through the continued formation of *uniones*, groups of enterprises, ordinarily not accounting units, which were joined to render more feasible the devolution of certain activities (e.g., research and development, repair and maintenance) from ministries to production units. Technical and economic personnel were also to be relocated to these lower levels (Zimbalist 1989:86–87; *Trabajadores* 4 Jun 88:3).

The rectification period also witnessed a series of miscellaneous changes relevant or potentially relevant to the democratization of production. These included, first, a move to decrease the number of meetings at work.[74] An outcome of this was that plan discussions began to be combined with the corresponding month's production or service assembly. Second, de-bureaucratization efforts were undertaken, resulting in the reported reduction of mid- and high-level administrators by 16,400 in 1988 (Rodríguez 1990: 96). Rectification also brought steps to equalize remuneration levels across the country. In 1987 salaries of the lowest-paid workers in Cuba were raised by 3 to 15 pesos a month (to between 100 and 118 pesos a month), and between 300,000 and 400,000 workers benefited. Pensions were also increased in 1987, and 725,000 people benefited (Zimbalist 1989:76; Rodríguez 1990:96, 100). Finally, a few changes occurred in the unions. For example, *Cuba Update* (summer 1990:24) reported a CTC Secretariat decision that all local trade union officials, presumably including *buró* officers, be elected by direct and secret vote.[75]

Review of the changes wrought under the rectification banner reveals that the campaign has had varied effects on the trend towards greater democratization of production begun in the 1970s. Largely positive were changes in the annual planning process and the brigades. Since the early 1970s Cuba has demonstrated a commitment to including producers in worksite-level planning, and the 1989 changes were intended to improve their participation by overcoming some of the procedure's main defects. These changes not only enhanced the role of the production unit vis-à-vis the center but they could also expand workers' opportunity for positive insertion in the formulation stage of the decision-making process. This in turn should heighten workers' interest in planning assemblies by increasing their influence over final form of their work-center's plan. Were the union's role in worksite-level planning also to be strengthened, democratization would advance further. The union, for example, might formulate a worksite plan independently of management, and workers could then debate the alternatives in planning assemblies.

The formation of brigades was also a positive step for democratization. Brigades have met with certain problems that have detracted from their ability to further majority control of production.[76] Nonetheless, they increased workers' opportunity to become involved in decision making in a direct fashion. Moreover, an explicit goal of brigade organization was to decrease the number of supervisorial personnel (*Trabajadores* 17 Jun 85:6). They therefore enhanced democratization by increasing the number of workers relative to non-workers who participated in decision making. The brigades also seem a positive move when arguments linking size and empowerment to democratization are recalled. In speaking of the brigades' potential and actual accomplishments, Cuban sources often made such connections explicitly: Brigades fostered collective work sentiment, better cooperation amongst producers, and a sense of identification with the goals of the larger community; they enhanced workers' understanding of production issues and their ability to interact with, learn from, and help one another; brigades strengthened a sense of responsibility and accountability among their members (Rabaza 1986; Veiga 1984; *Trabajadores* 15 Mar 85:1).

Yet together with these two hopeful developments, rectification had mixed effects in two areas that have proven problematic for the democratization of production: enterprise-center relations and the party.[77] First, while atrophy of the supraworksite decision-making arena dooms democratization, socialism's most common difficulty has been its inability to allow and to sustain adequate decision-making autonomy at the point of production. Although rectification does not represent a return to the hypercentralized economic management of the 1960s, in two critical areas, investment and enterprise control over earnings, it has spelled some retreat from levels of enterprise autonomy reached earlier under the SDPE. Second, from the point of view of non-members' influence on the party and internal party procedure, rectification, in my judgment, has not interfered with the democratization trend begun in 1970. Such considerations, however, are only part of the problem for the democratization of production posed by the party. The other concerns multiplicity. To what extent does the party monopolize other avenues through which workers might influence work and production, thereby becoming indistinguishable from other loci of authority? Or to what extent does the party represent one among a number of channels through which workers could exercise power over production? On balance, I find little evidence that nonparty avenues for workers' participation in decision making, especially essential ones such as the unions, have contracted under rectification. At the same time, the clear trend under rectification has been to enhance the role of the party in numerous areas of Cuban society. Such a trend bears close watching.

Glancing back over more than thirty years of production in Cuba, 1970 continues to stand out as a democratic watershed. Cuban workers had demonstrably more control over production in the 1970s and early 1980s than they did in the 1960s, and much of the explanation for this improvement lies in the politics through which socialism was instituted and consolidated on the island. Changes in the contemporary period of rectification, although limiting the democratization trend in some respects, offer no indication of a reversion to the patterns of production relations characteristic of the 1960s.

In the wake of the revolutions of 1989 and 1990, in the face of unremitting hostility from the United States, and pending the outcome of the continued struggles in the Soviet Union, Cuban socialism faces an uncertain future.[78] Whatever upcoming decades might bring, however, cannot detract from the imaginativeness, the boldness, the diligence, and the commitment displayed in Cuba's attempts to counter command by the few and obedience by the many in the realm of production. A world so backward in democratizing work relations can ill afford to ignore either its deficiencies or its unique and numerous accomplishments.

Notes

Preface

1. The revolutions in existing socialist countries have energized academic and political discussion of more deeply democratic alternatives in a way the re-forms of socialism did not. See, for example, Halliday 1990 and Kaldor 1990. A recent issue of *Socialist Review* (April–June 1990) was devoted to this topic. See especially articles by Cronin, Burawoy, Wainwright, and Ferleger and Mandel.

2. Dahl (1985) is one of those who argues that ownership and control can be separated. For the contrary position, see Anderson and Gibson 1978:200–204; Hill 1981:71–76; Zeitlin 1981:170–72; and Zeitlin 1977, esp. pt. 4.

3. See Bowles and Gintis 1986:83–90 and the multiple examples presented in Zwerdling 1978. This is also part of Burawoy's (1989*b*) contention that the democratization of production relations is more likely to occur under socialism than under capitalism. See also Burawoy and Lukács 1989, in which the authors argue the general point that capitalism is incompatible with the democratization of production.

4. For examples see Zwerdling 1978:12; Berman 1967:165–79; and MAHRO 1976:163. As Wood (1986:166) states it, "The political sphere in even the most 'liberal-democratic' capitalist society is itself constructed to maintain, bureaucratically and coercively whenever necessary, the barriers to democracy at the 'level' of production relations."

5. For example, drawing on Hungarian fieldwork, Burawoy (1989*a*) stresses how the gap between democratic socialist ideals and socialist practice, reproduced by the logic of existing socialism, deepens critical consciousness, high-lighting a vision of workers' self-organization in production.

6. For a more extensive discussion of conducting research in Cuba, see Fuller 1988.

7. The restrictions, enforced under the 1917 Trading with the Enemy Act, made travel to Cuba, outside certain narrow categories, punishable by up to ten years in prison and fines of up to ten thousand dollars. Travel to Cuba was also restricted from 1963 to 1977, except for persons with specific State Department authorization. Travel restrictions were relaxed between 1977 and May 1982.

8. Early surveillance was carried out by the National Security Agency,

203

which in 1978 had a secret budget estimated at fifteen billion dollars. See Bamford 1983.

9. From the beginning I requested permission to observe more worksites, as well as the meetings and assemblies I discuss throughout the book. But despite repeated efforts I was unable to make the necessary arrangements. (In fact, I am still trying.)

10. This bureau was the Instituto Cubano de Amistad con los Pueblos (ICAP). I asked ICAP to set up interviews with highly placed people who would have been inaccessible to me had I not gone through a semi-official channel. Although I supplied ICAP and other Cuban organizations with lists of topics I wanted to cover in interviews, as well as with drafts of some chapters, no one ever requested these materials before I spoke with them or asked that their content be changed in any way.

11. Thirty-six percent of the women I interviewed and 48 percent of the men I interviewed were of African descent.

12. These percentages are precisely those reported in 1962 by Zeitlin (1970:44) on the basis of more systematic attitudinal evaluations and sampling procedures.

13. This conclusion is shared by other researchers who have conducted interviews in Cuba. See Zeitlin 1970:17–18, 21; Seers et al. 1964:394 n. 70; and Benjamin, Collins, and Scott 1984:xi–xii.

Chapter 1

1. The importance of proportions is highlighted in the Bullock Report commissioned by the British Labour government in the 1970s (Kiloh 1986).

2. Mansbridge (1983, 1984) has devoted particular attention to these last characteristics in face-to-face decision-making forums.

3. See Wertheimer 1975 for a discussion of the idea of compulsory voting and Barber 1984, chap. 10, for a discussion of election by lot. Both authors focus on state politics.

4. See, for example, MacPherson 1977; Miller 1983; Duncan 1983; Held 1987; Barber 1984, 1986; Bowles and Gintis 1986; and Williams 1983.

5. Commonly cited critiques of direct democracy include the extra time it takes and the argument that many people are not intellectually prepared to make many decisions and could therefore easily be led astray by the more clever and knowledgeable. Less commonly voiced problems include the "intense minority" issue (Miller 1983:152), participants' competing time demands (Sirianni 1984:491–92), who formulates agendas and how (MacPherson 1977:95–98), and the denial or disappearance of the individual, private realm (Bowles and Gintis 1986:148). The complexity of the relation between direct and indirect forms of democracy at the workplace is evidenced in the following kinds of situations: the substitution of weak forms of direct democracy, such as suggestion boxes, for more substantial, though indirect, democratization efforts and the utilization of indirect worker representation on boards of directors to keep pressures for direct democracy at bay. Indirect democracy was introduced into the state arena in the late eighteenth century for a similar purpose. Finally, I am personally acquainted with an example, which is probably not unique, where management

blocked indirect worker participation on a board of directors indefinitely by adopting a radical, direct democracy position that workers' representatives should poll every worker before exercising their franchise on the board. Essentially, this came down to an insistence that all workers participate directly in board decision making—a position not favored by most workers because it was impractical—or that workers not participate at all.

6. For examples, see Espinosa and Zimbalist 1978:60; and ILO 1969:160.

7. MacPherson (1977:95–96) agrees. As early as 1920, Goodrich (1920: esp. 49–50, 239, 257–58), in his discussion of British workplaces, compared negative involvement with positive involvement. For an example of positive insertion into the decision-making process, see Sirianni's (1987:11–14) discussion of union and rank-and-file involvement in the design of technology.

8. Others have devised their own classification schemes based on different criteria. For example, see Herman 1982:20; Espinosa and Zimbalist 1978:57–58; International Labour Organization (ILO) 1969: 16, 117, 141–42; Stephens 1980: 14–15; and Bernstein 1976:52–54. Also, Bahro's (1978:295–98) work suggests an additional basis for classification: the level of challenge involved in making different types of decisions. The amount of managerial or owner resistance evoked when workers participate in making decisions of different types could be another interesting and useful basis for classifying production decisions. The three categories I propose are not mutually exclusive. For example, decisions about the employment of technology might have as much bearing on the relationship of the work center to its wider environment as on the relationship of workers to one another and to the physical features of work. Likewise, many aspects of production planning may be seen as simultaneously affecting the relationship between workers and owners or managers and the relationship between workers and the physical features of production, as well as the kind of relationship that distinguishes category one. In real-life situations, the categorization of a particular decision will thus always be approximate and depend on the specifics of the case.

9. Sirianni (1981: esp. 40–48) and Guarasci and Peck (1984) speak to this point.

10. Examples include Mansbridge 1983; Pateman 1970, 1989; Held 1987; Laclau and Mouffe 1985; and Barber 1984. This oversight is in contrast to the amount of attention some of these authors devote to the topic of how community and democracy are related.

11. For examples, see Rothschild-Whitt 1979a; Burawoy 1981; Bermeo 1983; Blair 1969; Clegg 1971; Espinosa and Zimbalist 1978; Moore 1978; and Cole 1987.

12. Some partial exceptions to this pattern include Algeria where, according to Clegg (1971:55), *autogestion* forced the fledgling Ben Bella government to withdraw large sectors of the economy from direct capitalist control and rendered the return of French settlers impossible. Also, Stephens (1980) points out that the institution of the enterprise-based Industrial Communities in Peru in the early 1970s sparked the formation of a national association of Industrial Communities that called for the supersession of capitalism. Stephens also recounts how recognition of the limitation of joint consultation at the enterprise level in Sweden in the 1960s spurred demands for increased workers' influence on decision making in

the macro arena. In the first two cases, the democratization of production was decisively halted soon thereafter. In Sweden, its further development currently faces severe challenges.

13. Bahro (1978:437–39) and Williams (1985:301) concur, as do Cohen and Rogers (1983), whose conception of what the democratization of the macro arena would entail, however, is more limited than Bahro's or Williams's.

14. Wood (1986) and Williams (1983, chap. 3) make the same point, despite substantial differences from Laclau and Mouffee (1985) in their overall perspectives.

15. See Sirianni 1984 for additional discussion of this point. Harris (1983) and Held (1987) present a third argument for multiplicity. It reduces the chances that unjust, immoral, or undemocratic decisions, which could sometimes be the product of democratized structures and practices, would be taken.

16. Havel, quoted in Wainwright 1990:31; Bahro (1978) clearly concurs.

17. Size in itself, however, is not the issue. Instead, how small is small enough depends not only on socially determined technological and economic considerations but also on which of the advantages associated with small size is assigned highest priority. Among those who cite specific numbers in their discussions of size and democracy, Albert and Hahnel (1981:289) envision workplaces from several to several thousand workers. Barber (1986:211) suggests one thousand to five thousand as a good size for strongly democratic neighborhood assemblies. Mansbridge (1984:478–79, 1983:286–87) writes that groups of six to twelve are best for self-development, assemblies of two hundred or fewer "can put each member palpably in touch with everyone else," that fifteen thousand is probably the largest group ever encompassed by face-to-face democracy, and that there is evidence suggesting degrees of unanimity differ between groups of two and thirty, groups of thirty and one thousand, and even nations with different size populations.

18. See Forester's (1989, esp. chap. 7) excellent discussion of the importance of listening for communication. This section should make clear why high-tech solutions, allowing large numbers of people to communicate directly by computer and television, are only very partial substitutes for small-group democratic activities and structures. Such proposals sharpen the conceptual distinction between the previously discussed issues of size and directness. Mansbridge (1983, 1984) presents the most extensive discussion of the drawbacks of face-to-face communication in democratic settings.

19. See Mansbridge 1983 and Cochrane 1986 on these points.

20. This is an important theme for Barber (1984) and Pateman (1970), and for Mansbridge (1983), who explores some of the tensions between democracy and community.

21. Albert and Hahnel's (1981) argument for democratization is based on the same premise, though they develop it less fully. In my view, Bowles and Gintis owe more to Marx on this point than their compartmentalized reading of him allows them to acknowledge.

22. Williams (1983:104) says, "In truth nobody can know exactly how any of it [new and expanded principles and practices of democracy] would work, until some of it has been tried. And it has certainly not, in any general way, been tried."

23. To read Albert and Hahnel's (1981, esp. chap. 7) detailed ideas on how economic planning could be democratized, is to get a sense for how much people would learn were they involved in the process.

24. The following sources expand on the points made briefly here: Harris 1983; Mansbridge 1983, 1984; Barber 1984; and Pateman 1970. Bahro (1978) and Albert and Hahnel (1981) devote much discussion to job restructuring and job rotation as central to empowerment through democratization.

25. Hartsock (1983, esp. chap. 9) understands these as important components of how women have theorized power.

Chapter 2

1. For examples of this argument about unions under capitalism, see Aronowitz 1973*a*, 1973*b*; Kolko 1976; Haydu 1985; Sirianni 1982; and Gramsci 1977. For similar analyses referring to the transition period, see Cardan 1974; Gorz 1973; Hyman 1974; and Panitch 1981. Finally, see Haraszti 1978 and Zukin 1981 for examples of analogous arguments about unions under socialism.

2. Blas Roca, quoted in Hernández and Mesa-Lago 1971:212.

3. The unions' production function was also set forth in the 1961 Law of Union Organization and in the union movement's 1966 Declaration of Principles. Many unions also agreed to a wage freeze to aid economic development (see Goldenberg 1965:206–7 and O'Connor 1970:201–2).

4. For additional information, see Cuban Economic Research Project (CERP) 1963:54 and Hernández and Mesa-Lago 1971:241–42.

5. Interview with a Central de Trabajadores de Cuba (CTC) official, Havana, 29 Sept 82.

6. Hernández and Mesa-Lago 1971:215. This description, which was published in 1962, also highlights the inclusiveness concern. The short-lived, early 1960s experiment with technical advisory councils (*consejos técnicos asesores*) is interesting in terms of democratization, even though unions did not play a large role in the development or functioning of the councils. For more, see Gilly 1965:42; O'Connor 1970:199–200; Zimbalist 1975:46; and Vilariño 1980:92–94.

7. The near unanimity of opinion in this regard is a rarity in the literature on postrevolutionary Cuba. This position is argued by Cuban-American social scientists of varying political persuasions, leftist critics of Cuban socialism, and foreigners generally supportive of the revolution, as well as by prominent Cuban Communists. See, for example, Hernández and Mesa-Lago 1971:242; Gilly 1965:20, 22; Domínguez 1978:273; Bonachea and Valdés 1972*b*:379; Dupuy and Yrchik 1978:54; Maurice Zeitlin and Carlos Rafael Rodríguez, quoted in Hernández and Mesa-Lago 1971:213–14; and Jorge Risquet, quoted in Bonachea and Valdés 1972*b*:379. The defense of workers' rights ordinarily includes decisions falling within content categories two and three.

8. Even though the defense of workers' rights was not a union priority during the first postrevolutionary decade, evidently, in isolated instances, the *secciones* were not totally passive where workers and the state differed over a particular policy or its implementation. Gilly (1965:20, 22), for example, has written that more than one base-level leader tried to represent workers before higher-level union leaders and the administration, and that unions could try to resolve

minor disputes between workers and administrators, though in doing so they were most likely to serve as umpires partial to the stronger team. Similarly, Mesa-Lago (1968:70–72) and Hernández and Mesa-Lago (1971:240–43) have shown that occasionally union locals joined workers to oppose certain output norms, thereby slowing their development and implementation on a widespread basis, even though higher levels of the union hierarchy sided with the state against the locals.

9. Three-fourths of the workers interviewed by Pérez-Stable (1976:43) in 1975 identified increasing production as a principal union function.

10. In October 1979 the National Council of the CTC reviewed the draft of a law governing the assemblies (*Trabajadores* 9 Oct 79:1). Roberto Veiga, the CTC's top official, reported in early 1980 that a government decree specifying administration responsibilities vis-à-vis the assemblies would soon be issued (Veiga 1980:29). "Still in many places," according to *Trabajadores* (22 Sept 81:2), "the director from the appropriate administrative level is conspicuous because of his or her absence at assemblies, and because he or she delegates other functionaries to represent him or her. This conduct is inadmissible. The director's presence at the assemblies is not a generous gift; it is a fundamental obligation."

11. Zimbalist (1975:51) reports that attendance at the assemblies ranged from 80 to 100 percent in the mid-1970s.

12. Interview with a member of the Tobacco Workers' Union, Havana, 30 Sept 82.

13. Interview with a member of the Health Workers' Union, Havana, 10 Oct 83. One worker told me that at his worksite the administration chaired the service assemblies, a procedure that would certainly change the character of the whole gathering (interview with a member of the Health Workers' Union, Havana, 27 Sept 82).

14. Workers' reports included those from union section officers and from workers elected to represent their departments or work groups at representative assemblies (*asambleas de representantes*) held every three months at the enterprise level.

15. Pérez-Stable 1975; Armengol and D'Angelo 1977. Contrast these surveys with one conducted in Romania, which reported that 63 percent of workers under thirty (the majority) said they never made proposals at union-organized production meetings and that almost half of the 37 percent who did said their proposals would have no effect (Nelson 1986:115).

16. See, for example, interview in a steel factory outside Havana, 1 Oct 82; Veiga 1980:29; *Trabajadores* 22 Sept 81:2 and 21 Mar 81:2; and Pérez-Stable 1976:40.

17. Interview with a member of the Light Industry Workers' Union, Havana, 9 Oct·83.

18. See *Trabajadores* 9 Dec 80:1, 31 Jan 81:1, 21 Feb 80:1, 21 Mar 81:2, and 2 Apr 86:1.

19. Interviews with members of the Public Administration Workers' Union, Havana, 13 Sept 82, and the Health Workers' Union, Havana, 27 Sept 82.

20. For example, the following story was related to me by a female employee of a light industrial plant: Because she was better educated and more artic-

ulate than most of her co-workers, they often asked her to present their complaints in the production assemblies, which she did along with her own. Consequently, she was branded a troublemaker by the administration. Mostly as a result, her position at the factory was eliminated, and she was forced to go six months without working before being reinstated (interview with a member of the Light Industry Workers' Union, Havana, 9 Oct 83).

21. Interview with a national CTC official, Havana, 29 Oct 82. See also *Trabajadores* 22 Sept 81:2.

22. Interview with a member of the Public Administration Workers' Union, Havana, 29 Sept 83.

23. The ideal concerning union involvement in management councils was expressed in the Theses of the 13th National CTC Congress: "The trade union representation to the management council shouldn't and can't be turned into a representation of the management council to the trade union. On the contrary, it should act in representation of the workers to the council. Without their consent, it can't be obliged or oblige itself to undertake administrative tasks agreed on by the council, especially if these touch on the specific interests of union members or on the functions or agreements of the union. . . . [It] is also absolutely necessary that [trade union representatives] not come up against an atmosphere of hostile self-sufficiency or condescending paternalism in the council" (*Granma Weekly Review*, 2 Sept 73:V.5.2).

Some are of the opinion that the ideal expressed in these statements had not completely eluded Cuban workers. Zimbalist (1975:51), for example, concluded in the mid-1970s that workers' input on the councils was "quite significant."

24. Interview with a member of the Cultural Workers' Union, Havana, 3 Oct 83.

25. Interview with a member of the Public Administration Workers' Union, Havana, 29 Sept 83.

26. Many have commented on the importance of union power in the supraworksite arena for the democratization of production. For example, see Sirianni 1987; Cole 1987; and Stephens 1979.

27. See Gilly 1965:39–42, 45, 47; Hernández and Mesa-Lago 1971:239–240, 243; Mesa-Lago and Zephirin 1971:165; and Mesa-Lago 1968.

28. The revolution's leaders, however, continued to use direct methods to solicit the opinions of working people (and of other groups as well) before making certain decisions affecting the entire nation. For example, they regularly discussed drafts of laws concerning workers in workplace assemblies, soliciting comments that were then used in formulating the final version of the law. The 13th National CTC Congress suggested improvements in this procedure, including (*a*) earlier distribution of the drafts and explanations of sections requiring elucidation; (*b*) clarification of the purpose of the assemblies in order to determine whether workers approved, disapproved, or wanted revisions in a proposed law; (*c*) precise notation of the number favoring each of these options, and (*d*) a more active role for the press in publicizing issues raised at the assemblies. See *Granma Weekly Review* 2 Sept 73:7–12.

29. See Mesa-Lago 1978:91 and *Granma Weekly Review* 2 Sept 73:7–12.

30. In addition to specifying union representation on the Council of Minis-

ters and its Executive Committee, the 1976 Constitution gave the National Committee of the CTC the right to initiate legislation in the National Assembly of People's Power (OPP). Workers I spoke with were familiar with this right, but they were unable to provide any details about its exercise. The original draft of the Constitution permitted any organ of the CTC to initiate such legislation (Domínguez 1978:530; see also Álvarez Tabío 1981:288–92, 426–27). The Constitution gave the same right to other social organizations in Cuba, as well as to ordinary voters who gathered ten thousand signatures. Union representation on Councils of Ministers has been neither unique nor universal in socialist countries. Also, after 1972, the union confederation was able to initiate incomes and social policy legislation in the German Democratic Republic (GDR) (Rueschemeyer and Scharf 1986:57). Polish unions enjoyed the same right in the 1970s (Pravda 1986:141).

31. According to Zimbalist (1975:51), Castro announced that representatives of the sectoral unions might also attend Council sessions at which Cuba's first five-year plan and the annual plan for 1975 were discussed.

32. The draft of this regulation was sent to the National Council of the CTC for review before final approval by the Council of Ministers (*Trabajadores* 9 Oct 79:1). The Council of Ministers was also empowered to form permanent or temporary commissions to facilitate the execution of its functions (Álvarez Tabío 1981:305–9).

33. See *Trabajadores* 7 Jul 79:2 and Veiga 1978:9. Remuneration and work interruptions were topics of much discussion at both the 14th and 15th National CTC Congresses.

34. Interview conducted by Sheryl Lutgens, Havana, 31 Mar 83. This regular, informal interaction between sectoral unions and their corresponding ministries is not unique in socialist countries, but it does not always occur either. For example, see Rueschemeyer and Scharf 1986:57 and Pravda 1986:142.

35. For additional examples, see *Trabajadores* 4 Oct 79:4; CTC 1984, art. 4.1.1; Gomez n.d.:8.

36. See Álvarez Tabío 1981:261–62, 338–41. For information on the process of choosing the Executive Bureaus of the municipal and provincial OPP assemblies, see Myers 1974:14. For information on the selection of delegates to the provincial and National OPP assemblies, see Harnecker 1980:85–88. A national CTC official told me that the secretaries-general of most sectoral unions were deputies of the National OPP Assembly. None of them, however, was guaranteed a position on this body, as they were, for example, in the GDR (interview, Havana, 29 Sept 82, Rueschemeyer and Scharf 1986:57). He also said that the provincial and municipal union leadership was well represented at the local OPP levels, even though these bodies did not have special chambers for socio-political organizations as in Yugoslavia (Carter 1986:212).

37. Ritter (1985:286) says there is a "strong impression" that "the Assembly usually performs what is essentially a rubber stamp function, approving or ratifying what is placed before it," though he does recognize that the National OPP Assembly wields some political power in Cuba. So does Domínguez (1982:33–38, 67), who admits that the "level of discussion" in the Assembly had been higher and the "policy consequences" more significant "than I had thought likely."

38. Zimbalist (1975:51) reports that elected union representatives participated directly in discussions of municipal, regional, and provincial plans. Barkin (1975:56) also mentions that direct collaboration occurred between the CTC and OPP at the provincial level around planning. See also Girling and Ruccio 1981:13.

39. Mesa-Lago 1978:83. Carlos Rafael Rodríguez explained that the unions had been "inadequately concerned with defending the interests of workers relative to their emphasis on spurring them to meet production targets." This is taken from Hernández and Mesa-Lago's summary (1971:214) of Zeitlin's 1969 interview with the Vice-President.

40. Pérez-Stable 1976:44. At the same time, however, 72 percent of Pérez-Stable's respondents said they would go to the union if they had a problem, while 11 percent had no clear idea of what the unions' role was. Pérez-Stable (1976:38) suggests that these somewhat contradictory responses reflected the fact that the people she interviewed "were living in a period of rapid change; a period during which the consequences of the disarray of the late 1960s were still fresh, but also one in which the first evidence of the order of things to come was everywhere apparent." For some related survey results from Czechoslovakia and Poland, see Porket 1986:98 and Pravda 1986:140.

41. Interview with two members of the Tobacco Workers' Union, Havana, 30 Sept 82.

42. Interview with a member of the Health Workers' Union, Havana, 27 Sept 82.

43. Interview with a member of the Cultural Workers' Union, Havana, 25 Sept 82.

44. Other rights, including those to maternity benefits, a healthy and safe working environment, social security, and a pension were mentioned less frequently.

45. Interview with a member of the Commercial and Restaurant Workers' Union, Havana, 5 Oct 82.

46. Interview with a member of the Public Administration Workers' Union, Havana, 13 Oct 83.

47. Interview with a member of the Cultural Workers' Union, Havana, 25 Sept 82.

48. Interview with a member of the Health Workers' Union, Havana, 10 Oct 83.

49. The case referred to in n. 20 (above), for example, was finally resolved through the intervention of an official from the national office of the CTC. Even though the employee was eventually reinstated through the help of high-level union officials, she was not pleased. She felt quite strongly that the injustice done her was obvious from the beginning, and the local union's inability, or unwillingness, to help her made her very angry. She also felt that her eventual reinstatement owed less to the justice of her cause than to the fact that someone in the administration at her worksite knew, and was possibly indebted to, someone in the national CTC office.

50. Included were workers' rights to have proper protective equipment, to be given pre-placement medical exams, to be retained when their capacity to work was reduced, and to refuse to perform unsafe work.

51. Union health and safety activities were buttressed by Cuba's penal code; managers who either exposed employees to dangerous or unhealthy working conditions or contributed to a worker's death or serious injury were subject to prison terms and fines. Cases in which managers were penalized under the code were publicized regularly in the union press. According to the union, job-related accidents increased between 1977 and 1980 because management used safety funds for other purposes. The unions criticized this practice, and accident rates declined (*Bohemia* 1981:55–56; Pérez-Stable 1985:300).

52. One of the proposals of the Theses of the 15th National CTC Congress, held in 1984, was the establishment of a legal basis for union inspections in areas other than health and safety (see CTC 1984, art. 4.2).

53. The CTC cited these investigations as an expression of the "authority and influence" of Cuban unions (*Trabajadores* 28 Mar 81:2). Preliminary to their inspection campaigns, the unions set up programs to train labor leaders and union members in labor and social legislation; 300,000 took part. Union inspections with a similar objective, but on a less extensive scale, were also conducted in 1981 (see *Trabajadores* 24 Sept 81:1).

54. See, for example, *Trabajadores* 26 Nov 80:3, 9 Dec 80:1, 23 Dec 80:1, 17 Jan 81:1, 30 Mar 81:1, and 28 Mar 81:2. Some of the errors and violations uncovered in the inspections, however, worked to the disadvantage of some workers. For example, improper promotions as well as promotions deserved but not granted and overpayments of wages or salaries as well as underpayments were all discovered.

55. For example, an administrator responsible for repeated infractions of social security regulations uncovered by the Metal Workers' Union was fined half his monthly salary (*Trabajadores* 8 Aug 82:3).

56. Compare this with Burawoy's (1985:63) experience in Hungary: "There's no point in going to the union with a grievance, as I discovered when I wasn't paid for three hours overtime I had worked. I talked to Anna about it, and she laughed at the idea of going to the union representative. We decided to do it as a joke. The two representatives we consulted, both women, thought it was a joke too." For survey data on the topic from Czechoslovakia, see Porket 1986:99.

57. Interview with a member of the Light Industry Workers' Union, Havana, 9 Oct 83.

59. Interview with a member of the Commercial and Restaurant Workers' Union, Havana, 12 Oct 83.

59. Interview with a member of the Light Industry Workers' Union, Havana, 9 Oct 83.

60. Pravda and Ruble's 1986 book on trade unions in Communist societies is organized entirely around this theme.

Chapter 3

1. See, for example, Mesa-Lago 1978:97.

2. Interview with a Central de Trabajadores de Cuba (CTC) official, Havana, 29 Sept 82. According to the Cuban Economic Research Project (CERP 1963:97), however, the "purpose behind this type of organization has been to imitate the Soviet structure of union organization."

3. Before 1961, union organization occurred by either craft or industry. According to Mesa-Lago (1978:86–87), however, as late as 1970, some workers were still organized by trade.

4. Hernández and Mesa-Lago's (1971:214) skepticism about organization by economic sector, which they feel gives unions "monopoly rights," is apparent in their contention that sectoral organization denies workers their "freedom of choice" (see CERP 1963:97).

5. Some workers I interviewed also supported industrial union organization because "there is sensitivity here [at the workplace] about status" (interview with a communications worker, Havana, 21 Sept 82). Organization by trade would tend to reinforce status differentials among workers; organization by sector would not.

6. Interview with a member of the Commercial and Restaurant Workers' Union, Havana, 5 Oct 82. The process, however, never went as far in Cuba as it did in China (PRC), where unions were completely disbanded between 1967 and 1974 (Walder 1986:201).

7. See *Trabajadores*, especially issues from 1972 and 1973, for accounts of these meetings.

8. *Trabajadores*, 2d half Feb 73. Green (1983:65) reports more than forty thousand *secciones* in 1982.

9. Hernández and Mesa-Lago 1971:215; *Trabajadores* 2nd half Sept 71. In 1961 the minimum number of members per section had been twenty-five (CERP 1963:99).

10. For information on People's Power (OPP), see Harnecker 1980; Bengelsdorf 1976; and Cockburn 1979:18–35. The principles that guided OPP elections and the conduct of OPP representatives were markedly different from those prevailing in most bourgeois democracies. All the authors cited above discuss these differences. For more information on the administrative reorganization, see Partido Comunista de Cuba 1978:155–64.

11. Although the commitment to sectoral unionism was clearly reiterated in the 1978 CTC Statutes, above the work-center level some sectoral unions began to represent producers from worksites falling under the jurisdiction of more then one ministry. Also, some ministries began to deal with more than one sectoral union (*Trabajadores* 1 Apr 77:2; CTC 1978, arts. 11, 31).

12. Two additional structural changes in the late 1970s were the formation of new municipal and provincial branches of the sectoral unions and the shifting of some sections from one industrial union to another. The objective was to establish more congruence between union membership and the type of work performed. For instance, the National Union of Basic Industry was abolished and its members were reassigned to more sectorally specific unions; workers in match factories were transferred from the Tobacco Workers' Union to the Chemical and Energy Workers' Union; people working in centers that *distributed* such diverse products as gasoline and eyeglasses were put into the Commercial and Restaurant Workers' Union instead of being scattered among various sectoral unions (*Trabajadores* 21 Oct 77:4, 5).

13. Some bureaus, however, apparently tended to take over the work of sections. Veiga publicly called for better communication between bureaus and their sections (*Trabajadores* 21 Oct 77:4–5, 26 Aug 77:1).

14. Stephens (1979:89, 105, 200–210), in a recent study of seventeen "developed Western capitalist democracies," offers several relevant observations. On the one hand, he finds a positive correlation between the percentage of the total labor force organized and the equality of income distribution. On the other, he notes that "the most discouraging" discovery of his research is the post-war stagnation or decline of unionism in the five largest democracies. Neither trend is characteristic of postrevolutionary Cuba. Stephens attributes the decline in unionism in large democracies primarily to "the exclusion of socialists from government."

15. See also CERP 1963:93–94; Bray and Harding 1974:64; and MacEwan 1981:25.

16. Pérez-Stable (1976:32) says the "vanguard movement" comprised 10 percent of the labor force during this period; according to Zimbalist (1975:49), the percentage of "exemplary workers" rose from 5 percent in 1966 to 17 percent in 1970. Domínguez (1978:275) counted approximately 120,000 "advanced workers" in May 1968 and 235,000, or about 18 percent of all organized workers, in February 1969. The different terms (vanguard, exemplary, advanced) applied to outstanding workers in both Spanish and English have confused the discussion. The Advanced Workers' Movement (Trabajadores de Avanzada) was a new program apparently initiated in 1966 or 1967; other groups of outstanding workers had been recognized before that time (see Mesa-Lago 1978:82; Martin 1974:30; Silverman 1973:165; Domínguez 1978:275; and Center for Cuban Studies 1976:15).

17. Interviews with two members of the Education and Science Workers' Union, Havana, 23 Sept 82, 3 Oct 82. Affiliation figures for some provinces lagged behind averages for the country as a whole. They also showed that workers in some sectors—transportation and merchant marine, ports and fishing, for example—were more resistant to joining unions.

18. *Trabajadores* 2 Apr 85:5. In comparison, Sweden's affiliation rate in the 1980s was 80 percent (Cole 1987:54). Except for China, where 85 percent of the workforce were union members (Wilson 1986:229), affiliation rates in most other socialist countries were reminiscent of Cuba's around the same period.

19. The concept of mass organization refers to more than sheer size. It also denotes a policy of open membership, unlike that of the party or the Advanced Workers' Movement. Mass organizations in general, not just the unions, assumed a more prominent role in Cuba in the 1970s, and the right of all Cubans to join them was specifically mentioned in the 1976 Constitution (Álvarez Tabío 1981:206–9). Such organizations were recognized as vehicles through which particular groups of citizens could express their special interests and concerns (Casal and Pérez-Stable 1981:81).

20. CERP 1963:97; my italics.

21. Interview with a member of the Public Administration Workers' Union, Havana, 13 Oct 83. *Gusano* (literally "worm") has been a common Cuban designation for opponents of the revolution. *Medio* means "half."

22. For more details of this period, see CERP 1963:72–74.

23. See, for example, Fantasia 1988:241 and Aronowitz 1973a:217–18).

24. Although the amount paid remained 1 percent of base wages, the 1978

CTC Statutes permitted the National CTC Council to change that percentage. Dues for retired workers were 0.5 percent of their income (CTC 1978, arts. 79–81). Any member who failed to pay dues for three months, without good cause, could have his or her membership revoked by the section's general assembly.

25. Interview with a member of the Commercial and Restaurant Workers' Union, Havana, 5 Oct 82.

26. Veiga 1978:29. The 1978 total was almost twenty-six million pesos (*Trabajadores* 27 Jan 79:5). In 1983 one peso was officially worth about 25 percent more than one dollar; since it is one of the least convertible currencies on the capitalist world market, however, the comparison defies straightforward interpretation.

27. For more information on *comisiones de glosas*, see *Trabajadores* 20 May 77:2.

28. For more information on review and control commissions, see CTC 1978. arts. 73–78.

29. Interview, Havana, 29 Sept 82.

30. The News and Book Publishing Union, for example, merged with the Arts and Entertainment Union to become the Cultural Workers' Union, and the Civil Aviation Union joined the Transportation Workers, Union. The merging process aroused some dissatisfaction among workers. One news worker, for instance, complained that joining publishing and news workers with artists and entertainers had caused some individuals in her work center to feel slighted. The national leadership of the Cultural Workers' Union, she said, was so beset by the problems of the "superstars" (art and entertainment workers) that it did not adequately attend to the concerns of the news and publishing workers (interview with a member of the Cultural Workers' Union, Havana, 25 Sept 82).

31. For accounts of the Cuban labor movement during the years of *mujalismo*, see Spalding 1977:231–33, 1974:6; Bray and Harding 1974:601; Ruiz 1968:133–34; MacEwan 1981:25; Baran 1961:17; Martin 1974:29; Domínguez 1978:96–97; Vilariño 1980:85–86; and Pérez-Stable 1975:64–65.

32. For a journalist's account of early Auténtico support for Castro, see Hinckle and Turner 1981, esp. 3–10.

33. According to Spalding (1974:8), the law applied to "all union officials," whereas the CERP (1963:107) claimed it applied only to "all executive members of the CTC."

34. For varying interpretations, see CERP 1963:107–8, esp. n. 54; Hernández and Mesa-Lago 1971:211; Martin 1974:29; Vilariño 1980:85; Morray 1962:71–74; and O'Connor 1966:14–15.

35. In O'Connor's (1966:17) view, "Worker reaction to the purges . . . was of course mixed, but there is little evidence of opposition." Suspicions of collusion between labor and counterrevolutionaries were not without foundation. By this time Mujal had set up a CTC-in-exile in Miami, which, along with other exile groups, was involved in a conspiracy against the revolution. Members of another group of labor exiles infiltrated the island before the Bay of Pigs invasion in an effort to spur a workers' uprising (Spalding 1977:241, 1974:9).

36. Gilly 1965:18. See also CERP 1963:112; Domínguez 1978:273; and Pérez-Stable 1975:65. Little information on the selection of local and intermediate

leaders at this time is available. The CERP (1963:100) mentions in passing that in 1962 sectoral unions and "their constituent bodies" met to appoint municipal bodies of the CTC. Domínguez (1978:273) stands alone in stressing the lack of labor support for the revolution evident at the 11th National CTC Congress. Most other observers—including one who was in Cuba about that time—are of the opinion that Cuban labor was by then firmly behind the revolution (see Pérez-Stable 1975:65; Spalding 1977:242; and Gilly 1965:17–24).

37. The Minister of Labor reported that the qualifications of more than three hundred thousand nominees were discussed in this way (*Granma Weekly Review* 24 Oct 71:4).

38. Mesa-Lago 1978:84; Domínguez 1978:272; Bonachea and Valdés 1972*b*:381; Pérez-Stable 1985:292, 304. Section elections were also held prior to the 13th National CTC Congress, which met in November 1973. Domínguez (1978:293) claims that these electoral procedures "regressed to pre-1966 forms," in that the number of candidates per post was not specified and voting could be done by acclamation or by show of hands. Section elections in the early 1970s attracted the attention of a number of widely cited Cuba scholars, many of them revealing obvious disappointment over what they judged was the continued lack of democracy in the union electoral process (Domínguez 1978; Mesa-Lago 1978; Bonachea and Valdés 1972*b*). Some of these observers reported on aspects of the 1970 section-level elections that deserve serious scrutiny. Domínguez (1978:292) and Mesa-Lago (1978:84–85), for example, present some evidence that the 1970 elections were not always contested. Mesa-Lago's figures (1978:84) indicate that only half of the workers expected to participate in assemblies to select candidates did so. Domínguez (1978:272, 293, 302) shows that, at least in one province, only about 75 percent of those eligible voted, and he claims that the party and the government still removed labor leaders that they did not like. Often, however, critics have tended to condemn through the tenor of their prose, rather than evidence, and their analyses have sometimes been misleading or rooted in unexamined and unacknowledged, yet controversial, definitions of democracy. For example, Mesa-Lago (1978:84–85) claims that "thousands" of workers who attended the assembles did not vote, even though, by his own figures, almost 98 percent of those attending did. Mesa-Lago was joined by Domínguez (1978:292) in faulting the elections because campaigning "by any means" was prohibited. Certainly, the costly and often uninformative advertising blitzes that are the hallmark of electoral campaigns in many places did not characterize these elections. But workers did have opportunities to learn about candidates' qualifications. Finally, Domínguez (1978:271–73, 292), who apparently sees an advantage in having the same people hold office for extended periods, viewed the large election turnover as evidence of "instability." An equally reasonable interpretation would stress the necessity of periodic leadership changes for the viability of union democracy. Domínguez's (1978:293) concern about leadership instability, however, did not keep him from later criticizing the 13th National CTC Congress for voting to hold local elections "only" biennially. For further criticisms, see Bonachea and Valdés 1972*b*:381–82; Mesa-Lago 1978:86, 114; and Domínguez 1978:273.

39. According to Mesa-Lago (1978:90), Peña was elected by 99 percent of the vote. Whether other candidates also sought the post is unclear.

40. Domínguez (1978:293–95), however, is not satisfied with the procedures for either selecting delegates or choosing the national CTC leaders. Characterizing delegate elections at the local level as "poorly contested," he provides data indicating that the largest industrial unions and those whose delegations contained the highest proportions of rank-and-file members were underrepresented at the Congress according to the worker-to-delegate ratio. He claims that representation was unequal to ensure that "labor bureaucrats who had not faced the electorate" were well represented at the Congress. Because my major concern is change, two points about his commentary need to be made. First, as Domínguez supplies no comparable data on delegations to prior congresses, it is impossible to say whether the situation at the 13th National CTC Congress constituted an improvement or a digression. Second, if for no other reason than because union membership had begun to increase markedly in the early 1970s, in 1973 a larger percentage of Cuban workers had more voice in selecting national CTC leadership than in previous years.

41. Both the National Committee of the CTC and the National Organizing Commission for the 14th National CTC Congress approved the procedures and the timetable for the entire electoral process, from the grass-roots to the national level. The relevant documents were apparently drafted by the CTC's Department of Organization.

42. One thing assembly participants were asked to consider was the importance of selecting a group of leaders representative of the section in terms of certain demographic characteristics. See, for example, *Trabajadores* 13 May 77:4, 7 Aug 79:2.

43. The Statutes approved at the 1978 National CTC Congress stipulated that no top administrator could be a union leader and that each industrial union was to decide which job classifications were thereby ineligible (see CTC 1978, art. 3). The remaining section officers were in charge of organization, education, voluntary work, salaries and work organization, women, youth, social and labor matters, finances, health and safety, sports, culture and recreation, emulation, and *divulgación*. Those elected decided among themselves who would focus on which of these areas. In small sections, officers were responsible for more than one task.

44. One worker suggested this regulation may have been adopted because some workers failed to attend nominating assemblies because they wanted to avoid being elected a section officer, a job most agreed took a lot of time (interview with a member of the Education and Science Workers' Union, Havana, 11 Oct 83).

45. Figures reported in *Trabajadores* (3 Jun 77:4) and by workers I interviewed indicated that these guidelines were followed.

46. For more information on the 1977 section elections, see Veiga 1978:4; CTC 1978, esp. arts. 18–21; *Trabajadores* 13 May 77:4. Domínguez's (1978:295) large volume, *Cuba: Order and Revolution*, was completed in time for him to comment on these elections, and his interpretation is reminiscent of his accounts of earlier section contests. Castro's derisive assessment of elections in which campaigners tote signs saying "Vote for George" or "Vote for Sam" brought chuckles from delegates to the 14th National CTC Congress (*Trabajadores* 4 Dec 78:3). The contrast between electoral procedures in Cuban *secciones* and those at the lowest

level of the union hierarchy in some other socialist countries is often striking. For example, see Nelson 1986:110 (Romania); Ruble 1986:30–31 (USSR); Carter 1986:206 (Yugoslavia); Kemény 1986:187–88 and Haraszti 1978:92 (Hungary); and Rueschemeyer and Scharf 1986:68 (German Democratic Republic [GDR]).

47. The more sections there were under a bureau, the smaller the proportion of each section's officers who participated in the bureau election. The range was from 40 to 100 percent. If all section leaders did not take part in bureau elections, the section officers themselves decided who would participate (*Trabajadores* 13 May 77:4).

48. *Trabajadores* 13 May 77:4; CTC 1978, esp. arts. 25, 28, 29; and Veiga 1978:4, 6. For some comparative information on electoral procedures at analogous union levels in Poland and the GDR, see Pravda 1986:133 and Rueschemeyer and Scharf 1986:67.

49. A CTC official I interviewed in 1982 pointed out that most municipal, provincial, and national union officers had begun their careers as production or service workers and had then served as leaders at the grass-roots level before advancing to leadership positions at higher organizational levels. "Coming up through the ranks," he said, was one of the most important prerequisites for holding intermediate- and national-level union office (interview with a national CTC official, Havana, 29 Sept 82).

50. The National Committees managed the affairs of the sectoral unions in accordance with broad policies decided at the national congresses. The Executive Secretariats carried out the dictates of the National Committees. In the early 1980s neither the number of Secretariat members nor their selection by open vote was specifically stipulated (CTC 1984:189).

51. The organizing commission for each union's national congress decided the number of nominees-per-delegate.

52. The delegate-to-worker ratio varied from about 1 to 150 in the Cultural Workers' Union to about 1 to 1,100 in the Farmworkers' Union.

53. See *Trabajadores* 5 Aug 77:1, 11 Oct 77:5. For more information on the selection of the national leaders of sectoral unions, see *Trabajadores* 13 May 77:4 and CTC 1978, esp. arts. 32, 34, 37, 39.

54. Provincial committees mentioned in *Trabajadores* had between fifteen and thirty members. In the early 1980s neither the number of Executive Secretariat members nor their selection by open vote was specifically stipulated.

55. For more information on selection of intermediate-level leaders in industrial unions, see Veiga 1978:4 and CTC 1978, esp. arts. 41–51.

56. See *Trabajadores* 27 Feb 79:3 for a report on the 38th meeting of the CTC's National Council.

57. CTC 1978, arts. 59–72. Green (1982:65) says that the CTC Secretariat was elected by secret ballot. The National Council also elected the other members of the Review and Control Commission, but they did not have to be members of the Council. Roberto Veiga, who took over as secretary-general when Lázaro Peña died in 1974, was elected to the office in 1978. Domínguez (1978:272) says it was the "Political Bureau" that "brought in" Veiga as secretary-general on Peña's death. As Castro explained it to the 14th National CTC Congress, the party met with union leaders in an "absolutely free manner" and asked them to con-

sider the question of Peña's successor until they were able to arrive at a consensus (see *Trabajadores* 4 Dec 78:3).

58. Domínguez 1978:293; Veiga 1978:7. Each sectoral union was allotted delegates in accordance with its size (Green 1983:65). There were 126 fewer delegates to the 14th National CTC Congress than to the 13th. This was probably due, in part, to a decrease in the number of sectoral unions, but it also undoubtedly meant an increase in the worker-to-delegate ratio. The importance of the growth in the number of grass-roots delegates was publicly noted by one worker before the Congress (*Trabajadores* 2 Nov 78:3). Fifty-nine percent of the delegates were party or Communist Youth League (UJC) (*Trabajadores* 29 Nov 78:1).

59. See CTC 1978, esp. arts. 68, 71, 72. One Municipal Committee mentioned in *Trabajadores* had twenty-five members, and another had twenty-nine.

60. In 1975, however, Pérez-Stable (1976:40) found that only about 40 percent of the rank-and-file workers and union leaders she interviewed mentioned their right to recall a leader.

61. *Trabajadores* 14 Jul 79:3; CTC 1978, arts. 9, 89, 90. The importance of the right to recall was underscored by its specific mention in a program for union reform in a Hungarian *samizdat* publication (Kemény 1986:187).

62. Additional examples of electoral democratization in the unions include (1) increases in attendance at nominating assemblies for section leaders from roughly 50 percent of eligible voters in 1970 to about 87 percent in 1977, (2) the 1977 provision that nominations for section officers could not be made unless 75 percent of the members showed up, and (3) the increased use of secret ballots. The 1978 CTC Statutes limited voting by acclamation or by show of hands to special situations.

Chapter 4

1. The lack of attention to production as a political issue can often be traced either to researchers' rejection of Marx's idea of fundamental class antagonism under capitalism or to their acceptance of his suggestion that classes, class antagonism, and thus politics itself, will disappear in post-capitalist societies.

2. For the party's character before 1970, see Enzensberger 1976; Domínguez 1978, 1982; Mesa-Lago 1978; Casal and Pérez-Stable 1981; LeoGrande 1978, 1979*a*, and 1979*b*; Matthews 1969:321–23; and González 1976.

3. For the development of party structure after 1970, see LeoGrande 1978, 1979*a*, 1979*b*, and 1980; Casal and Pérez-Stable 1981; and Cuban Communist Party 1981*a* and 1981*b*. For differentiation of the party from the state administration, see Raúl Castro 1975*a*; LeoGrande 1979*b*, 1980; Domínguez 1978; and Harnecker 1980. Maintaining a clear division between the party and the administration was easier said than done (Domínguez 1978, 1982). Confusion and uncertainty over who was responsible for what often fostered tension between bureaucrats and party members (see Domínguez 1978:328 and Garzón's [1980:26–27] discussion of Domínguez's statement). Rigby (1976:46, 61), unlike Domínguez, suggests that the absence of a clear-cut distinction between party and state roles is essential to the proper functioning of Communist systems.

4. The Cuban Communist party (PCC) instituted a formal nomenclature system about the time of the 1st Party Congress in 1975 (see Partido Comunista

de Cuba 1978:57–99 and Cuban Communist Party 1981*a*:297–300). Different-level positions in the nomenclature were the responsibility of different-level party organs. Some fell under the purview of the Central Committee; probably many more were the responsibility of party organs at provincial and municipal levels. For further discussion of the nomenclature, see Hough 1969; esp. 116, 151–4; Nove 1982:591; and Ionescu 1967: esp. 60–64.

5. Partido Comunista de Cuba 1978:44. Doubtless the same procedure also applied to higher-level union bodies. According to *Trabajadores* (17 Jan 83:3), the national CTC bureaucracy had 294 party members in twenty-five nuclei.

6. Raúl Castro 1975*a*:74. Although 2d Party Congress documents called for an improvement in the nuclei's work in these areas, a prominent party member argued that the party's base organs should devote more attention to political activities as opposed to productive tasks and internal functioning (see Cuban Communist Party 1981*a*:295 and Harnecker 1981:33).

7. Cuban Communist Party 1981*a*:84.

8. I used total population figures in the calculations for Table 2. When party membership is calculated as a percentage of the labor force the approximate figures are 1.3 percent for 1963, 2.4 for 1964, 3.4 for 1965, 3.8 for 1966, 6.4 for 1971, 7.2 for 1972, 7.6 for 1973, 8.1 for 1974, 8.9 for 1975, and 17.7 for 1980. The 1966 figure is from LeoGrande 1980:400; labor-force figures for 1963–65 and for 1971–75 are from Mesa-Lago 1981:115; 1980 calculations are based on the number of union members reported in 1980 (2,383,000) or 97.1 percent of the active labor force (see Cuban Communist Party 1981*a*:60). Despite the steady growth of the Cuban party, it was, and probably still is, among the smallest in terms of the percentage of members in the total population. In 1975 the PCC represented 2.3 or 2.4 percent of the population, whereas in the same period the Communist party in Albania encompassed 4 percent of the population, in Hungary about 7 percent, and in Romania 12 or 13 percent (see Prifti 1979:15 for 1976 Albanian figures; Molnár 1979:214 for 1979 (?) Hungarian figures; and Gilberg 1979:296 for 1976 Romanian figures).

9. The importance of the numerical increase in party membership is demonstrated more fully in a later section of this chapter, when I discuss the informal mechanisms through which non-members could influence the party.

10. For data on the size and number of party nuclei, see Domínguez 1978:334; LeoGrande 1980:400 and 1979*b*:467, 469, 474; and Cuban Communist Party 1981*a*:77–78. In contrast, the average size of the basic party unit in Czechoslovakia was thirty-two (Toma 1979:114); in the German Democratic Republic (GDR) it was twenty-nine, counting candidate-members (Grote 1979:190).

11. Interview with a member of the Commercial and Restaurant Workers' Union, Havana, 5 Oct 82.

12. Interview with a member of the Education and Science Workers' Union, Havana, 3 Oct 83.

13. Interview in a steel factory outside Havana, 1 Oct 82.

14. See Cuban Communist Party 1981*a*:290–91 and Fidel Castro 1975*c*: 112–13.

15. Interviews with a member of the Education and Science Workers' Union, Havana, 9 May 82, 23 Sept 82.

16. Interview with a member of the Cultural Workers' Union, Havana, 27 Sept 83.

17. Like everything else in Cuba, income differentials have undergone modification over the course of the revolution. For more details, see Mesa-Lago 1981, esp. chaps. 7, 8; MacEwan 1981, chap. 12; and Mesa-Lago 1982:154–55.

18. The calculations for 1980 and 1985 should be considered best approximations, as they where figured from data not exactly comparable to those from 1975 (Partido Communista de Cuba 1978:19; Pérez-Stable 1985:295; Azicri 1988:80).

19. LeoGrande (1979a:45, 50) is in basic agreement, though he does not attribute every single appointment specifically to Fidel Castro and a few men around him. There is little doubt, however, that the highest-level appointments (Central Committee, Political Bureau, Secretariat) were made by these leaders. For concurring opinions, see Dumont 1970a:75, 193; Mesa-Lago 1978:70; González 1976:4; and Domínguez 1978:329.

20. LeoGrande 1979a:51. There are no general data on the number of candidates per post. According to Domínguez (1978:334), however, in 1974 one province had 1.1 candidates ($N = 77$) for the sixty-seven positions on the Provincial Committee. This candidate-to-post ratio is about the same as that reported by Dumont (1970a:76) for the late 1960s.

21. Additionally, each Provincial Committee elected a Provincial Control and Revision Commission. The duties of the Provincial Control and Revision commissions (as well as of the Commission at the national level) included reviewing party finances and overseeing activities of *militantes*, both within the party and within other organizations in which they were active (Cuban Communist Party 1981b:22). Only the chairs of these commissions had to be members of a provincial committee. The Central Committee ratified the election of all provincial control and revision commission members (Cuban Communist Party 1981b:21). For a comparative discussion of the roles assumed by analogous organs in other socialist countries, see Cocks 1975:236–44.

22. Despite the stipulation that provincial party leaders be elected, Domínguez (1978:314) reports that in 1976 they were appointed by the Political Bureau. Although the source of his pronouncement is not clear, this possible departure from specified procedure could have been necessitated by the administrative reorganization of the island that followed the 1st Party Congress (see Chap. 3). This reorganization changed provincial boundaries and created eight new provinces. As a result, the provincial party apparatus throughout the country had to be completely reorganized (or established), and it is conceivable that the leaders Domínguez refers to served in an interim capacity until provincial parties could be re-formed.

23. Cuban Communist Party 1981a:7; Casal 1976:27. I do not know why this occurred. By contrast, in Hungary, whose population was approximately the same as Cuba's but whose party was more than three times larger in the mid-1970s, congresses were convened with only five hundred or six hundred delegates (see Molnár 1979:216).

24. In Hungary, by contrast, Central Committee candidates were chosen by the Political Bureau and the Secretariat (Molnár 1979:216).

25. Cuban Communist Party 1981*b*:16. The number of candidates per post for provincial, municipal, and work center committees was decided by the corresponding assembly at each level.

26. Fidel Castro 1976:236. The inclusion of women in the party has been slow (see Table 4). The goal set by the 1st Party Congress—to have women's party membership equal their proportion of the paid labor force (41 percent in 1985)—remained elusive (Partido Comunista de Cuba 1978:29; *Trabajadores* 25 Feb 85:4).

27. Fidel Castro 1976:236; Cuban Communist Party 1981*a*:81. Domínguez (1978:302) says that in 1975 party rules called for 40 to 50 percent of municipal assembly delegates to be directly linked to production, and that 31 percent of the members of Executive Bureaus of municipal committees fell into this category.

Table 4
Female Participation in the Cuban Communist Party: Selected Years, 1962–86 (In percentages)

	Party Membership	Nuclei Officers	Municipal Officers	Regional Officers	Provincial Officers	National Officers	Central Committee/National Directorate	Congressional Delegates
1962	15						4	
1963	13–15							
1964	11							
1965							5	
1967	10							
1972	12							
1973	13							
1974	13		3	4	6	6		
1975	13–15	17	13	13	6–13	6–9	5	15
1976	17							
1979	18							
1980	19–20							15
1981	19							
1982	20							
1983	21							
1984	21	24	19			17	13	
1985	22							
1986	22						14	

Sources: LeoGrande 1980:403–5; Casal 1976:26; Cuban Communist Party 1981*a*:78; Pérez-Stable 1983:7; Partido Comunista de Cuba 1978:28–29; Domínguez 1978:324, 502–3; *Trabajadores* 20 Dec 80:1; Fidel Castro 1976:235–36; Enzensberger 1976:126; Azicri 1988:80–81; Bengelsdorf 1988*b*:127.

28. Cuban Communist Party 1981*a*:406–7. Later Castro remarked that the same principles were observed in electing the Political Bureau. See Casal and Pérez-Stable 1981:90 for a reference to Castro's words at the 1st Party Congress.

29. Assessments of this type are scattered throughout Dumont 1970*a*; see, for example, 185–86, 202, 225–26, 247–48.

30. LeoGrande's (1979*a*:45, 1980:406) few comments on early party functioning have a slightly different emphasis. Instead of stressing pervasive top-down control, he notes the lack of mechanisms for controlling subordinates as well as superiors. In his view, lack of accountability characterized the party.

31. See, for example, Domínguez 1978: esp. 316–38.

32. The Secretariat membership rose from seven to eleven in the early 1970s, and the Political Bureau, from thirteen to sixteen in 1980. Also, at the 2d Party Congress a new rank, Political Bureau alternate, was created, of which there were eleven. Originally, the Political Bureau had eight members (González 1976:4).

33. Counting both members and alternates, of which there were seventy-nine in 1980, the Central Committee nearly doubled in size between the 1st and 2d Party Congresses. Domínguez (1982:24) believes the Central Committee's growth was probably owing to the "difficulty in deciding who might be dropped." From his own figures on the changing composition of the Central Committee as it grew, however, it seems likely that the decision to *include* more representatives, especially of mass organizations, was also responsible for the increase.

34. Further indication that the party decision-making pyramid was leveled off is that additional high-level bodies also began to function. Party congresses were convened at approximately five-year intervals. The Political Bureau and the Secretariat began to meet regularly even before the Central Committee did, the Secretariat usually weekly, and the Political Bureau almost as often.

35. LeoGrande offers additional evidence that the party elite in Cuba expanded: Only rarely in the 1970s did Central Committee members head up the departments that made up its administrative apparatus, whereas in earlier years that was almost always the practice. For more information, see LeoGrande 1980:410–13 and Casal and Pérez-Stable 1981:94.

36. Cuban Communist Party 1981*b*:8, 15. The notable exception to this proscription against factions in a Communist party was found in the statutes of the Czechoslovak party in 1968 (Croan 1976:152).

37. See, for example, Fidel Castro 1976:241 and Raúl Castro 1975*a*:80. The Party Statutes also stipulated that every member had the right to vote on matters that were discussed and that party decisions at all levels were to be adopted by a majority of eligible voters, provided a quorum (50 percent) was present (see Cuban Communist Party 1981*b*:11, 15). This last item was added to the statutes at the 1st Party Congress in 1980.

38. Cuban Communist Party 1981*b*:9. Molnár (1979:220) noted a subtle shift in Hungary, where criticism, formerly a member's duty according to Party Statutes, later became only a right.

39. Interviews with members of the Education and Science Workers' Union (11 Oct 83) and with members of the Public Administration Workers' Union (29 Sept 83).

40. LeoGrande (1980:398) suggests that familiarity with such materials is valuable also because it lessens the possibility that party policies will be distorted during implementation by members who do not understand their intent.

41. Interview with a member of the Public Administration Workers' Union, 29 Sept 83.

42. Interviews with two members of the Light Industry Workers' Union, 9 Oct 83.

43. In 1973 Raúl Castro (1975a:79) noted that when criticism/self-criticism was used correctly, an errant party member would be consulted privately and individually before being criticized by the collective. Western observers often note that top-level pronouncements on the necessity for more open discussion and criticism within Communist parties do not necessarily bring any changes in party practice (see, for example, Prifti 1979:24, 26).

44. Domínguez 1978:330–31, 338. Statutes approved at the 2d Party Congress gave the delegates an opportunity to "suggest and rule on modifications, deletions, and/or additions" to the agenda of the Congress before the meeting began (Cuban Communist Party 1981b:18). During the Congress the language of the article was strengthened. See Guerra 1976:119.

45. Delegates to the 1st Party Congress, for example, approved almost unanimously the main report, the Party Statutes, the Programmatic Platform, the draft of the Constitution, and the members of the Central Committee (Domínguez 1978:332; González 1976:4).

46. For details on the preparation of these statutes, see Malmierca 1976: 83–99, from which my account is largely drawn.

47. Domínguez (1978:331) says the Political Bureau approved the provisional statutes after they were drafted.

48. Simultaneously, the commission in charge of elaborating the statutes studied certain of their aspects more closely, with the collaboration of lower-level party leaders. According to Malmierca (1976:86), these leaders made important contributions to sections relating to the functioning of grass-roots party bodies.

49. Even if a member's suggestion were not accepted by her or his nucleus, the member could still personally take it to the commission in charge of preparing the final draft for consideration. See Raúl Castro 1976:19–20 for an example.

50. Malmierca (1976) does not specify whether 1,365 was the number of *substantively different* suggestions or the *total number* of suggestions, many of which may have had the same content. If substantively similar suggestions were counted as only one, the calculations presented here probably underestimate the amount of mid- and base-level input at this stage of the process.

51. One clue to the significance of this issue is provided by an observer of the Yugoslav party, who wrote that the option of leaving the party voluntarily "substantially" increased a member's "freedom of action" if his or her views clashed with the official party position (Shoup 1976:188). See also Bahro 1978:370.

52. Interview with a member of the Health Workers' Union, Havana, 27 Sept 82.

53. Dumont (1970a:76) notes that three-fourths of the workers had to be present to make the assembly valid.

54. For example, interviews with members of the Cultural Workers' Union, Havana (25 Sept 82), and with members of the Education and Science Workers' Union, Havana (23 Sept 82).

55. One worker, however, told me that in her center it was the administrators who proposed workers for party membership and that workers had nothing to do with the process (interview with a member of the Commercial and Restaurant Workers' Union, Havana, 29 Sept 82).

56. See, for example, Bray and Harding 1974:681; Enzensberger 1976: 125; and MacEwan 1975:128.

57. Interviews at a steel factory outside Havana, 1 Oct 82, and with a member of the Commercial and Restaurant Workers' Union, Havana, 29 Sept 82.

58. For examples, see Harnecker 1980:20–21.

59. Interview with a member of the Commercial and Restaurant Workers' Union, Havana, 12 Oct 83. Two workers I interviewed disagreed that party membership held no advantage. They said that some people joined the party, not because they really believed in its mission and purpose, but because party membership was the best way to improve one's situation and to make one's children's lives easier (interviews with two members of the Light Industry Workers' Union, Havana, 9 Oct 83). Some years earlier Dumont (1970a:188, 258) offered relevant comments.

60. Domínguez (1978:214) says that 30 percent of exemplary workers were selected as party members in 1962–63. Matthews (1969:321–22) gives a somewhat different and, from what I learned, an incorrect account of the process through which exemplary workers became party members.

61. Cuban Communist Party 1981b:5–7. An addition to the Party Statutes approved at the 2d Party Congress allowed anyone denied membership to appeal the decision to the Revision and Control Commission at the provincial or national level (Cuban Communist Party 1981b:22).

62. Interview with a member of the Education and Science Workers' Union, Havana, 9 May 82.

63. Interviews in a steel factory outside Havana, 1 Oct 82, and with a member of the Cultural Workers' Union, Havana, 4 Oct 83. Dumont (1970a:76) and Domínguez (1978:212–13) both indicate that this procedure was followed in the early and late 1960s as well.

64. Interview with a member of the Health Workers' Union, Havana, 27 Sept 82.

65. The youth was then evaluated by the Communist Youth League (UJC), resulting in admission, rejection, or future reconsideration. A candidate who was admitted had to spend at least three years in the UJC before being endorsed by it for membership in the party. The minimum age for party membership was eighteen; the maximum UJC age was thirty (Cuban Communist Party 1981b:6, 1981a:74). For more information on UJC admission, see Harnecker 1980:154–55, 200, and Domínguez 1978:315. For the first time in 1979, ninth-graders in the Pioneers (the Cuban children's organization) were evaluated and the most outstanding were admitted directly into the UJC (see Cuban Communist Party 1981a:71). For information on the UJC, see Domínguez 1978:321–23; Cuban Communist Party 1981a:73–76; and Sutherland 1969:119.

66. Fidel Castro (1976:228) reported in 1976 that almost 40 percent of the party's new members came from the UJC. Domínguez (1978:315) cites 55 percent as the corresponding figure for 1976. Yet the 2d Party Congress reported that only 36 percent of all new members in 1975–80 came from the UJC (Cuban Communist Party 1981a:78).

67. Documents from the 1st Party Congress show that improving the worker composition of the party also took precedence over improving members' educational level. At this Congress the party leadership rejected base-level proposals to make a sixth-grade education an entrance requirement, arguing that it would disqualify many workers and thus interfere with the goal of increasing the party's worker composition (Camacho 1975:135).

68. On other occasions union leaders, rather than rank-and-file workers, were brought into such discussions. For example, in 1979 the Political Bureau issued a resolution on the functioning of base-level party organs and recommended that union leaders at all levels examine it (*Trabajadores* 14 Jul 79:1). Likewise, one of the Theses debated by the delegates to the 1st National Congress of Maritime Workers in 1977 concerned the party's role "as the vanguard of the working class," presumably in that sector of the economy (*Trabajadores* 5 Aug 77:4).

69. A better-known example of this formalized assembly process occurred in the crisis period following the failure of the 1970 sugar harvest. At that time prominent party figures held numerous meetings at which ordinary workers could discuss the causes of and possible solutions to the complicated economic and social problems facing the nation. The purpose of such assemblies went beyond examination and analysis of party work by direct producers: They also served a legitimizing function (LeoGrande 1980:398), and they gave the party an opportunity to educate non-members about its policies and positions.

70. See *Granma Weekly Review* 24 Oct 71:4; and Bengelsdorf 1976:3; and Bengelsdorf and Locker 1974:7. The Programmatic Platform covered the history of the revolution, as well as the principles and objectives of its policies on economic, social, cultural, educational, and ideological development; international politics; and the relations among the party, the state, and mass organizations (see Partido Comunista de Cuba 1982). See Casal 1976:23 for a brief discussion of the difference between the Programmatic Platform and party platforms in the United States.

71. Raúl Castro 1976:18. At party meetings to discuss the platform, however, 1,429 proposals for change were made (Raúl Castro 1976:17). As a result of all these discussions, the draft of the Programmatic Platform was amended 147 times (Casal 1976:27).

72. See Raúl Castro 1976: esp. 17–25 for complete details on discussions of the platform, including proposals not included in the final draft.

73. See Partido Comunista de Cuba 1981.

74. Interview with a member of the Public Health Workers' Union, Havana, 3 Oct 83.

75. Interview with a member of the Public Health Workers' Union, Havana, 3 Oct 83.

76. This opinion was also expressed by one of Harnecker's (1980:137) informants.

77. Interview with a member of the Cultural Workers' Union, Havana, 4 Oct 83.

78. On Laws 32 and 36, see Chapter 7; on stimulation funds see Chapter 5.

79. On this point an interesting reference was made at the 2d Party Congress to "People's Opinion Teams." These presumably party teams were briefly described as mechanisms for soliciting people's opinions about specific problems. Although I have no further information about them, they perhaps represented a party attempt to routinize and institutionalize informal mechanisms for gathering opinions from non-members (see Cuban Communist Party 1981a:91).

80. Domínguez (1978:317) makes some rather pessimistic comments on this point.

Chapter 5

1. Bernardo 1971:189, 195. Bernardo's description of the period of budgetary finance in Cuba is the most inclusive.

2. Interview at the Institute of Internal Demand, Havana, 21 Sept 82.

3. The meanings of these concepts and the roles they played under the SDPE (El Sistema de Dirección y Planificación de la Economía), however, are not precisely equivalent to their meanings and roles in capitalist economies.

4. For some examples, see Fitzgerald 1989:289–91.

5. For more thorough discussions of problems encountered in the implementation of the SDPE, see Mesa-Lago 1982:130–32; Junta Central de Planificación (JUCEPLAN) 1980b; Castro 1986:5–6. Reform of the price structure, one priority of the SDPE, was badly needed because prices were often unrelated to production costs, rendering other goals of the SDPE unrealistic. The State Price Committee (Comité Estatal de Precios) was to implement this reform. For more general discussions of the difficulties of decentralization in a socialist context, see Medvedev 1977, esp. chap. 11; Kornai 1959, esp. 168ff.; Bornstein 1977.

6. Quesada 1980b:95–96; interview in a steel factory outside Havana, 1 Oct 82.

7. Cuba had not just one type of economic plan; it had many. They covered various time periods (one-, five-, and twenty-year forecasts), and planning occurred for many geographic and economic levels (nation, territory, economic sector, central administrative body, local government organ, and individual enterprise). For more details, see Quesada 1981:17–21; López and Santiago 1975:21–22; and JUCEPLAN 1980b:6–8. With the institution of the SDPE, the government focused on coordinating the various plans and expanding the scope of planning to encompass longer periods, larger geographic areas and more economic levels. For more information, see López and Santiago 1975:16; Rodríguez 1980:251–55; JUCEPLAN 1980b: esp. 51–63; and Partido Comunista de Cuba 1981:43. Nove (1987:458) quotes a Soviet economist who emphasizes the importance for heightening enterprise autonomy of expanding the temporal scope of plans.

8. Although the topic falls outside the scope of my analysis, the SDPE was also intended to strengthen the participation of municipal and provincial organs of People's Power (OPP) and central state administrative bodies in the planning process (Partido Comunista de Cuba 1981:24, 41). For information on how the OPP organs took part in planning, see Dupuy and Yrchik 1978:57; Girling and Ruccio 1981:10–15; and JUCEPLAN 1980b:52–55.

9. See White (1987) for more details. White describes the position of the Junta Central de Planificación (JUCEPLAN) in the planning process as "awkward" because it is "sandwiched between the demands of the Party leadership on one side and the pressures of economic and social agencies on the other" (255).

10. JUCEPLAN 1980*b*:121. Five-year plans were also discussed at the enterprise level (Girling and Ruccio 1981:12, 26; Domínguez 1978:300).

11. For further information on things the work units were supposed to consider at this stage see Quesada 1981:23–25.

12. According to Zimbalist (1985:223), about "34 percent of locally oriented enterprises in services, commerce, and industry are responsible to the local organ of Popular Power." The head of JUCEPLAN offered the following figures: 75 percent of all commercial and eating establishments, 86 percent of all educational institutions, and 92 percent of all health-delivery facilities were under local OPP direction (*Trabajadores* 24 Feb 79:2). Domínguez (1982:41) notes that in 1978 enterprises under subnational government jurisdiction accounted for only 9 percent of state sector gross production. *Bohemia* 1984 reports that OPP-subordinate local industries tripled the value of their output between 1977 and 1983 (from 500 to 1500 million pesos).

13. Interview with an adviser to the president of JUCEPLAN, Havana, 28 Sept 82. Regulations governing secondary production were published in *Trabajadores* 28 Jun 82. Possibly the salary limitation was prompted less by concern over the proportion of enterprise activities dedicated to secondary production than by the prices at which enterprises sold their secondary goods. For more information on aspects of the planning process discussed above, see Martell 1979; Quesada 1981; Girling and Ruccio 1981:10–16; Domínguez 1978:419; Mesa-Lago and Zephirin 1971:145–84; López and Santiago 1975:8–25; and Ayala and Hidalgo-Gato 1980:36–59 and 1975:229–41.

14. Quesada (1980*b*:94–95), who was in charge of improving SDPE functioning, said that in planning, the enterprise is subordinate to the center, whereas in production, it has autonomy.

15. Zimbalist 1989:74. Additionally, Zimbalist (1990*b*:13) notes that, "in at least one important respect" the SDPE resulted in further centralization: Material supplies came to be implemented in a more centralized fashion after its introduction.

16. For example, enterprises were supposed to conduct ongoing studies aimed at perfecting the organization and norming of work; they had to guarantee that workers' wages bore a satisfactory relationship to productivity and to cost. Enterprises had also to adhere to Cuban labor legislation specifying wage scales and grades; health and safety standards; and accident, death, illness, and maternity benefits, among other things. Additionally, enterprises were responsible for improving their remunerative systems, for providing job training, and for giving professional and technical students practical work experience while they were in school (Consejo de Ministros 1980:119–20).

17. I was told by enterprise managers and state functionaires, however, that under no circumstances could National Bank control over enterprise salary funds result in workers' receiving less than the wages stipulated for their job ranks and categories (interviews in a steel factory, at the Institute of Internal Demand, and with an adviser to the president of JUCEPLAN, Havana, 1 Oct 82, 21 Sept 82,

and 28 Sept 82). The second appraisal of the SDPE revealed difficulties with the National Bank's control over wage and salary disbursement, and a number of changes were recommended (JUCEPLAN 1980*b*:239–46).

18. In 1981, recently graduated middle- and high-level technical workers were excepted from this system. Also, 1 percent of the openings in enterprises could still be filled centrally to ensure that disabled workers had employment and to alleviate problems faced by women seeking work outside the home. See *Trabajadores* 19 Jan 81:4, 3 Apr 82:2.

19. For more detailed information see Quesada 1981:145–49, and *Trabajadores* 16 Jan 81:1, 30 Dec 80:2, 5 Jan 81:1, 3 Apr 82:3. This number represented 67 percent of all workers supposed to be covered by the new contract system. At that time, workers in the city and province of Havana and those in the education, art, and health sectors were not yet incorporated into the system (*Trabajadores* 5 Jan 81:1, 16 Jan 81:1). The system was implemented in Havana in 1986.

20. Consejo de Ministros 1980:111–13 has more details.

21. See Partido Comunista de Cuba 1978:199. National enterprises that were not self-sufficient were to be subsidized by national administrative bodies. Local enterprise financing was different: They were subordinate, not to any central branch of government, but to local OPP organs, and their budgets were linked to these bodies. The SDPE also stipulated that state organs were expected to cover losses incurred above the enterprise level with revenues generated by profitable enterprises under their jurisdiction. If those revenues were insufficient, the difference was made up from the national budget. After 1986, it was announced that firms not operating in the black, instead of having their deficits cancelled annually, would begin to see them held over from year to year (*Trabajadores* 17 Apr 86:5).

22. Interview with a JUCEPLAN official, 28 Sept 82.

23. Quesada 1981:98; *Trabajadores* 3 Aug 78:4, 9 Aug 79:2; White 1987: 159. State organs and administrative bodies could also finance the purchase of working capital assets, particularly for enterprises planning to increase such assets. The appropriate central organism attempted to cover planned increases in working capital in some enterprises under its jurisdiction by decreasing the value of these resources in others. Only when the two did not balance were funds diverted from the state budget to cover the difference. The second review of SDPE implementation revealed difficulties with this process (JUCEPLAN 1980*b*:226–28).

24. For a critique of financial planning in Cuban enterprises, see JUCEPLAN 1980*b*:173–75, 233–37. One difficulty, bearing directly on the issue of autonomy, was that an enterprise's financial plan could easily be invalidated by changes in supply, salaries, production figures, and so forth, originating at a higher level.

25. Some enterprises experienced difficulties in this regard (JUCEPLAN 1980*b*: esp. 192–93, 203, 205).

26. Interview with a JUCEPLAN official, 28 Sept 82.

27. For more details on the arbitration panels, see *Trabajadores* 31 Jan 81:4; see also JUCEPLAN 1980*b*:123–30.

28. For this and other problems that arose, see *Trabajadores* 7 Oct 81:2, 22

Oct 81:3, 2 Mar 82:3; and JUCEPLAN 1980*b*:113–19. Kornai (1959: esp. 95–96, 156, 159) also discusses the relationship between contracts and worksite autonomy under socialism.

29. For more information on the variety of ways the national government laid claim to firm earnings, see Pérez 1980*a*:32; JUCEPLAN 1980*b*:160, 170–72; Quesada 1981:102–3; Santiago 1980; and Gómez 1986.

30. Interview with a member of the Education and Science Workers' Union, Havana, 11 Oct 83. For prescriptions governing distribution of both funds, see JUCEPLAN 1980*a* and 1980*c*. Although the stipulation basing distribution of the prize fund partly on wages meant that higher-paid employees could receive more, the inequality of the system did not approach that of the one instituted in Hungary in 1968 that restricted bonuses (based on profitability) to 15 percent of workers' earnings yet 85 percent of top management's (Burawoy n.d.:16).

31. Gómez (1986) and Zimbalist and Brundenius (1989:136–37) detail some of the later modifications.

32. Kornai (1959:103, 133–34) notes the incentive to adopt loose plans when bonuses depend on overfulfillment. For more details, see Comisión Nacional 1980:142; *Trabajadores* 19 Jun 81:4, 22 Dec 79:2; Quesada 1980*a*; and Nove 1980:6–7.

33. According to Partido Comunista de Cuba (1978:203), profits remaining after the stimulation funds were formed reverted to the national government. Other Cuban sources explain that excess profits were subject to a surcharge.

34. In 1984, 1275 Cuban enterprises were profitable, up 20 percent from 1983 (*Trabajadores* 16 May 85:1).

35. The first steps toward forming stimulation funds in units that were totally dependent on state subsidies were to be taken in 1980 (JUCEPLAN 1980*b*:48–49). As in profitable work units, other performance indicators besides a decrease in the planned subsidy could alter the amount of nonprofitable enterprises' stimulation funds. They could be adversely affected by non-fulfillment of production plans or of contractual obligations or by a failure to increase productivity. If an enterprise underfulfilled its plan by more than 5 percent in any of these areas, or if the absolute value of what it produced was less than the year before, it could not form stimulation funds (see Comisión Nacional 1980:143–44 and Quesada 1981:188–89).

36. *Trabajadores* 20 Jul 82:3. For discussions of other problems with the *fondos*, see Quesada 1980*a*: esp. 110–12; Veiga 1984:16–17; *Trabajadores* 2 Jun 81:1; JUCEPLAN 1980*b*:385–40; Gómez 1986:87–89; and Zimbalist and Brundenius 1989:135–37.

37. Questions have been raised about the efficacy of the prizes as stimuli for workers. Together, the two funds could not exceed the amount an enterprise paid in salaries for 30.2 days; they were distributed only once a year, and they represented only a small portion of a worker's basic wage (Zimbalist and Brundenius 1989:135). According to Mesa-Lago (1982:155), in 1979 an individual worker received between 37 and 103 pesos from the *fondo de premios*. Articles in *Trabajadores*, referring to 1980, reported on firms in which each producer received 43 to 110 pesos from the prize fund. In 1979 the median wage in Cuba was 150 pesos per month. See *Trabajadores* 2 Jun 81:1, 3 Apr 81:3, 11 Mar 81:3.

38. White 1987:154–55. According to one government official, the SDPE was an effort to achieve "restrained centralization" (interview at the Institute of Internal Demand, Havana 21 Sept 82). The contrast between the SDPE and Yugoslav decentralization is marked. In Yugoslavia, state participation in production planning was halted very early. Enterprises soon came to decide what to produce, what production methods to use, and what their production targets would be. Centralized control over investment began to erode somewhat later. From the early 1960s until at least the mid-1970s, the trend was for banks and individual enterprises to finance ever-larger proportions of the country's investments, thus minimizing the role of the center. Hunnius (1973:294) reports that in 1967 banks held 43.8 percent of Yugoslavia's investment resources, enterprises held 33.4 percent, and the government, 13.4 percent. Stephens (1980:68, 74) gives data for 1971, when banks controlled 51 percent of gross investment and enterprises had been granted the right to lend one another money at flexible interest rates. In 1975, according to Lee (1976:112), banks controlled 90 percent of investment resources, and firms, the other 10 percent. For more information, see Singleton 1976:150–59 and Zukin 1984: esp. 254–56. Yugoslav enterprises also fixed prices for their own products (Singleton 1976:159–62, 285). As self-management developed, the Yugoslav state claimed less and less of the economic surplus. Despite yearly variations, the percentage of earnings retained by production units grew substantially, as enterprise taxes were reduced (1965) and interest payments on social capital and rental fees on capital equipment were abolished (Blumberg 1968:233; Stephens 1980:69). Moreover, the state was only minimally concerned with determining how surplus was divided within enterprises, which themselves decided how their earnings would be allocated among different work units. Although the state established a minimum wage and a maximum ratio between the highest- and lowest-paid workers (Blumberg 1968:203), firms had wide latitude in determining which workers were paid how much and how profits were divided among wages, investment, collective consumption funds, and so forth (Singleton 1976:270). In addition, Yugoslavia eliminated state subsidies to "inefficient" enterprises as enterprise autonomy increased. Critiques of the Yugoslav self-management system link decentralization to other ills, which limited both directly and indirectly, the full democratization of production: persistent unemployment, migration, monopolistic practices of banks and enterprises, income inequality, uneven development among regions, and over-investment in sectors of the economy where short-term, high profits were made at the expense of investment in longer-term, lower-yield, yet more socially useful projects. See Blumberg 1968:211–12; Stephens 1980:68; Sachs 1981:13; Kunitz 1979:524, 525; Medvedev 1977:267; Lee 1976:112–14; and Singleton 1976:163, 307, 311.

Chapter 6

1. Boorstein (1968:159) describes the situation: *"Hay que arar con los bueyes que hay*—You've got to plow with the oxen you have. So those who could run calculating machines became statisticians, and bookkeepers became experts on finances and the balance of payments."

2. For more history of early planning in Cuba, see Mesa-Lago 1981; Mesa-

Lago and Zephirin 1971; Dumont 1970b; esp. 68–72, 79–81; Ritter 1974; Beauvais 1983:57–58; Huberman and Sweezy 1969: esp. chap. 9; Vilariño 1980; and Boorstein 1968.

3. Zimbalist and Brundenius 1989:126. As the history of the 1985 plan, however, demonstrates, the planning system remained vulnerable to Castro's personal interventions (White 1987:155–56).

4. Interview with a member of the Education and Science Workers' Union, Havana, 11 Oct 83.

5. Complaints emerged about the negative impact of overly ambitious plans on some workers under the SDPE (El Sistema de Dirección y Planificación de la Economía). See, for example, Trabajadores 28 Nov 81:1 and CTC 1984:123–24.

6. See JUCEPLAN 1980b:27, 121; Trabajadores 18 Mar 81:2; Cuban Communist Party 1981a:60; Domínguez 1978:300; and Zimbalist 1985:221.

7. Cuban Communist Party 1981a:387. The decree is Decree 42, article 85 (Hernández 1980:19–20).

8. A member of the Commercial and Restaurant Workers' Union told me that at her worksite 75 percent attendance was required at planning discussions (interview, Havana, 30 Sept 82).

9. Trabajadores 7 Oct 80:3. The 1980 figures do not include the proposals from workers in five sectoral unions, which apparently did not keep adequate records.

10. Interviews with a member of the Council of Ministers and a JUCEPLAN (Junta Central de Planificación) official, Havana, 21 Sept 82, 28 Sept 82. See also an interview conducted by Sheryl Lutgens with a national officer of the Education and Science Workers' Union, Havana, 31 Mar 83. The CTC (1984: 122) also called for a reduction in the number of plan indicators.

11. Interview with a JUCEPLAN official, Havana, 28 Sept 82.

12. Armengol and D'Angelo 1977:174. The precise question concerned participation in the formulation of work or production plans. Many respondents also agreed that workers spoke out in these forums and that they made proposals in them.

13. Interview in a steel factory outside Havana, 1 Oct 82.

14. Interview with a member of the Cultural Workers' Union, Havana, 4 Oct 83.

15. A JUCEPLAN official claimed that higher figures were most commonly proposed by supraworksite bodies when production units were just beginning operations and no one was sure how they would function (interview, Havana, 28 Sept 82).

16. Interview with a JUCEPLAN official, Havana, 28 Sept 82.

17. In 1986 Castro claimed that "until recently" no progress was made to facilitate the practical participation of workers' collectives in designing the plan (Fitzgerald 1989:16).

18. Ninety-three percent of the planned work-center and 88 percent of the planned enterprise-level assemblies were convened to discuss control figures for the 1980 plan (Trabajadores 13 Oct 79:6).

19. For example, see Trabajadores 5 May 81:1, 15 Jul 80:3, 25 Mar 80:2; Bohemia 1983:55.

20. CTC 1984:121–23. In 1979 the union bureau of *Cubana*, the national airline, refused to discuss the control figures with the administration because workers had been given figures for only two of the plan's indicators (*Trabajadores* 18 Nov 79:1).

21. Interview with a JUCEPLAN official, Havana, 8 Sept 82. Harnecker (1980:8) reports that the union at one worksite, through talks with workers, produced its own estimates of some of the control figures, and then, in conjunction with management, devised a set of control figures that were eventually discussed and compared with JUCEPLAN's figures in the larger workers' assembly.

22. See *Granma Weekly Review* (4 Aug 74:9) for a brief description of a planning assembly in which the union chair did a good job performing these tasks.

23. See Williams's (1985:298–301) interesting comments on this topic.

Chapter 7

1. A fifth plan was drafted and published but never became law because of turnover in the Ministry of Labor (Cuban Economic Research Project [CERP] 1963:127–28).

2. CERP 1963:127–33. It is not clear, however, whether the bipartite commissions were in full operation before the revolution (Hernández and Mesa-Lago 1971:219; CERP 1963:123; Grupo Cubano de Investigaciones 1963:1457–58).

3. Reports on how the three commission members were chosen are inconsistent. Zimbalist (1975:46) says the management representative was usually appointed by the relevant ministry and the Ministry of Labor, and worker representatives were elected by the workers. CERP (1963:134), however, says the union appointed one member, management selected the second, and the union and management had to agree on the Ministry of Labor representative. Grupo Cubano de Investigaciones (1963:1467) says that the workers and management each designated a representative and that together management and the union chose the Ministry of Labor member. If union and management could not agree, the ministry itself selected one of the workers at the center as its delegate. See also Zeitlin 1970:191–92.

4. This provision, which was retained in later arbitration systems, also counteracted pressures toward the professionalization of conflict resolution, such as have appeared in Yugoslavia (Hayden 1985).

5. CERP 1963:134. Zeitlin (1970:192) presents a slightly different list of kinds of cases the *comisiones* were empowered to hear.

6. Two sources claim that the Ministry retained final authority to hand down decisions, which could not be appealed (CERP 1963:135; Hernández and Mesa-Lago 1971:220). See Zeitlin (1970:192) for an indication of how the union might be involved.

7. Unconvinced of the positive value of the change, Bonachea and Valdés (1972b:371) say that the "workers . . . now had the progressive right of coercing themselves." The all-worker composition of the councils distinguished them from worksite dispute commissions in the Soviet Union, which were composed of both union and management representatives. Bodies analogous to the Cuban *consejos*

were not established in Poland until 1982 (*Trabajadores* 3 Dec 86:9; *Pravda* 1986:137).

8. According to Hernández and Mesa-Lago (1971:221) and Bonachea and Valdés (1972b:370), council members had to have a socialist attitude toward work, to be disciplined, to have compiled a good attendance record, and to have escaped previous sanction by a labor justice organ.

9. Interviews with a member of the Education and Science Workers' Union, Havana, 9 May 82, 23 Sept 82. In 1978, 3,218 council members (of a total of nearly 88,000) received five- or ten-year service awards (*Trabajadores* 14 Oct 78:3, 13 Sept 77:6, 20 Sept 77:4, 12 Jun 79:2).

10. In 1976 the National Farmworkers' Union, the largest union in Cuba, reported that roughly 42 percent of its council members had received such training (*Trabajadores* 16 Aug 77:2).

11. This list was compiled from ones provided by Hernández and Mesa-Lago (1971:221), Bonachea and Valdés (1972b:370), Ritter (1974:267), and *Trabajadores* (1st half Nov 73:2).

12. Zimbalist (1975:47), who visited Cuban worksites in 1974, says that in cases of disciplinary infractions council members, before applying a sanction, commonly spoke personally with workers and their families in an effort to determine the cause of the problem.

13. Hernández and Mesa-Lago 1971:221. Other possible sanctions at this time were loss of work merits, disqualification for certain posts, wage deductions, transfers, and temporary discharges. Bonachea and Valdés (1972b:370) also report that imprisonment was a possible penalty in extreme cases, but it is unlikely that it could have been imposed solely by a work council.

14. Zimbalist 1975:47; Hernández and Mesa-Lago 1971:222, 224. In any event, material sanctions would then have had only limited effect, since the amount of money in circulation far exceeded the quantity of goods available for purchase.

15. For examples see *Trabajadores* 16 Apr 76:2, 18 Mar 77:2, 30 Aug 77:2, 16 Sept 77:2, 18 Oct 77:2, 18 Apr 77:4, 31 May 77:2. The work councils, however, were not permitted to order certain salary adjustments without the approval of the Regional Appeal and National Review Councils.

16. For examples see *Trabajadores* 25 Jan 77:4, 18 Mar 77:2, 27 Sept 77:2, 30 Sept 77:2, 14 Oct 77:2, 26 Aug 77:2. Judging from the remedies and sanctions that the *consejos* imposed or withheld, their power to resolve worker-management conflicts outstripped that of some comrades' courts in East European countries that depended largely on social pressure as a sanction (Hayden 1985: 232–24).

17. Without providing details, Hernández and Mesa-Lago (1971:221) report that in some instances during the 1960s managers could discipline a worker without council intervention and could even, in exceptional cases, dismiss a worker, who had no right to appeal.

18. The full title of Law 8 is "Ley #8 de la Organización y Funcionamiento de los Consejos del Trabajo." Article 10 states that a council member can be recalled only by the workers' assembly that originally elected him or her. As part of a governmental reorganization, the Ministry of Labor was eliminated about the

same time; some of its activities were taken over by the new State Committee of Labor and Social Security (CETSS).

19. As the unions began to perform these four tasks, they distributed responsibilities among different levels of the Central de Trabajadores de Cuba (CTC) and the sectoral unions, especially their secretaries and departments of labor and social affairs. Special commissions and groups of union activists were also appointed at enterprise, municipal, and provincial levels to help with the work (*Trabajadores* 15 Aug 78:1). *Trabajadores* (1 Aug 78) reported that in Santiago de Cuba province twenty-eight union commissions with 270 members were set up to serve the needs of 1,351 councils.

20. Law 8 specified that worksites with more than 150 workers could form more than one work council and that those with fewer than 25 workers elected representatives to nearby councils.

21. About a year after assuming supervision of the work councils, the unions had made 2,022 such visits (*Trabajadores* 14 Oct 78:3).

22. The reports were later forwarded to upper levels of the CTC and the sectoral unions.

23. Two alternates could also be elected as observers, but they could not vote. This gave additional workers council experience, preparing them to replace regular members who did not serve their full terms (Law 8, 1977, art. 7). For additional information on council electoral proceedings, see Harnecker 1980:41–42. Tenure continued at three years, though some members still served more terms (*Trabajadores* 25 Sept 79:3). Of more than 110,000 council members in 1979, some 6,000 had served more than ten or even fifteen years.

24. The draft of the law specified a sixth-grade education, but its final version was not precise on this point.

25. Interview with a member of the Cultural Workers' Union, Havana, 25 Sept 82.

26. Articles 20 and 22 of the new law merely stated that the union section should be informed of upcoming council hearings and that attention should be paid to what its representative had to say during council proceedings. Contrast this to Yugoslavia, where the law required the union to represent workers before the disciplinary commissions and the local courts of associated labor. The unions could also bring cases before this last body themselves (Carter 1986:208–9).

27. According to one worker, "The real challenge is to try to solve the problem elsewhere first, before resorting to the work council" (interview with a member of the Education and Science Workers' Union, Havana, 23 Sept 82). Preferably, a worker who had a complaint against management should first approach rank-and-file union leaders, who were to initiate informal discussions in an effort to settle the dispute. Only when this procedure had failed should a union suggest taking the issue to a work council. Similarly, interviewees felt that an administrator, before disciplining a worker and notifying the council, should discuss the situation with the worker. As one woman saw it, "A worker has to be given many chances before the work council gets involved" (interview with a member of the Commercial and Restaurant Workers' Union, Havana, 5 Oct 82).

28. Interview with a member of the Health Workers' Union, Havana, 27 Sept 82.

29. Interview with a member of the Cultural Workers' Union, Havana, 25 Sept 82.

30. Interview with a member of the Commercial and Restaurant Workers' Union, Havana, 5 Oct 82.

31. Interview with a member of the Light Industry Workers' Union, Havana, 9 Oct 83.

32. About the same time other changes were made in the Cuban judicial system. See Berman and Whiting, Jr., 1980:478–79; Domínguez 1978:257; and Álvarez Tabío 1981:363–95 for more details.

33. Interview with a member of the Cultural Workers' Union, Havana, 25 Sept 82.

34. For details of tribunal procedures, see "Proyecto de Ley de Procedimiento Civil, Administrativo y Laboral" 1977, art. 702.

35. The Cuban judicial system included both professional and lay judges at all tribunal levels, with the latter outnumbering the former on municipal and provincial benches. Only the assembly that elected a judge had recall power (Álvarez Tabío 1981:390–91).

36. During their tenure, Cuban judges could not simultaneously hold administrative or executive positions, a restriction that apparently applied to both lay and professional judges (Álvarez Tabío 1981:376). For some comparative information on appellate bodies in Yugoslavia, see Carter 1986:209.

37. Other disciplinary cases commonly heard by the councils were the appropriation of worksite property for personal use; damage to property or waste of materials; disrespect to or abuse of fellow workers or superiors; and negligence or carelessness at work. A member of the Education and Science Workers' Union told me that teachers who engaged in amorous relationships with their students, thus flouting rules laid down by the Ministry of Education, had occasionally been brought before a work council (interview, Havana, 12 Jul 83).

38. The administration had from fifteen to ninety days to bring a case to the council, depending on the gravity of the alleged violation (Law 8, 1977, art. 17).

39. The top fine was 500 cuotas; the longest prison term was three years (Trabajadores 19 Dec 78:3, 23 Dec 78:2, 10 Nov 79:2).

40. Workers had 180 days in which to bring such cases before a work council (Law 8, 1977, art. 18). The councils were also responsible for processing workers' applications for long-term pensions and forwarding them to the CETSS (Law 8, 1977, art. 31).

41. For details of some cases of this kind, see Trabajadores 16 Nov 78:3, 20 Feb 79:3, 22 Feb 79:3, 23 Aug 79:3.

42. Some workers got higher pay than others doing the same job simply because they held the job at a particular historical period, often before the revolution, when wages for that job were above the current rate; these were termed "historical wages."

43. For examples, see Trabajadores 7 Nov 78:3, 4 Jan 79:3, 5 Jun 79:3.

44. For examples, see Trabajadores 20 Mar 79:3, 25 Aug 79:4.

45. Interview with a member of the Education and Science Workers' Union, Havana, 12 Jul 82.

46. *Trabajadores* 13 Oct 79:5, 3 Oct 78:3. Although I lack definitive data on non-existent or non-functioning councils, my feeling, based on workers' widespread familiarity with these bodies, is that this problem was not a serious one.

47. Interview with a member of the Public Administration Workers' Union, Havana, 29 Sept 83.

48. For examples, see Veiga 1980:30–31; *Trabajadores* 6 Oct 79:1, 24 Feb 79:4, 25 Aug 79:4.

49. For examples, see *Trabajadores* 17 Aug 78:2, 19 Dec 78:3.

50. For examples, see *Trabajadores* 23 Aug 79:3, 29 May 79:3, 4 Jan 79:3, 8 Jul 77:4, 22 Mar 77:2, 19 Mar 76:2; Veiga 1978:25.

51. Actions that violated workplace discipline were discussed in detail in *Trabajadores* 24 Nov 81:3, 25 Nov 81:3. See *Trabajadores* (9 Dec 86:9) for a breakdown of disciplinary violations by type. One worker, who was a party member, told me that minor infractions, such as having someone else punch your time card or arriving late for work, were still being handled by the work council at his worksite (interview with a member of the Health Workers' Union, Havana, 27 Sept 82).

52. The worker had to submit his or her case in writing within ten days; the form used was very simple (Decreto-Ley, art. 5).

53. After 1980 retirement pensions were no longer handled by the *consejos* either (CTC 1984:13).

54. For example see CTC 1984:100.

55. The preliminary report was published in *Trabajadores* 29 Dec 79:4. The problems cited in this report included deficiencies in labor legislation; defects in work councils; ignorance of labor legislation among administrators, council members, and unions; slack and overly mechanical use of the grievance procedures among administrators; and delays in settling cases by both work councils and appeals bodies. For other difficulties in the system of resolving disputes, see *Trabajadores* 15 Mar 80:2.

56. Interview with a member of the Cultural Workers' Union, Havana, 25 Sept 82.

57. Interview with a member of the Cultural Workers' Union, Havana, 6 Oct 83.

58. These are Pérez-Stable's (1983:7) terms.

59. Indeed, *Trabajadores* (9 Apr 85:5, 17 Apr 85:4, 28 Feb 85:4) reported that the preparation of appeals caused workers and unions continued difficulties.

60. *Trabajadores* 31 Mar 81:2, 17 Jun 81:2, 1 Apr 85:4, 24 Jun 85:4, 5 Jul 86:1. In a fifteen-month period in 1984–85, approximately 58 percent of the appeals of disciplinary sanctions that incurred the range of possible penalties were upheld by appeal tribunals (*Trabajadores* 11 Dec 86:9). For additional critiques of Law 32, see *Trabajadores* 1 Jun 81:1, 27 Mar 82:3, 14 Mar 81:3, 15 Mar 80:2, 22 Apr 85:4, 18 Jun 85:4, 5 Jul 86:1, 11 Dec 86:9.

61. Interview with a member of the Public Administration Workers' Union, Havana, 13 Oct 83.

62. Interview with a member of the Commercial and Restaurant Workers' Union, Havana, 12 Oct 83.

63. Pérez-Stable 1983:7; *Trabajadores* 3/23 Mar 82:3. See *Trabajadores* 9

Mar 82:3 and 11 Mar 82:3 for the infractions of administrative discipline listed in Law 36. *Trabajadores* (11 Mar 82:3) specified several penalties that could be imposed for violations of Law 36, including private warnings, fines from 5 to 100 percent of a manager's monthly salary, transfer, demotion, or firing.

64. Interview with a member of the Public Health Workers' Union, Havana, 25 Sept 83; *Trabajadores* 17 Jun 81:2, 15 Sept 81:3, 28 Nov 84:4. See also Veiga's comments on the imbalance in *Trabajadores* 14 Mar 81:3.

65. Interview with a member of the Public Health Workers' Union, Havana, 25 Sept 83.

66. Interview with a member of the Agricultural Workers' Union, Havana province, 8 Oct 83.

67. Interview with a member of the Education and Science Workers' Union, 12 Jul 83.

68. Union participation in grievance resolution or in any other decision-making forum does not, of course, guarantee democratization. A union may be too weak in numbers, or have too little power at the national level, effectively to counter management advantages. Or ironically, as we have seen in this chapter, active unions may create pressures that cause workers' power to decline in certain ways. Also, unions may support the status quo rather than advocate more power for workers. Under capitalism this occurs with company unions or when unions become a pillar of what Burawoy (1979, esp. chap. 6) has labeled the internal state. In like fashion, some observers of socialist countries argue that unions there merely transmit state and party directives and that therefore "the transfer of the grievance procedure to the trade-union organization is not the concession to labor that it appears to be" (Hazard 1968:195). See also Markovits (1982) for a discussion of unions and workplace conflict commissions in the German Democratic Republic.

69. See Ruble 1986:33.

70. Interview with a member of the Agricultural Workers' Union, Havana province, 8 Oct 83.

71. The downward trend in appeal activity before 1970 has also been attributed to (1) a decline in wage disputes because of the policy of equalizing wages regardless of effort; (2) an increase in consciousness owing to the emphasis on the development of the "new person"; and (3) expansion of government control over or elimination of conflict resolution procedures and other channels of worker protest (Hernández and Mesa-Lago 1971:224; Domínguez 1978:274, 278). In opposition to my argument, Hernández and Mesa-Lago (1971:213) suggest that union decline in this period was caused partly by the establishment of the *consejos* in 1965.

72. The councils heard an average of eighty thousand cases a year between 1974 and 1978, but only around thirty-one thousand cases in 1981 and twenty thousand in 1985 (Pérez-Stable 1985:301; *Trabajadores* 9 Jun 86:4).

Chapter 8

1. See, as examples, Pérez-Stable 1975:66–68, 1976:32; Mesa-Lago 1978:3; Martin 1974:30; MacEwan 1981:152; Zeitlin 1970:xxv–xxvi; Bengelsdorf and Locker 1974:8; and Munck 1984:232–34.

2. Reckord 1971:101–6. In this meeting only Communist Youth League (UJC) members supported the worker's complaint. Descriptions of Cuban unions and their leaders in the 1960s are similar to comments and observations of unions in the 1970s and 1980s in Hungary (Haraszti 1977:93–94; Burawoy and Lukács 1985:733–34; Burawoy 1985:65), the Soviet Union (Ruble 1986:35), Czechoslovakia (Porket 1986:89), Romania (Nelson 1986:114), and China (Walder 1986: 84, 88).

3. Interview with a national CTC (Central de Trabajadores de Cuba) official, Havana, 9 Sept 82.

4. For a further sense of the change in worksite union autonomy, compare Harnecker's (1980:5–6) report on a union leader's intervention in a production assembly in the 1970s with Reckord's (1971) and Gilly's (1965) accounts from the 1960s.

5. Interview with a member of the Public Administration Workers' Union, Havana, 13 Sept 82. According to this woman, the union never did play a more active role, even though the many dissatisfied workers could have replaced the leadership, because too many workers had learned to "shut up under capitalism and still shut up." Another difficulty was the disunity caused by the combination of day- and night-shift workers in the union section. Thus, at election time most members were unfamiliar with many of the candidates.

6. Interview with a member of the Health Workers' Union, Havana, 27 Sept 82.

7. *Granma Weekly Review* 24 Oct 71:4–5. Eugenio Balari (1985:182–83), head of the Institute of Internal Demand, made similar comments over a decade later. For a comparison of different levels of workplace conflict in Cuba and the German Democratic Republic, see Fuller 1990.

8. Interview in a steel factory outside Havana, 1 Oct 82.

9. The Labor Code was published in *Trabajadores* on 4 Mar 85. See also Pérez-Stable 1985:299–300. Although some provisions of the SDPE (El Sistema de Dirección y Planificación de la Economía) increased conflict between workers and management, others may have mitigated or relocated it. For example, workers and managers who shared in a firm's profits developed some common interest in lowering costs and increasing output. Moreover, because the supply of production inputs consistently fell below demand, inter-firm contracting for these inputs tended to heighten conflict between workers and managers in one enterprise and those in another.

10. Interview with a member of the Health Workers' Union, Havana, 10 Oct 83.

11. According to Wilson (1987:314), this remained a problem in China into the 1980s.

12. Interview with a member of the Cultural Workers' Union, Havana, 21 Sept 82.

13. Interview with a member of the Health Workers' Union, Havana, 27 Sept 82.

14. See also, LeoGrande 1979*b*:476. From Harnecker's (1980:xxxvii, 1, 2), Roca's (1986:169), and Ghai, Kay, and Peek's (1988:63) work, we see that in practice the ideal of spreading factory leadership posts among different individuals

was not always achieved. A member of the Education and Science Workers' Union told me the overlap between party membership and union leadership occurred because party members were, "the only ones who couldn't refuse" when they were nominated for union office (interview, Havana, 11 Oct 83). Precise data on leadership overlap is difficult to secure, but a few interesting comparisons emerge from research in other socialist countries. In China, "most" members of the enterprise trade union leadership were party members in the early 1980s. In the 1960s in Czechoslovakia and in the 1970s in Poland, around one-third of trade union leaders at the enterprise level were party members. The heads of enterprise trade union committees in the German Democratic Republic (GDR), Poland, and China were usually party members, if not leaders. At the lower levels, analogous to Cuban *secciones*, one-quarter of trade union officers were party members in the GDR in the 1980s, and one-fifth of the shop stewards in Poland in the 1970s were party members. Moreover, one-third of factory directors were reported to be enterprise trade union officers in Poland in the 1970s; in the GDR, however, this rarely happened. In China, party and managerial positions reportedly often overlapped (Wilson 1986:230–31; Porket 1986:89; Pravda 1986:133, 135; Fuller 1990; Rueschemeyer and Scharf 1986:68).

15. Both Domínguez (1978:328) and Rabkin (1985:261) discuss the confusion between the workplace roles of the party and management.

16. Interview with a member of the Health Workers' Union, Havana, 6 Oct 82. For further discussions of the relationship among unions, management, and party, see Partido Comunista de Cuba 1978:42–46; Harnecker 1980:xxxvii–xxxix; and Raúl Castro 1975a:87–88.

17. Interview in a steel factory outside Havana, 1 Oct 82. For another example, see Rabkin 1988:42.

18. Interviews in a steel factory outside Havana, 1 Oct 82; with a member of the Education and Science Workers' Union, Havana, 23 Sept 82; and with an official of the CTC, Havana, 29 Sept 82.

19. Interview with a member of the Cultural Workers' Union, Havana, 21 Sept 82.

20. Interview with a member of the Cultural Workers' Union, Havana, 25 Sept 82; Reckord 1971:96.

21. Interview with a member of the Cultural Workers' Union, Havana, 25 Sept 82. See also *Trabajadores* (9 Nov 78:3), for a report on how a union played its counterpart role when management blamed a worker's own negligence for an accident that caused his death. One worker I interviewed argued that sometimes unions had too much power at the workplace: "The administration has to talk to them [unions] about everything. They can't do anything without talking to the union. For the administration the union is a big burden" (interview with a member of the Construction Workers' Union outside Havana, 7 Oct 82).

22. See for example, Zeitlin (1970:xxx, 193). Zeitlin (1970:xxxix) also reports that in a late 1960s experiment, administrators of some plants were elected by the workers. Since the mid-1970s, Soviet workers in certain locales have elected administrators. At the Party Congress in 1986, Gorbachev envisioned the expansion of this practice (Moses 1987:205, 221).

23. Interview with a member of the Health Workers' Union, Havana, 27 Sept 82.

24. Interview with a national CTC official, Havana, 29 Sept 82. Ghai, Kay, and Peek's (1988:64) research in the agricultural sector corroborates my contention that workers have informal influence in removing a bad boss.

25. Interview with a national CTC official, Havana, 29 Sept 82.

26. Interview with a member of the Education and Science Workers' Union, Havana, 3 Oct 82. See also Harnecker 1980:25–26.

27. For Castro's speech see *Trabajadores* 6 Feb 79:2. For the editorial, entitled "La Contrapartida Sindical: 'una obligación, una convicción,'" see ibid. 7 Jul 79:1.

Chapter 9

1. The first of these approaches, which in my view has little to recommend it, emphasizes the character and personal style of Fidel Castro. According to Ernst Halperin (1966:viii), "the modern sociological interpretation of history, according to which the course of events is determined not by the decisions of individuals but by the clash of powerful social forces," which is, "dubious when applied to the French and Russian revolutions," is "inapplicable to Cuba. One man alone, Fidel Castro, is responsible for the course of events in Cuba." Understanding Cuban socialism is thereby reduced to understanding Castro, vastly and unrealistically simplifying postrevolutionary reality: Castro's distaste for institutions and organizations explains the weakness of the party and the unions before 1970; his need for power and control explains the hypercentralization of economic and political decision making during the same period; these personal qualities, because they checked the entrenchment of a bureaucratic stratum, allowed the development of participatory institutions and programs in the post-1970 era; the willingness of the masses to take part in such institutions and programs can be explained by Castro's magnetism and charisma.

The second approach draws attention to the Soviet Union, viewing it as the principal determinant of many aspects of the Cuban revolution. Although analyses of this sort vary in how they perceive Soviet influence on Cuba (e.g., Cuba voluntarily copies the Soviet Union; Cuba reacts in opposition to the Soviet Union and does things differently; the Soviet Union determines, indirectly or directly, what happens in Cuba; what happens in Cuba is analogous to what previously went on in the Soviet Union), they all direct attention away from the Cuban revolution in their attempts to explain it: The unions in the 1960s are viewed as imitations of their Soviet counterparts; tensions between the Soviet Union and Cuba during the same decade help to account for the hesitancy to form a vanguard party and for the outcome of the Great Debate; after 1970 the stability and expansion of economic and political links with the Soviet Union brought changes in numerous Cuban institutions, including the government, the party, the military, and the unions, a dynamic summed up by Mesa-Lago (1978:115) as a "trend characterized by central controls, dogmatism, administrative-bureaucratic features, and limited mass participation." For a critique of this vein of analysis, see Fitzgerald 1978.

The third approach is, in my view, superior to the first two. This perspective, informed by dependency and world systems theory, highlights the importance of Cuba's external economic relationships in explaining internal change. Eckstein and Zimbalist's (1987) interpretation of Cuban development, for example, points to the salience of such factors for understanding postrevolutionary Cuban political economy. Thus, according to these authors, a balance-of-payments deficit in the 1960s led to an emphasis on exports that required heavy centralization of decision making. Though the authors do not overlook "domestic sources of surplus accumulation," and though I am convinced that attention to international economic factors is important for understanding postrevolutionary Cuba, any such approach should be viewed with skepticism insofar as it reduces everything that happens inside Cuba to a reflection of some external economic tie. Not only does this underplay Cuba's historical autonomy, just as do the Soviet-centered analyses, but it also tends to reduce politics to economics, obscuring the many important instances in which political decisions and forces have held the key to understanding social change. For additional discussions of models commonly employed to study Cuba, see Valdés 1988 and Bengelsdorf 1988a.

2. For example, in one reported instance a ministry official had to intervene at a worksite to solve a minor supply problem and a management-labor dispute (Dumont 1970b:19).

3. According to Karol (1970:464), in the late 1960s rumor had it that many of Castro's closest advisers "were urging him to proceed to the militarization of the whole economy."

4. For discussions of the militarization of work in the latter half of the 1960s, see Dumont 1970a: esp. 144–45, 151–53, 156–58; Dumont 1970b: 231–33; Karol 1970:444–45; Huberman and Sweezy 1969:146–49; Valdés 1972a: 41–58; LeoGrande 1978:28; Malloy 1971:37–41; and San Martín and Bonachea 1981:554–59.

5. White (1987:158–59) notes that some of these same arguments were used by Cuban planners and economists to justify the degree of centralization that existed in the late 1980s.

6. MacEwan 1981:34. For additional information on the skill drain in the 1960s, see Fitzgerald 1985; O'Connor 1970:260; Valdés:1972b:441–42; and Portes and Bach 1985:85–86, 141–52. Boorstein (1968:55–58, 63–64) gives several examples of how the flight of skilled personnel affected the functioning of various production sites.

7. Some of Che Guevara's comments are relevant here (Fitzgerald 1985: 259). Some observers argue, however, that decentralization demands fewer skilled personnel because the market "makes decisions" that people must make in a more centralized system. See Ritter 1974:92–94.

8. Farber (1983:59, 60) writes that the Communist party had engaged in "electoral horse-trading and unprincipled politicking" dating to the early 1940s, and that in the mid-1940s it was one of the few Communist parties criticized by the Soviet Union for touting the "right-wing line of the U.S. Communist leader Earl Browder." See also Farber 1976:137–38.

9. Suárez 1967:26. According to Fidel Castro, Raúl Castro, who had joined the Communist Youth as a university student, actually broke party discipline by joining the Moncada attack (Lockwood 1969:163).

10. Farber 1983:63. For more information on the relations of the Communists to the July 26 Movement, see Zeitlin and Scheer 1963:117–20; Thomas 1971:136–37, 159–60, 198–99, 223–35, 296–98; and Sims 1985:54–56. The

following are some of the assessments of this relationship contained in these sources: "The Communists never helped the 26th of July Movement until the 26th of December—five days before the fall of the Batista regime" (a guerrilla fighter quoted in Zeitlin and Scheer 1963:120). "In the struggle against Batista it [the Communist party] played a less prominent part than the Catholic laity" (Thomas 1971:297). "Where had most party secretaries been in the epic days of Moncada or the *Granma*? 'Under the bed,' as Castro later said" (Thomas 1971:298). For another source of information on the pre-victory relationship between the Communists and the July 26 Movement, see Goldenberg 1965: esp. 165–170.

11. Matthews 1969:176. Matthews (1969:144) and Thomas (1971:535) share the opinion that Fidel Castro was merely "using" the Communists at this time. See also Matthews 1969:167, 182; Farber 1983:73; and Goldenberg 1965: 182 for indications of the level of suspicion that clouded the relationship between the Communists and Castro's movement during this period.

12. In respects both Zeitlin and Scheer (1963: esp. 97–98, 109–10) and Farber (1983) offer a more harmonious account of the early relationship of the Communists and Cuba's new political leadership. See also Farber 1976:229–33.

13. See also Matthews 1969:315–16; Enzensberger 1976:124; Thomas 1971:601; Morray 1962:170–71; Goldenberg 1965:265–66; and LeoGrande 1979*b*:457–65).

14. Enzensberger 1976:123. The expulsions associated with the purge affected between 29 and 82 percent of the party membership (Domínguez 1978:212–13).

15. That Mujal was, however, primarily an opportunist rather than a devotee of Batista is illustrated by Ambassador Earl Smith's revelation that Mujal sent an emissary to him, "to say that if the U.S. attitude was changing towards Cuba he, Mujal, would like to know, since he would not be likely to stand firm behind Batista" (Thomas 1971:203). See Thomas 1971:228 and Zeitlin and Scheer 1963:119 for information on opposition to Batista within the unions.

16. For a worker's graphic description of the prerevolutionary leadership of his union, see Zeitlin 1970:xxvi–xxvii. Morley (1980:409–11) notes that the anti-Communist segment of the July 26 labor leadership also sought external support from the Inter-American Regional Organization of Workers (ORIT) and the AFL-CIO.

17. For more information on some of these events, see O'Connor 1970:191; Morray 1962:60–68, 75–76; Woodward 1963:37–38; and Martin 1974:29. Thomas (1971:673) also refers to a "major challenge" to the government by construction workers in September 1963, citing a few details offered by exile sources.

18. In contrast, over the years 1971–75 the two figures were 7.5 and 5.7 percent. In 1976–80 the increases were 4.0 and 3.1 percent, and in 1981–85 the figures were 7.3 and 6.4 percent (Eckstein and Zimbalist 1987:8).

19. Mesa-Lago 1978:59. Eckstein and Zimbalist (1987:9) report that between 1959 and 1968 output of more than one-fourth of Cuba's important industrial items increased by *at least* 100 percent, but that in 1969 production fell even in the sectors where it had previously risen.

20. The above figures on absenteeism may be found in MacEwan 1981: 145; Fitzgerald 1978:11; Domínguez 1978:275–76; Ritter 1974:282; and Bonachea and Valdés 1972b:375. For information on absenteeism in the early part of the decade, see O'Connor 1970:205–6 and Ritter 1974:266–67.

21. Mesa-Lago 1981:134. In contrast, rates of change for 1974 and 1975 were 5.0 and 7.1 percent.

22. Valdés 1972a:37, Karol 1970:426; Huberman and Sweezy 1969:143. In addition, Fitzgerald (1985:121) cites a 1968 study of ninety-nine work centers that found low productivity responsible for a loss of 8,755 labor hours.

23. Nove (1983:91–92) notes how this course has been followed time and again in other socialist countries, usually with detrimental economic and political results.

24. Mesa-Lago 1981:44. Investment rates in the late 1960s are the topic of some debate. See Mesa-Lago 1981:44; Zimbalist 1985:216, 227; and Brundenius 1984:32–33, 71, 78.

25. FitzGerald 1976:159. See also Zeitlin's (1970:xi–xii) description of scarcity during this period.

26. Dumont (1970b:117–18) notes that under these circumstances microlevel managers often chose either to follow the orders of the center, even if they knew them to be mistaken, or to ignore them and do as they pleased.

27. The stress on equality of reward clashed with another observable kind of inequality. Certain individuals, for example, party, military, and administrative elites, were the recipients of perks not available to ordinary workers. Ritter (1974:288ff.) lists housing, autos, better food, and foreign travel among these. And although the degree of material inequality was probably not high, even in comparison with other socialist countries, the widespread scarcity of consumer items rendered even the smallest material privilege more obvious and more significant, contributed to the population's diffuse but growing dissatisfaction, and fostered attitudes and behaviors that suppressed production. Fitzgerald (1985:118–19) argues that the pay inequities that did exist during the period lessened the efficacy of moral incentives.

28. Quoted in Fitzgerald 1978:11. Castro reported that in one textile plant, sixty of one hundred workers were lost because they had enough savings to make working unnecessary. See ibid.

29. Fitzgerald 1978:12. The Minister of Labor also recognized the potentially destructive political symptoms of the crisis (Zeitlin 1970:xxi).

30. See, for example, Pérez-Stable 1975:62; Mesa-Lago 1978:156; Huberman and Sweezy 1969:217–18, and Casal 1976:24. Zeitlin (1970:xvi–xvii), however, does not concur.

31. Besides instituting changes that expanded majority control over production, the leadership's response to the crisis of the late 1960s also included a new electorally based governmental system (People's Power [OPP]), the revitalization of mass organizations, an emphasis on material incentives and income differentials, the production of more consumer goods, and some price hikes.

32. FitzGerald (1976:157) sensed this tendency in 1973 when she wrote, "Cuba remains on a rightward swing that it entered in mid-1968, and for the moment it shows no sign of returning."

33. Although these labor records clearly helped the government keep closer tabs on the workforce, they were also the primary documents used to determine workers' social security and disability claims and to decide promotion and wage increases.

34. Before the law was promulgated, vagrants were given two months to sign up for work without penalty. Over 100,000 people took advantage of this amnesty provision. See also Fitzgerald's (1985:315–17) discussion of this law.

35. In Szelenyi's (1982:315) words, "Decentralization in itself is only the delegation of power to lower echelons of the power-structure and does not affect the relationship between the powerful and the powerless."

36. In the opinion of some, the 1948 elections were canceled because the Communists could not have done as well (see Toma 1979:99). The Eastern European country that fits this pattern least well is Yugoslavia, which also made an innovative, widespread, and long-lasting attempt to further the democratization of production.

37. Balari (1985:35) estimates the combined numbers in the Rebel Army and the underground to have been ten thousand to fifteen thousand. Controversy surrounds the issue of who supported the July 26 Movement during the institution process in the 1950s. Some observers contend it received very little help from anyone in Cuba, whereas others, in an effort to accentuate the importance of one sector's support, de-emphasize the contribution made by other sectors. The picture painted by such accounts often highlights the small size of the Rebel Army, the mistrust and cynicism of the peasantry, the passivity of the workers, the weakness of the Havana resistance, and/or the noninvolvement or overt hostility of the middle and upper classes. For examples, see Dumont 1970b:22; Goldenberg 1965:162, 295; O'Connor 1972:75; and Lockwood 1969:165–67.

38. Huberman and Sweezy (1960:78) report that three-fourths to four-fifths of the soldiers in the final campaign of 1958 were peasants. On peasant support for Castro's forces, see also O'Connor 1972:74–75; Blackburn 1963:77–79; Matthews 1969:134, 185; Dumont 1970b:22; and Wolf 1969: esp. 267–73.

39. For information on the *territorio libre*, see Blackburn 1963:79 and Thomas 1971:167, 192, 198, 261–62.

40. On this attack, see Bianchi 1987 and Thomas 1971, chap. 10.

41. Morley 1980:274–75. It is difficult to determine how much actual support for the resistance was indicated by these contributions. Castro told Lockwood (1969:167) that the July 26 Movement received "large and immediate help" from sugar-mill and plantation owners, once the guerrilla forces had gained control of the territory where their establishments were located and had instituted a taxation system.

42. MacEwan (1985:423, 425) makes a similar point.

43. Nary an observer of the Cuban revolution in its early years has failed to remark on the widespread popularity of the new government (O'Connor 1970: 316; Suárez 1967:12; Karl 1975:28; Goldenberg 1965:236). Two studies in particular reinforce this point. One was a survey of urban and semi-urban residents that reported that 86 percent of the respondents were supporters of the new regime and that half of them could be classified as fervent supporters (Fagen 1972a:159–61; Goldenberg 1965:211–12). The second, based on interviews with

workers all over the country, concluded that the majority, whether working in small or large plants, whether unskilled or skilled, old or young, and regardless of race or class origins, were revolutionaries (Zeitlin 1970). Certainly, the revolution had die-hard opponents from the beginning, and, inevitably, more surfaced as time went on. Nevertheless, the depth of social support for the new government was impressive; it contrasts even with the situation in the Soviet Union, where during the initial period of War Communism the signs of dissatisfaction and demoralization were strong, even among the urban working class.

44. Blackburn 1963:91. Brundenius (1985:200–201) cites an estimate that 20 percent of the average annual national income was redistributed in 1959–60. *Revolución* (19 Aug 59:1) notes that in the first eight months of 1959 domestic purchasing power expanded by two hundred million pesos.

45. On these and other popular policies and actions, see O'Connor 1970:302–3; Blackburn 1963:90; Goldenberg 1965:210; Fitzgerald 1985:103; Thomas 1971:420–22, 574; Zeitlin and Scheer 1963:74–76, 124, 162; and Morray 1962:24–26, 155–56.

46. See also MacEwan (1985:427–28) on this point. In Zeitlin's (1970: 269) words, "The workers in Cuba have entered massively and decisively into the political process since the revolution." Or, as Zeitlin and Scheer (1963:212) put it, "The Cuban Revolution has been a fundamentally democratic experience for the Cuban people." There is an additional, less direct, sense in which mass participation in the consolidation process reinforced the leadership's growing trust in the citizenry, helping to create the possibility of democratization as an alternative in the 1970s. Just as the egalitarian economic and social policies implemented by the political leaders gave many Cubans a material stake in the revolution, the varied forms through which they participated in the construction of socialism expanded their basic education and job-related skills, their confidence, their organizational, administrative, and oratorical abilities, and their understanding of the problems facing their country. Numerous Cubans thus came to have an added personal stake in the revolution. And because so many citizens had acquired these kinds of strengths and skills through participation in the 1960s, the country's political leaders could contemplate democratization in the early 1970s with some assurance that the population was prepared to handle the new responsibilities that would be crucial to its success.

47. For more information on this period in Hungarian history, see Donáth 1981:221–46.

48. Additional examples of mass involvement during consolidation include the Cuban Women's Federation (FMC) formed in August 1960 and the Committees for the Defense of the Revolution (CDR) formed in September 1960.

49. Domínguez 1978:207–8. Both Woodward (1963:46) and Grupo Cubano de Investigaciones (1963:1579) have suggested that the major impetus behind the formation of the militias was Castro's fear that the Rebel Army would turn against him. The militias, however, never took such a role.

50. Sugar workers were apparently strongly represented (see O'Connor 1970:305). Woodward (1963), however, says the militias were mainly composed of urban members of the Central de Trabajadores de Cuba (CTC). Militia members were paid their regular wages during mobilizations. There is always the possibility that many people joined out of opportunism or because they were pressured to do

so. Zeitlin (1970:39), however, who was in Cuba in 1961 and 1962, came away convinced that the proportion of militia members who signed up for these reasons was insignificant. Goldenberg (1965:208, 237), who stayed until July 1960, would not agree; nor probably would Thomas (1971:586), who reports that of the 150 militia members captured at Playa Girón, 50 joined the invaders.

51. Zeitlin 1970:39; Fagen 1972*b*:208. Some militia members apparently had to buy their own uniforms and weapons (Frank 1985:416).

52. Zeitlin 1970:20. The National Revolutionary Militia, so far as I know, did not have a precise analogue in the countries of Eastern Europe. According to Frank (1985:418), "No other modern government . . . has ever permitted so many or so large a proportion of its civilians (Cuban population is 6.5 million [1960]) to have arms." The militia was disbanded in the mid-1960s. After being reformed in the 1980s, it initially attracted more volunteers than there were arms available, though I do not know how closely the organization paralleled the original one.

53. MacEwan 1981:115. It is difficult to know exactly how many Cubans participated in voluntary labor throughout the economy. Detailed records were not kept, and published figures often include unpaid but not voluntary workers, such as prisoners and students, for whom work was included as part of their overall school program. See Matthews 1969:251–52 for a first-hand account of Cubans' feelings about voluntary work.

54. Valdés 1972*b*:426; Huberman and Sweezy 1969:23. See also Fitzgerald 1985:161.

55. The student *brigadistas* represented about 36 percent of the total primary school enrollment, about 47 percent of the total basic secondary school enrollment, about 24 percent of the total pre-university school enrollment, about 30 percent of the total teacher training enrollment, and about 19 percent of all students enrolled in commercial colleges (Seers et al. 1964:202).

56. When the literacy campaign formally ended in December 1961, adult education programs were established throughout the country. Of the workers Zeitlin interviewed in 1962, 41 percent were receiving some kind of schooling; 15 percent (650,000) of the people over age fourteen were enrolled in adult education programs around the same time; by the mid-1960s the absolute number had risen to one million (Zeitlin 1970:269; Seers et al. 1964:218; Lockwood 1969: 108). The regular education system also grew rapidly. Scholarship opportunities expanded, more facilities were constructed, and more teachers were trained. In the mid- and late 1960s, approximately 28 to 30 percent of the population was receiving some kind of formal educational instruction, more than twice the percentage in 1957 (Huberman and Sweezy 1969:47–48; Lockwood 1969:108; Valdés 1972*b*:429–38; Fitzgerald 1985, chap. 6; Seers et al. 1964:205–19).

57. The beginning of the process is sometimes dated earlier—to late 1984. The full title of the campaign is "rectification of errors and negative tendencies." Castro's sense of rectification is nicely captured in the following statements: "It cost much blood to leave the past behind. It cost much blood to do away with capitalism. And what we got rid of through the front door we don't want sneaking back in on us through the windows" (Castro 1989:82). "It's what we could call a revolution within a revolution" (Castro 1988:34).

58. For example, Castro cited gender inequality as a problem deserving

attention under rectification (Castro 1989:167). There were, of course, other factors prompting some rectification measures that were related only tangentially, if at all, to the SDPE (El Sistema de Dirección y Planificación de la Economía). One example is Cuba's worsening foreign exchange deficit, due largely to depressed world market prices for its sugar and re-exports of Soviet petroleum.

59. Bonuses (*primas*) began to be introduced in 1979 along with the *fondos de estimulación*. The use of piece rates was extended under the SDPE (Zimbalist 1989). For a fuller discussion of piece rates and problems associated with them, see Domínguez 1987.

60. See *Trabajadores* 2 Dec 87:12 and 28 Dec 88:1 for discussions of *fondo* problems. As a result of inequities associated with the socio-cultural and housing funds, a move began among enterprises with such funds to donate money from them to projects outside the firm. By early 1988, 87 percent of the enterprises with socio-cultural and housing funds had donated 38 million pesos in such a fashion (*Trabajadores* 30 Jan 88:12). Added to such inequalities were much more dramatic ones resulting from legal and illegal opportunities to earn income outside the state sector that grew or were created in post-SDPE Cuba. Some people could apparently earn 100,000 to 300,000 pesos annually through such activities and sometimes significantly reduced the effort expended at their state jobs to do this. Castro pointed out that 100,000 pesos was twenty times the annual salary earned by a surgeon performing heart transplants (Castro 1989:2).

61. García 1989:31. See also García 1989:23 and Torrado 1990:96.

62. This method was referred to as the party's cadre policy (*política de cuadros*). For information on party efforts in this area, see Machado 1988.

63. The party had 500,000 members in 1986 and an estimated 511,000 members in 1988 (*Trabajadores* 8 Dec 86:3; Azicri 1988:79). The former figure represented 1 out of every 20 Cubans. Twenty-three percent of the party's members were women around 1988 (Abelardo 1988:43).

64. Abelardo 1988:46–47. Three percent (350) of the nominees for municipal committees were rejected before the elections took place.

65. Bengelsdorf 1988*b*:127; Domínguez 1988:7; Abelardo 1988:49. Abelardo's article also notes that 23 percent of the secretaries-general of the party nuclei were women (a 13 percent improvement between 1985 and 1987), that in 1987 five first secretaries of municipal committees were women (compared to two in 1985), and that women comprised 23 percent of the provincial committee members in 1987 (an improvement of 3 percent over 1985).

66. This coincided closely with similar moves in other socialist countries. See Ivanova (1989) and Slider (1987) on brigades in Bulgaria and the USSR, respectively. Rabaza (1986) provides a brief overview of brigades in other Eastern European countries.

67. See *Trabajadores* 24 Jun 85:6; Rabaza 1986; and Codina 1987 for information on details of these payments.

68. *Trabajadores* 5 Jun 89:3. Serious delays continued to plague worksite planning. The discussions of the directive figures for the 1989 plan should have been completed by March 6 of that year. Yet by March 9, only half of them had even been convened (*Trabajadores* 15 Mar 89:1).

69. During the month of June 1989, *Trabajadores* ran regular articles ex-

plaining the new planning process, which had been tried out previously in 177 selected enterprises. It was to be evaluated in October of the same year, and at the 16th National CTC Congress.

70. Seasoned Cuba watchers have recently hinted, however, that enterprise autonomy is likely to increase following the Fourth Party Congress in 1991 (Benjamin 1990a:19; Zimbalist 1990b:19).

71. For example, León (1987:127) writes that part of rationalizing the planning system was a reduction in the types of investments determined centrally from twenty-three hundred to eight hundred. See also Zimbalist 1990b:13.

72. *Trabajadores* 2 Mar 89:2). Also, Zimbalist (1990b:28) reports that, "Direct supplies contracting was established between enterprises for 518 different products during 1988."

73. Apparently, it was also announced in 1986 or 1987 that enterprise losses would no longer be covered automatically by the center (Fitzgerald 1989:307; Mesa-Lago 1988:67).

74. In one speech Castro also argued that meetings should not be held during work (Castro 1989:46).

75. In addition, the following topics were considered in the workplace discussions of the draft of the CTC Statutes to be approved at the 16th National CTC Congress: (a) increasing the time between union elections and (b) expanding the CTC Secretariat's functions and creating another national-level CTC organ, smaller than the National Council and larger than the National Committee, to carry on CTC business between congresses (*Trabajadores* 10 May 89:12; 15 May 89:1). By 1989 the number of union sections in the country had grown to over sixty-four thousand from the more than forty thousand reported in 1982 (*Trabajadores* 4 May 89:1).

76. See *Trabajadores* 16 May 86:4 and CTC 1990:22 for some of these. See also Moses's (1987:223–24) interesting comments on the shortcomings of brigades in the Soviet Union.

77. The miscellaneous changes sparked by rectification mentioned earlier are also likely to have mixed effects on the democratization of production.

78. For recent examples of U.S. aggression against Cuba, see Benjamin 1990c:22; some economic repercussions of the changes in Eastern Europe are discussed in Benjamin: 1990a; adding to the uncertainty, both Benjamin (1990a, 1990b) and Pérez-Stable (1990) report an increase in discontent among the Cuban population.

References

Abelardo Álvarez, Gil. 1988. "Las asambleas de balance del partido en 1987, continuación del proceso de rectificación de errores y tendencias negativas." *Cuba socialista* 31, no. 1 (January–February):38–50.

Albert, Michael, and Robin Hahnel. 1981. *Socialism Today and Tomorrow.* Boston: South End Press.

Álvarez Tabío, Fernando. 1981. *Comentarios a la constitución socialista.* Havana: Editorial de Ciencias Sociales.

Ambursley, Fitzroy, and Robin Cohen, eds. 1983. *Crisis in the Caribbean.* New York: Monthly Review Press.

Anderson, Charles, and Jeffry Gibson. 1978. *Toward a New Sociology.* 3d ed. Homewood, Ill.: Dorsey Press.

Armengol Rios, Alejandro, and Ovidio D'Angelo Hernández. 1977. "Aspectos de los procesos de comunicación y participación de trabajadores en la gestión de las empreses." *Economía y desarrollo,* no. 42 (July–August):157–80.

Aronowitz, Stanley. 1973*a. False Promises.* New York: McGraw-Hill.

———. 1973*b.* "Trade Unionism and Workers' Control." Pp. 62–106 in Hunnius, Garson, and Case 1973.

Ayala Castro, Hector, and Frank Hidalgo–Gato. 1975. "Cuba económica." *Economía y desarrollo,* no. 30 (July–August):229–41.

———. 1980. "Aspectos teóricos del sistema de dirección y planificación de la economía." *Economía y desarrollo,* no. 57 (May–June):36–59.

Azicri, Max. 1988. *Cuba: Politics, Economics and Society.* London: Pinter.

Bahro, Rudolf. 1978. *The Alternative in Eastern Europe.* London: Verso Editions.

Balari, Eugenio. 1985. *Cuba-USA: Palabras Cruzadas.* Havana: Editorial de Ciencias Sociales.

Bamford, James. 1983. *The Puzzle Palace.* Harmondsworth, Eng.: Penguin.

Baran, Paul. 1961. *Reflections on the Cuban Revolution.* New York: Monthly Review Press.

Barber, Benjamin. 1984. *Strong Democracy.* Berkeley: University of California Press.

———. 1986. "Voting Is Not Enough." Pp. 210–17 in Stinebrickner 1986.

Barkin, David. 1975. "Popular Participation and the Dialectics of Cuban Development." *Latin American Perspectives* 2, no. 4 (supplement):42–59.

251

252   *References*

Barkin, David, and Nita R. Manitzas. 1973. *Cuba: Camino abierto*. Mexico City: Siglo Veintiuno Editores.

Beauvais, Jean-Pierre. 1983. "Achievements and Contradictions of the Cuban Workers' State." Pp. 49–71 in Ambursley and Cohen 1983.

Belousov, Rem, Nikolai Gritsenko, and Sergei Shkurko. 1988. "Participation of Work Collectives in Managing Production." Pp. 188–204 in USSR Academy of Sciences 1988.

Bendix, Reinhard. 1956. *Work and Authority in Industry*. Berkeley: University of California Press.

Bengelsdorf, Carolee. 1976. "A Large School of Government." *Cuba Review* 6, no. 3 (September):3–18.

———. 1988a. "Cubanology and Crises: The Mainstream Looks at Institutionalization." Pp. 212–26 in Zimbalist 1988.

———. 1988b. "On the Problem of Studying Women in Cuba." Pp. 119–136 in Zimbalist 1988.

Bengelsdorf, Carolee, and Michael Locker. 1974. "Perfect Identification of Government and Community." *Cuba Review* 4, no. 4 (December):3–9.

Benjamin, Medea. 1990a. "Things Fall Apart." *NACLA Report on the Americas* 24, no. 2 (August):13–22.

———. 1990b. "Soul Searching." *NACLA Report on the Americas* 24 no. 2 (August):23–31.

———. 1990c. "The War Goes On." *NACLA Report on the Americas* 24, no. 2 (August):22.

Benjamin, Medea, Joseph Collins, and Michael Scott. 1984. *No Free Lunch: Food and Revolution in Cuba Today*. San Francisco: Institute for Food and Development Policy.

Berman, Harold, and Van Whiting, Jr. 1980. "Impressions of Cuban Law." *American Journal of Comparative Law* 28 (summer):475–86.

Berman, Katrina. 1967. *Worker-Owned Plywood Companies: An Economic Analysis*. Pullman: Washington State University Press.

Bermeo, Nancy. 1983. "Worker Management in Industry: Reconciling Representative Government and Industrial Democracy in a Polarized Society." Pp. 181–97 in Graham and Wheeler 1983.

Bernardo, Roberto. 1971. "Managing and Financing the Firm." Pp. 185–208 in Mesa-Lago, ed., 1971.

Bernstein, Paul. 1976. *Workplace Democratization: Its Internal Dynamics*. Kent, Ohio: Kent State University Press.

Bianchi Ross, Ciro. 1987. "Five Bullets over a Dream." *Cuba internacional* 3, no. 3 (March):21–23.

Blackburn, Robin. 1963. "Prologue to the Cuban Revolution." *New Left Review*, no. 21 (October):52–91.

Blair, Thomas. 1969. *The Land to Those Who Work It: Algeria's Experiment in Workers' Management*. Garden City, N.Y.: Doubleday.

Blumberg, Paul. 1968. *Industrial Democracy: The Sociology of Participation*. New York: Schocken Books.

Bohemia. 1981. "Accidentes." Vol. 73, no. 46 (November): 55–56.

———. 1983. "Las tesis se discutieron de verdad." Vol. 75, no. 38 (September):55–57.

————. 1984. "Nos enfrentamos al futuro en condiciones favorables." Vol. 76, no. 28 (July): 48–58.

Bonachea, Rolando, and Nelson Valdés, eds. 1972a. *Cuba in Revolution*. Garden City, N.Y.: Anchor Books.

————. 1972b. "Labor and Revolution: Introduction." Pp. 357–83 in Bonachea and Valdés 1972a.

Boorstein, Edward. 1968. *The Economic Transformation of Cuba*. New York: Monthly Review Press.

Bornstein, Morris. 1977. "Economic Reform in Eastern Europe." In *East European Economies Post–Helsinki*, pp. 102–34. Washington, D.C.: U.S. Government Printing Office.

Bowles, Samuel, and Herbert Gintis. 1986. *Democracy and Capitalism*. New York: Basic Books.

Braverman, Harry. 1974. *Labor and Monopoly Capital: The Degradation of Work in the Twentieth Century*. New York: Monthly Review Press.

Bray, Donald, and Timothy Harding. 1974. "Cuba." Pp. 583–734 in Chilcote and Edelstein 1974.

Brundenius, Claes. 1984. *Revolutionary Cuba: The Challenge of Growth with Equity*. Boulder, Colo.: Westview.

————. 1985. "Cuba: Redistribution and Growth with Equity." Pp. 193–212 in Halebsky and Kirk 1985.

Brus, Wlodzimierz. 1975. *Socialist Ownership and Political Systems*. London: Routledge and Kegan Paul.

Burawoy, Michael. 1979. *Manufacturing Consent: Changes in the Labor Process under Monopoly Capitalism*. Chicago: University of Chicago Press.

————. 1980. "The Politics of Production and the Production of Politics: A Comparative Analysis of Machine Shops in the United States and Hungary." *Political Power and Social Theory* 1:261–99.

————. 1981. "Terrains of Contest: Factory and State under Capitalism and Socialism." *Socialist Review* 11, no. 4 (July–August):83–124.

————. 1985. "Piece Rates, Hungarian Style." *Socialist Review* 15, no. 1 (January–February):43–69.

————. 1989a. "Reflections on the Class Consciousness of Hungarian Steelworkers." *Politics and Society* 17, no.1 (March):1–34.

————. 1989b. "Should We Give Up on Socialism?" *Socialist Review* 19, no. 1 (January–March):59–74.

————. 1990. "Marxism Is Dead, Long Live Marxism!" *Socialist Review* 20, no. 2 (April–June):7–19.

————. n.d. "Workers in Workers' States." University of California, Berkeley. Mimeo.

Burawoy, Michael, and János Lukács. 1985. "Mythologies of Work: A Comparison of Firms in State Socialism and Advanced Capitalism." *American Sociological Review* 50, no. 6 (December):723–37.

Burawoy, Michael, and Theda Skocpol, eds. 1982. *Marxist Inquiries*. Chicago: University of Chicago Press.

Camacho Aguilera, Julio. 1976. "Informe presentado a la comisión de vida interna y cuadros." Pp. 133–37 in Partido Comunista de Cuba 1976.

Cardan, Paul. 1974. *Workers' Councils and the Economics of a Self-Managed Society*, November. Philadelphia: Philadelphia Solidarity.

Carter, Bernard. 1986. "Yugoslavia: Unions in a Self-Managed Society." Pp. 193–218 in Pravda and Ruble 1986.

Casal, Lourdes. 1976. "The Cuban Communist Party: The Best Among the Good." *Cuba Review* 6, no. 3 (September):23–30.

Casal, Lourdes, and Marifeli Pérez-Stable. 1981. "The Party and State in Post-1970 Cuba." Pp. 81–103 in Holmes 1981.

Case, John, and Rosemary Taylor, eds. 1979. *Co-ops, Communes and Collectives: Experiments in Social Change in the 1960s and 1970s*. New York: Pantheon.

Castro Ruz, Fidel. 1973. *El socialismo en Cuba*. Buenos Aires: Editorial Anteo.

———. 1975a. "Discurso pronunciado en el acto central por el XXI aniversario del ataque al cuartel Moncada." Pp. 141–91 in Castro and Castro 1975.

———. 1975b. "Fragmento del discurso pronunciado en la clausura del acto de la juventud en Las Villas." Pp. 21–26 in Castro and Castro 1975.

———. 1975c. "Versión del discurso pronunciado en la asamblea de balance de la provincia de la Habana." Pp. 109–22 in Castro and Castro 1975.

———. 1976. *La primera revolución socialista en América Latina*. Mexico City: Siglo Veintiuno Editores.

———. 1986. "The Main Report of Cuba's Third Party Congress." *Cuba Update*. Vol. 7, nos. 1–2 (winter–spring):5–7.

———. 1988. "En la clausura de la asamblea provincial del partido de Ciudad de La Habana." *Cuba socialista* 8, no. 1 (31) (January–February):1–37.

———. 1989. *Por el camino correcto*. Havana: Editora Política.

Castro Ruz, Fidel, and Raúl Castro Ruz. 1975. *Selección de discursos acerca del Partido*. Havana: Editorial de Ciencias Sociales.

Castro Ruz, Raúl. 1975a. "Discurso pronunciado ante los cuadros y funcionarios del Comité Central el 4 de mayo de 1973." Pp. 55–88 in Castro and Castro 1975.

———. 1975b. "Discurso pronunciado en la clausura del seminario a los delegados del Poder Popular que se celebró en Matanzas el 22 de agosto de 1974." Pp. 193–242 in Castro and Castro 1975.

———. 1976. "Informe presentado a la Comisión de la Plataforma Programática." Pp. 17–23 in Partido Comunista de Cuba 1976.

Center for Cuban Studies. 1976. *Center for Cuban Studies Newsletter* 3, nos. 2–3 (March–June).

Central de Trabajadores de Cuba (CTC). 1978. *Estatutos de la Central de Trabajadores de Cuba*.

———. 1983. *XV Congreso de la CTC. Proyecto de Tesis*.

———. 1984. *XV Congreso de la CTC memorias*. Havana: Editorial de Ciencias Sociales.

———. 1990. *Estatutos y resoluciones aprobados en el XVI Congreso*.

CERP. *See* Cuban Economic Research Project.

Chilcote, Ronald, and Joel Edelstein, eds. 1974. *Latin America: The Struggle with Dependency and Beyond*. New York: John Wiley and Sons.

Clegg, Ian. 1971. *Workers' Self-Management in Algeria*. New York: Monthly Review Press.

Cochrane, Allan. 1986. "Community Politics and Democracy." Pp. 51–77 in Held and Pollitt 1986.

Cockburn, Cynthia. 1979. "People's Power." Pp. 18–35 in Griffiths and Griffiths, eds., 1979.

Cocks, Paul. 1975. "Bureaucracy and Party Control." Pp. 215–48 in Mesa-Lago and Beck 1975.

Codina, Alexis. 1987. "Worker Incentives in Cuba." *World Development* 15, no. 1 (January):127–38.

Cohen, Joshua, and Joel Rogers. 1983. *On Democracy.* Harmondsworth, Eng.: Penguin.

Cole, Robert. 1987. "The Macropolitics of Organizational Change: A Comparative Analysis of the Spread of Small-Group Activities." Pp. 34–66 in Sirianni, ed., 1987.

Comisión Nacional de Implantación del Sistema de Dirección y Planificación de la Economía de la República de Cuba. 1980. "Metodología para la formación de los fondos de estimulación económica." *Cuestiones de la economía planificada* 3, no. 2 (March–April):140–45.

Comité Estatal de Trabajo y Seguridad Social. 1980. "Resolución No. 457/1980 para la aplicación de la reforma general de salarios." *Cuestiones de la economía planificada* 3, no. 3 (May–June):138–44.

Consejo de Ministros. 1980. "Reglamento general de la empresa estatal." *Cuestiones de la economía planificada* 3, no. 1 (January–February):109–24.

Croan, Melvin. 1976. "The Leading Role of the Party: Concepts and Contexts." Pp. 151–75 in János 1976.

Cronin, Jim. 1990. "Western Socialism after the Cold War." *Socialist Review* 20, no. 2 (April–June):20–30.

CTC. *See* Central de Trabajadores de Cuba.

Cuba internacional. 1974. "A los trabajadores organizados el máximo de la participación en la gestión económica." January, p. 17.

Cuba Update. New York.

Cuban Communist Party. 1981*a*. *2d Congress of the Communist Party of Cuba: Documents and Speeches.* Havana: Political Publishers.

———. 1981*b*. *Statutes of the Communist Party of Cuba.* Havana: Political Publishing House.

Cuban Economic Research Project (CERP). 1963. *Labor Conditions in Communist Cuba.* Miami: University of Miami Press.

Dahl, Robert. 1985. *A Preface to Economic Democracy.* Berkeley: University of California Press.

"Decreto-Ley #32 sobre la Disciplina Laboral." 1980. *Trabajadores* 21 Feb 80: 3.

Domínguez, Jorge. 1976. "Institutionalization and Civil-Military Relations." *Cuban Studies* 6, pt. 1 (January–July):39–65.

———. 1978. *Cuba: Order and Revolution.* Cambridge, Mass.: Belknap.

———. 1982. "Revolutionary Politics: The Demands for Orderliness." Pp. 19–70 in Domínguez, ed., 1982.

———. 1988. "Blaming Itself, Not Himself: Cuba's Political Regime After the Third Party Congress." Pp. 3–10 in Roca 1988.

Domínguez, Jorge, ed. 1982. *Cuba: Internal and International Affairs.* Beverly Hills, Calif.: Sage.

Domínguez, Lázaro. 1987. "Para un análisis de las deficiencias en la normación del trabajo en Cuba." *Cuba socialista* 28, no. 4 (July–August):86–102.

Donáth, Ferenc. 1981. "Istaván Bibó and the Fundamental Issue of Hungarian Democracy." Pp. 221–46 in Miliband and Saville 1981.

Dumont, René. 1970a. *Cuba: Es socialista?* Caracas: Editorial Nuevo Tiempo.

———. 1970b. *Cuba: Socialism and Development.* New York: Grove Press.

Duncan, Graeme, ed. 1983. *Democratic Theory and Practice.* Cambridge: Cambridge University Press.

Dupuy, Alex, and John Yrchik. 1978. "Socialist Planning and Social Transformation in Cuba: A Contribution to the Debate." *Review of Radical Political Economics* 10, no. 4 (January):48–60.

Eckstein, Susan, and Andrew Zimbalist. 1987. "Patterns of Cuban Development: The First Twenty-five Years." *World Development* 15, no. 1:5–22.

Edelstein, Joel. 1985. "Economic Policy and Development Models." Pp. 177–92 in Halebsky and Kirk 1985.

Enzensberger, Hans Magnus. 1976. "Portrait of a Party: Prehistory, Structure, and Ideology of the PCC." Pp. 102–37 in Radosh 1976.

Espinosa, Juan, and Andrew Zimbalist. 1978. *Economic Democracy: Workers' Participation in Chilean Industry 1970–1973.* New York. Academic Press.

Evenson, Debra. 1990. "Channeling Dissent." *NACLA Report on the Americas* 24, no. 2 (August):26–28.

Fagen, Richard. 1972a. "Charismatic Authority and the Leadership of Fidel Castro." Pp. 154–68 in Bonachea and Valdés 1972a.

———. 1972b. "Mass Mobilization in Cuba: The Symbolism of Struggle." Pp. 201–23 in Bonachea and Valdés 1972a.

Fantasia, Rick. 1988. *Cultures of Solidarity.* Berkeley: University of California Press.

Farber, Samuel. 1976. *Revolution and Reaction in Cuba, 1933–60.* Middletown, Conn.: Wesleyan University Press.

———. 1983. "The Cuban Communists in the Early Stages of the Cuban Revolution: Revolutionaries or Reformists?" *Latin American Research Review* 18:59–83.

Fejtö, François. 1974. *A History of the People's Democracies: Eastern Europe Since Stalin.* Harmondsworth, Eng.: Penguin.

Ferleger, Lou, and Jay Mandle. 1990. "The Economic Future of Socialism in Eastern Europe." *Socialist Review* 20, no. 2 (April–June):125–30.

Fischer, Frank, and Carmen Sirianni, eds. 1984. *Critical Studies in Organization and Bureaucracy.* Philadelphia: Temple University Press.

Fischer-Galati, Stephen, ed. 1979. *The Communist Parties of Eastern Europe.* New York: Columbia University Press.

Fišera, Vladimir. 1978. *Workers' Councils in Czechoslovakia 1968–1969.* New York: St. Martin's Press.

FitzGerald, Frances. 1976. "A Reporter at Large: Slightly Exaggerated Enthusiasms." Pp. 138–72 in Radosh 1976.

Fitzgerald, Frank. 1978. "A Critique of the 'Sovietization of Cuba' Thesis." *Science and Society* 42, no. 1 (spring):1–32.

———. 1985. "Politics and Social Structure in Revolutionary Cuba: From the

Demise of the Old Middle Class to the Rise of the New Professionals." Ph.D. diss., SUNY Binghamton.

———. 1989. "The Reform of the Cuban Economy, 1976–86: Organisation, Incentives, and Patterns of Behaviour." *Journal of Latin American Studies* 21, no. 2 (May):283–310.

Forester, John. 1989. *Planning in the Face of Power*. Berkeley: University of California Press.

Frank, André Gunder. 1985. "Cuba: A Revolution of the People (November 23, 1960)." Pp. 413–19 in Halebsky and Kirk 1985.

Fuller, Linda. 1988. "Fieldwork in Forbidden Terrain: The U.S. State and the Case of Cuba." *The American Sociologist* 19, no. 2 (summer):99–120.

———. 1990. "Union Autonomy at the Socialist Workplace: A Comparison of Cuba and the German Democratic Republic." *Socialism and Democracy* 11 (September):75–108.

García Valdés, Carlos. 1989. "El proceso de rectificación: motivación y fuente para el desarrollo de la economía política del socialismo en Cuba." *Cuba socialista* 38, no. 2 (March–April):13–36.

Garzón, José. 1980. "Administration and Politics in the Evolving Cuban Revolution." Paper prepared at University of California, Berkeley, April 2.

Ghai, Dharam, Cristóbal Kay, and Peter Peek. 1988. *Labour and Development in Rural Cuba*. New York: St. Martin's Press.

Giddens, Anthony, and David Held. 1982. *Classes, Power, and Conflict*. Berkeley: University of California Press.

Gilberg, Trond. 1979. "The Communist Party of Romania." Pp. 281–335 in Fischer-Galati 1979.

Gilly, Adolfo. 1965. *Cuba: coexistencia o revolución*. Buenos Aires: Ediciones Monthly Review.

Girling, Robert, and David Ruccio. 1981. "The Cuban Economy Today: An Appraisal of Its Planning and Management System, 1970–1980." Occasional Paper no. 1, Institute for the Study of a Democratically Managed Society, California State University, Sonoma, July.

Goldenberg, Boris. 1965. *The Cuban Revolution and Latin America*. New York: Praeger.

Gomez, Manuel. n.d. "Cuban Occupational Health and Safety Law." Abbreviated 8-page translation.

Gomez Rodríguez, Félix. 1986. "Fondos de estimulación económica en las empresas de la economía cubana." *Economía y desarrollo*, no. 90 (January–February):77–89.

González, Edward. 1976. "The Party Congress and *Poder Popular*." *Cuban Studies* 6, pt. 2 (January–July):1–14.

———. 1981. "Political Succession in Cuba." Pp. 396–428 in Horowitz 1981.

Goodrich, Carter. 1920. *The Frontier of Control: A Study of British Workshop Politics*. New York: Harcourt, Brace, and Howe.

Gorz, André.1973. "Workers' Control Is More than Just That." Pp. 325–43 in Hunnius, Garson, and Case 1973.

Graham, Lawrence, and Douglas Wheeler, eds. 1983. *In Search of Modern Portugal*. Madison: University of Wisconsin Press.

Gramsci, Antonio. 1977. *Selections from Political Writings (1910–1920)*. New York: International Publishers.

Granma. Havana.

Granma Weekly Review. Havana.

Green, Gil. 1983. *Cuba at Twenty-five*. New York: International Publishers.

Grenier, Guillermo. 1988. *Inhuman Relations: Quality Circles and Anti-Unionism in American Industry*. Philadelphia: Temple University Press.

Griffiths, John, and Peter Griffiths. 1979. "Cuba: The Second Decade." Pp. 1–17 in Griffiths and Griffiths, eds., 1979.

———, eds. 1979. *Cuba: The Second Decade*. London: Writers and Readers Publishing Cooperative.

Grote, Manfred. 1979. "The Socialist Unity Party of Germany." Pp. 167–200 in Fischer-Galati 1979.

Grupo Cubano de Investigaciones. 1963. *Un estudio sobre Cuba*. Miami: University of Miami Press.

Guarasci, L. Richard, and Gary Peck. 1984. "Beyond the Syndicalism of Workplace Democracy: Worker Self-Management in an Age of Degraded Labor." Typescript.

Guerra Hidalgo, Secundino. 1976. "Palabras al presentar la resolución sobre los Estatutos del Partido." Pp. 103–29 in Partido Comunista de Cuba 1976.

Guevara, Ernesto, Charles Bettelheim, Ernest Mandel, Marcelo Fernández Font, and Alberto Mora. 1974. *El debate cubano*. Barcelona: Editorial Laia.

Halebsky, Sandor, and John Kirk, eds. 1985. *Cuba: Twenty-five Years of Revolution, 1959–1984*. New York: Praeger.

Halliday, Fred. 1990. "The Ends of Cold War." *New Left Review*, no. 180 (March–April):5–23.

Halperin, Ernst. 1967. "Foreword." Pp. vii–xii in Suárez 1967.

Hamberg, Jill. 1983. "New Census Data." *Cubatimes* 3 (spring–summer):37–38.

Haraszti, Miklós. 1978. *A Worker in a Workers' State*. New York: Universe Books.

Harding, Neil, ed. 1984. *The State in Socialist Society*. Albany: State University of New York Press.

Harnecker, Marta. 1980. *Cuba: Dictatorship or Democracy?* Westport, Conn.: Lawrence Hill.

———. 1981. "A Cuban Leader Answers Tough Questions." *Cubatimes* 2 (spring):19–24, 31–34.

Harris, David. 1983. "Returning the Social to Democracy." Pp. 218–34 in Duncan 1983.

Hartsock, Nancy. 1983. *Money, Sex, and Power*. Boston: Northeastern University Press.

Hayden, Robert. 1985. "Who Wants Informal Courts? Paradoxical Evidence from a Yugoslav Attempt to Create Workers' Courts for Labor Cases." *American Bar Foundation Research Journal*, no. 2:293–326.

Haydu, Jeff. 1985. "Factory Politics in Britain and the United States: Engineers and Machinists, 1914–1919." *Comparative Studies in Society and History* 27, no. 1 (January):57–85.

Hazard, John. 1968. *The Soviet System of Government*. Chicago: University of Chicago Press.

Held, David. 1987. *Models of Democracy*. Stanford, Calif.: Stanford University Press.

Held, David, and Christopher Pollitt. 1986. *New Forms of Democracy*. Beverly Hills, Calif.: Sage.

Herman, Andrew. 1982. "Conceptualizing Control: Domination and Hegemony in the Capitalist Labor Process." *Insurgent Sociologist* 11, no. 3 (fall):7–22.

Hernández, Roberto E., and Carmelo Mesa-Lago. 1971. "Labor Organization and Wages." Pp. 209–49 in Mesa-Lago, ed., 1971.

Hernández González, Enrique. 1980. "Participación de los trabajadores en la dirección de la producción socialista." *Cuestiones de la economía planificada* 3, no. 5 (September–October):11–35.

Herrera, Antonio José, and Hernan Rosenkranz. 1979. "Political Consciousness in Cuba." Pp. 36–52 in Griffiths and Griffiths, eds., 1979.

Hill, Stephen. 1981. *Competition and Control at Work*. Cambridge, Mass.: MIT Press.

Hinckle, Warren, and William Turner. 1981. *The Fish Is Red: The Story of the Secret War Against Castro*. New York: Harper and Row.

Holmes, Leslie, ed. 1981. *The Withering Away of the State? Party and State Under Communism*. London: Sage.

Horowitz, Irving, ed. 1981. *Cuban Communism*. 4th ed. New Brunswick, N.J.: Transaction Books.

Hough, Jerry. 1969. *The Soviet Prefects: Local Party Organs in Industrial Decision-making*. Cambridge, Mass.: Harvard University Press.

————. 1979. "Policy Making and the Worker." Pp. 367–96 in Kahan and Ruble 1979.

Huberman, Leo, and Paul Sweezy. 1960. *Cuba: Anatomy of a Revolution*. New York: Monthly Review Press.

————. 1969. *Socialism in Cuba*. New York: Monthly Review Press.

Hunnius, Gerry. 1973. "Workers' Self-Management in Yugoslavia." Pp. 268–321 in Hunnius, Garson, and Case 1973.

Hunnius, Gerry, G. David Garson, and John Case, eds. 1973. *Workers' Control: A Reader on Labor and Social Change*. New York: Vintage Books.

Hyman, Richard. 1974. "Workers' Control and Revolutionary Theory." Pp. 241–78 in Miliband and Saville 1974.

ILO. *See* International Labour Organization.

International Labour Organization (ILO). 1969. *Participation of Workers in Decisions Within Undertakings*. Labour-Management Relations Series, no. 33. Geneva: International Labour Office.

Ionescu, Ghiţa. 1967. *The Politics of the European Communist States*. New York: Praeger.

Ivanova, Slavka. 1989. "Les brigades en Bulgarie et la participation." *Sociologie du travail* 31 (March):301–13.

János, Andrew, ed. 1976. *Authoritarian Politics in Communist Europe: Uniformity and Diversity in One-Party States*, Research Series, no. 28. Berkeley: Institute of International Studies.

JUCEPLAN. *See* Junta Central de Planificación.

Junta Central de Planificación (JUCEPLAN). 1980a. "Resolución 322. Reglamento para la distribución del fondo de premios." *Cuestiones de la economía planificada* 3, no. 2 (March–April):128–35.

————. 1980b. *Segunda plenaria nacional de chequeo de la implantación del SDPE*. Havana: Ediciones JUCEPLAN.

———. 1980c. "Resolución 576. Reglamento general para la utilización del fondo para medidas socioculturales y construcción de viviendas." *Cuestiones de la economía planificada* 3, no. 2 (March–April):136–39.

Kaldor, Mary. 1990. "After the Cold War." *New Left Review*, no. 180 (March–April):25–37.

Kanter, Rosabeth. 1977. *Men and Women of the Corporation*. New York: Basic Books.

Karl, Terry. 1975. "Work Incentives in Cuba." *Latin American Perspectives* 2, no. 4 (summer supplement):21–41.

Karol, K. S. 1970. *Guerrillas in Power*. New York: Hill and Wang.

Kemény, István. 1986. "Trade Unions and Workers' Interests in Hungary." Pp. 173–91 in Pravda and Ruble 1986.

Kiloh, Margaret. 1986. "Industrial Democracy." Pp. 14–50 in Held and Pollitt 1986.

Kolko, Gabriel. 1976. *Main Currents in Modern American History*. New York: Pantheon.

Kornai, János. 1959. *Overcentralization in Economic Administration*. London: Oxford University Press.

Kozol, Jonathan. 1978. *Children of the Revolution*. New York: Delta.

Kunitz, Stephen. 1979. "Health Care and Workers' Self-Management in Yugoslavia." *International Journal of Health Services* 9, no. 1:521–37.

Laclau, Ernesto, and Chantal Mouffe. 1985. *Hegemony and Socialist Strategy: Towards a Radical Democratic Politics*. London: Verso Editions.

Law 8, Organización y Funcionamiento de los Consejos del Trabajo. 1977. *Trabajadores* 30 Sept 77:5–6.

Lee, Michele. 1976. "Yugoslavia in 1975." *Critique* 6 (spring):112–18.

LeoGrande, William. 1978. "Continuity and Change in the Cuban Political Elite." *Cuban Studies* 8, no. 2 (July):1–31.

———. 1979a. "The Theory and Practice of Socialist Democracy in Cuba: Mechanisms of Elite Accountability." *Studies in Comparative Communism* 12 (spring):39–62.

———. 1979b. "Party Development in Revolutionary Cuba." *Journal of Interamerican Studies and World Affairs* 21, no. 4 (November):457–80.

———. 1980. "The Communist Party of Cuba Since the First Congress." *Journal of Latin American Studies* 12, no. 2 (November):397–419.

———. 1981. "A Bureaucratic Approach to Civil-Military Relations in Communist Political Systems. The Case of Cuba." Pp. 603–25 in Horowitz 1981.

León Bilbao, Idalberto. 1987. "Apuntes sobre el perfeccionamiento organizativo y metodológica de la planificación." *Cuestiones de la economía planificada* 2, no. 3 (July–September):87–130.

Lockwood, Lee. 1969. *Castro's Cuba, Cuba's Fidel*. New York: Random House.

Lopez, Juan. 1972. "Cuba's Workers Steeled in Struggle." *People's World* (June 17):6–7.

López Coll, Armando, and Armando Errasti Santiago. 1975. "Notas sobre el proceso de planificación en Cuba." *Economía y desarrollo*, no. 29 (May–June):8–25.

MacEwan, Arthur. 1975. "Incentives, Equality, and Power in Revolutionary Cuba." *Socialist Revolution* 23 (April):117–30.

——. 1981. *Revolution and Economic Development in Cuba*. London: Macmillan.

——. 1985. "Why Is Cuba Different?" Pp. 420–28 in Halebsky and Kirk 1985.

Machado Ventura, José. 1988. "La política de cuadros: una tarea priorizada." *Cuba socialista* 34, no. 4 (July–August):1–7.

MacPherson, C. B. 1977. *The Life and Times of Liberal Democracy*. Oxford: Oxford University Press.

MAHRO (The Radical Historians Organization). 1976. *Visions of History*. New York: Pantheon.

Malloy, James. 1971. "Generation of Political Support and Allocation of Costs." Pp. 23–42 in Mesa-Lago, ed., 1971.

Malmierca Peolí, Isidoro. 1976. "Informe presentado a la Comisión de Estatutos." Pp. 83–99 in Partido Comunista de Cuba 1976.

Manitzas, Nita R. 1973. "El marco de la revolución." Pp. 13–59 in Barkin and Manitzas 1973.

Mansbridge, Jane. 1983. *Beyond Adversary Democracy*. Chicago: University of Chicago Press.

——. 1984. "Feminism and the Forms of Freedom." Pp. 472–81 in Fischer and Sirianni 1984.

Markovits, Inga. 1982. "Law or Order—Constitutionalism and Legality in Eastern Europe." *Stanford Law Review* 34:513–613.

Martell, Raúl. 1979. *La empresa socialista*. Havana: Editorial de Ciencias Sociales.

Martin, Lionel. 1974. "Reestructuración sindical en Cuba." *Cuba internacional* 4, no. 56 (April):28–30.

Matthews, Herbert. 1969. *Fidel Castro*. New York: Simon and Schuster.

Medvedev, Roy. 1977. *On Socialist Democracy*. Nottingham, Eng.: Spokesman Books.

Mesa-Lago, Carmelo. 1968. *The Labor Sector and Socialist Distribution in Cuba*. New York: Praeger.

——. 1971. "Economic Policies and Growth." Pp. 277–338 in Mesa-Lago, ed., 1971.

——. 1972. "Economic Significance of Unpaid Labor in Socialist Cuba." Pp. 384–412 in Bonachea and Valdés 1972a.

——. 1978. *Cuba in the 1970s: Pragmatism and Institutionalization*. Albuquerque: University of New Mexico Press.

——. 1981. *The Economy of Socialist Cuba: A Two-Decade Appraisal*. Albuquerque: University of New Mexico Press.

——. 1982. "The Economy: Caution, Frugality, and Resilient Ideology." Pp. 113–66 in Domínguez, ed., 1982.

——. 1988. "The Cuban Economy in the 1980s: The Return of Ideology." Pp. 59–100 in Roca 1988.

Mesa-Lago, Carmelo, ed. 1971. *Revolutionary Change in Cuba*. Pittsburgh: University of Pittsburgh Press.

Mesa-Lago, Carmelo, and Carl Beck, eds. 1975. *Comparative Socialist Systems: Essays on Politics and Economics*. Pittsburgh: University of Pittsburgh Center for International Studies.

Mesa-Lago, Carmelo, and Luc Zephirin. 1971. "Central Planning." Pp. 145–84 in Mesa-Lago, ed., 1971.

Miliband, Ralph, and John Saville, eds. 1974. *The Socialist Register*. London: Merlin Press.

———. 1979. *The Socialist Register*. London: Merlin Press.

———. 1981. *The Socialist Register*. London: Merlin Press.

Miller, David. 1983. "The Competitive Model of Democracy." Pp. 133–55 in Duncan 1983.

Mills, C. Wright. 1959. *The Sociological Imagination*. London: Oxford University Press.

Molnár, Miklos. 1979. "The Communist Party of Hungary." Pp. 201–44 in Fischer-Galati 1979.

Moore, Barrington, Jr. 1978. *Injustice: The Social Bases of Obedience and Revolt*. New York: M. E. Sharpe.

Morley, Morris. 1980. "Toward a Theory of Imperial Politics: United States Policy and the Processes of State Formation, Disintegration and Consolidation in Cuba, 1898–1978." Ph.D. diss., SUNY Binghamton.

Morray, J. P. 1962. *The Second Revolution in Cuba*. New York: Monthly Review Press.

Moses, Joel. 1987. "Worker Self-Management and the Reformist Alternative in Soviet Labour Policy, 1979–1985." *Soviet Studies* 39, no. 2 (April):205–28.

Munck, Ronaldo. 1984. *Politics and Dependency in the Third World*. London: Zed Books.

Myers, Barbara. 1974. "The Eyes and Ears of the People." *Cuba Review* 4, no. 4 (December):10–11, 14–15, 25.

Nelson, Daniel. 1986. "The Politics of Romanian Trade Unions." Pp. 107–23 in Pravda and Ruble 1986.

Nicolić, Miloš, ed. 1985. *Socialism on the Threshold of the Twenty-first Century*. London: Verso Editions.

Nove, Alec. 1980. "The Soviet Economy: Problems and Prospects." *New Left Review*, no. 119 (January–February):3–19.

———. 1982. "Is There a Ruling Class in the USSR?" Pp. 588–604 in Giddens and Held 1982.

———. 1983. *The Economics of Feasible Socialism*. London: George Allen and Unwin.

———. 1987. "'Radical Reform': Problems and Prospects." *Soviet Studies* 29, no. 3 (July):452–67.

Nuti, Domenico Mario. 1979. "The Contradictions of Socialist Economies: A Marxian Interpretation." Pp. 228–73 in Miliband and Saville 1979.

O'Connor, James. 1966. "The Organized Working Class in the Cuban Revolution." *Studies on the Left* 6 (March–April):3–30.

———. 1970. *The Origins of Socialism in Cuba*. Ithaca, N.Y.: Cornell University Press.

———. 1972. "Cuba: Its Political Economy." Pp. 52–81 in Bonachea and Valdés 1972*a*.

Padula, Alfred, and Lois Smith. 1985. "Women in Socialist Cuba, 1959–1984." Pp. 79–92 in Halebsky and Kirk 1985.

Panitch, Leo. 1981. "Trade Unions and the Capitalist State." *New Left Review*, no. 125 (January–February):21–43.

Partido Comunista de Cuba. 1976. *Primer Congreso del Partido Comunista de Cuba. Memorias.* Vol. 2. Havana: Departamento de Orientación Revolucionaria del Comité Central del Partido Comunista de Cuba.

———. 1978. *Tesis y Resoluciones. Primer Congreso del Partido Comunista de Cuba.* Havana: Editorial de Ciencias Sociales.

———. 1981. *Lineamientos económicos y sociales para el quinquenio 1981–1985.* Havana: Editora Política.

———. 1982. *Plataforma programática del Partido Comunista de Cuba: Tesis y resolución.* Havana: Editora Política.

Pateman, Carole. 1970. *Participation and Democratic Theory.* Cambridge: Cambridge University Press.

———. 1989. *The Disorder of Women.* Cambridge: Polity Press.

Pennock, J. Roland, and John Chapman, eds. 1975. *Participation in Politics.* New York: Lieber-Atherton.

Pérez González, Humberto. 1979. "Clausura del congreso constituyente de la asociación nacional de economistas de Cuba." *Publicaciones* (October):1–56.

———. 1980a. "Sobre el proyecto de plan de la economía nacional para 1980." *Cuestiones de la economía planificada* 3, no. 1 (January–February):12–34.

———. 1980b. "Sobre la implantación del sistema de dirección y planificación de la economía de la provincia ciudad de La Habana." *Cuestiones de la economía planificada* 3, no. 2 (March–April):9–23.

Pérez-Stable, Marifeli. 1975. "Whither the Cuban Working Class?" *Latin American Perspectives* 2, no. 4 (supplement):60–77.

———. 1976. "Institutionalization and Workers' Response." *Cuban Studies* 6, nos. 1–2 (January and July):31–54.

———. 1983. "Cuba en los 80." *Areíto* 8, no. 32:4–9.

———. 1985. "Class, Organization and *Conciencia*: The Cuban Working Class after 1970." Pp. 291–306 in Halebsky and Kirk 1985.

———. 1990. "In Pursuit of Cuba Libre." *NACLA Report on the Americas* 24, no. 2 (August):32–39.

Porket, Joseph. 1986. "Czechoslovak Trade Unions Under Soviet-Type Socialism." Pp. 85–106 in Pravda and Ruble 1986.

Portes, Alejandro, and Robert Bach. 1985. *Latin Journey: Cuban and Mexican Immigrants in the United States.* Berkeley: University of California Press.

Pravda, Alex. 1986. "Poland in the 1970s: Dual Functioning Trade Unionism Under Pressure." Pp. 125–47 in Pravda and Ruble 1986.

Pravda, Alex, and Blair Ruble, eds. 1986. *Trade Unions in Communist States.* Boston: George Allen and Unwin.

Prifti, Peter. 1979. "The Labor Party of Albania." Pp. 5–48 in Fischer-Galati 1979.

"Proyecto de Ley de Organización y Funcionamiento de los Consejos del Trabajo." 1977. *Trabajadores* 1 Jul 77:4.

"Proyecto de Ley de Procedimiento Civil, Administrativo y Laboral." 1977. *Trabajadores* 15 Jul 77:2.

Quesada Pérez, Felino. 1980a. "Acerca de los fondos de estimulación material." *Cuestiones de la economía planificada* 3, no. 4 (July–August):94–120.

———. 1980b. "La autonomía de la empresa en Cuba y la implantación del Sistema de Dirección y Planificación de la Economía." *Cuestiones de la economía planificada* 3, no. 1 (January–February):91–99.

———. 1981. *El sistema de dirección y planificación de la economía en las empresas.* Havana: Editorial de Ciencias Sociales.

Rabaza Peñalver, Francisco. 1986. "Las brigadas de producción en el sector de construcciones básicas." *Economía y desarrollo*, no. 91 (March–April):119–43.

Rabkin, Rhoda. 1985. "Cuban Political Structure: Vanguard Party and the Masses." Pp. 251–69 in Halebsky and Kirk 1985.

———. 1988. "Cuba: The Aging of a Revolution." Pp. 33–56 in Roca 1988.

Radosh, Ronald, ed. 1976. *The New Cuba: Paradoxes and Potentials.* New York: William Morrow.

Reckord, Barry. 1971. *Does Fidel Eat More than Your Father?* London: Andre Deutsch.

Revolución. Havana.

Rigby, T. H. 1976. "Politics in the Mono-Organizational Society." Pp. 31–80 in János 1976.

Ritter, Archibald. 1974. *The Economic Development of Revolutionary Cuba.* New York: Praeger.

———. 1985. "The Organs of People's Power and the Communist Party: The Nature of Cuban Democracy." Pp. 270–90 in Halebsky and Kirk 1985.

Robertson, Ian, ed. 1981. *The Social World.* New York: Worth.

Roca, Sergio. 1986. "State Enterprises in Cuba Under the New System of Planning and Management (SDPE)." *Cuban Studies* 16:153–79.

Roca, Sergio, ed. 1988. *Socialist Cuba: Past Interpretations and Future Challenges.* Boulder, Colo.: Westview.

Rodríguez, Gonzalo M. 1980. *El proceso de industrialización de la economía cubana.* Havana: Editorial de Ciencias Sociales.

Rodríguez, José Luis. 1990. "Aspectos económicos del proceso de rectificación". *Cuba socialista* 44, no. 2 (April–June):86–101.

Rojas, Marta. 1986. "Literacy—The Leap into the Light." *Cuba internacional* 2, no. 12 (December):18–21.

Rothschild-Whitt, Joyce. 1979a. "The Collectivist Organization: An Alternative to Rational-Bureaucratic Models." *American Sociological Review* 44, no. 4 (August):509–27.

———. 1979b. "Conditions for Democracy: Making Participatory Organizations Work." Pp. 215–44 in Case and Taylor 1979.

Rowbotham, Sheila. 1986. "Feminism and Democracy." Pp. 78–109 in Held and Pollitt 1986.

Ruble, Blair. 1986. "Industrial Trade Unions in the USSR." Pp. 23–52 in Pravda and Ruble 1986.

Rueschemeyer, Marilyn, and C. Bradley Scharf. 1986. "Labor Unions in the German Democratic Republic." Pp. 53–84 in Pravda and Ruble 1986.

Ruiz, Ramón Eduardo. 1968. *Cuba: The Making of a Revolution.* Amherst: University of Massachusetts Press.

Sachs, Stephen. 1981. "Yugoslav Economy in Difficulty." *Workplace Democracy* 7 (summer):12–13.

San Martín, Marta, and Ramón Bonachea. 1981. "The Military Dimension of the Cuban Revolution." Pp. 531–62 in Horowitz 1981.

Santiago Errasti, Armando. 1980. "Algunas consideraciones acerca del ingreso neto, la ganancia y la rentabilidad." *Cuestiones de la economía planificada* 3, no. 3 (May–June):111–30.

Seers, Dudley, Andrés Bianchi, Richard Jolly, and Max Nolff. 1964. *Cuba: The Economic and Social Revolution.* Chapel Hill: University of North Carolina Press.

Shalom, Steve, ed. 1983. *Socialist Visions.* Boston: South End Press.

Shoup, Paul. 1976. "The Limits of Party Control: The Yugoslav Case." Pp. 176–96 in János 1976.

Silverman, Bertram. 1973. "Organización económica y conciencia social: Algunos dilemas." Pp. 142–85 in Barkin and Manitzas 1973.

Sims, Harold. 1985. "Cuban Labor and the Communist Party, 1937–1958: An Interpretation." *Cuban Studies* 15, no. 1 (winter):43–58.

Singleton, Fred. 1976. *Twentieth Century Yugoslavia.* New York: Columbia University Press.

Sirianni, Carmen. 1981. "Production and Power in a Classless Society: A Critical Analysis of the Utopian Dimensions of Marxist Theory." *Socialist Review* 11, no. 59 (September–October):33–82.

———. 1982. *Workers' Control and Socialist Democracy: The Soviet Experience.* London: Verso Editions and NLB.

———. 1983. "Councils and Parliaments: The Problems of Dual Power and Democracy in Comparative Perspective." *Politics and Society* 12, no. 1:83–123.

———. 1984. "Participation, Opportunity, and Equality: Toward a Pluralist Organizational Model." Pp. 482–503 in Fischer and Sirianni 1984.

———. 1987. "Worker Participation in the Late Twentieth Century: Some Critical Issues." Pp. 3–33 in Sirriani, ed., 1987.

Sirianni, Carmen, ed. 1987. *Worker Participation and the Politics of Reform.* Philadelphia: Temple University Press.

Slider, Darrell. 1987. "The Brigade System in Soviet Industry: An Effort to Restructure the Labour Force." *Soviet Studies* 39, no. 3 (July):388–405.

Smith, Earl. 1962. *The Fourth Floor.* New York: Random House.

Spalding, Hobart, Jr. 1974. "The Workers' Struggle: 1850–1961." *Cuba Review* 4, no. 1 (July):3–10, 31.

———. 1977. *Organized Labor in Latin America.* New York: New York University Press.

Stephens, Evelyne. 1980. *The Politics of Workers' Participation: The Peruvian Approach in Comparative Perspective.* New York: Academic Press.

Stephens, John D. 1979. *The Transition from Capitalism to Socialism.* London: Macmillan.

Stinebrickner, Bruce, ed. 1986. *American Government 86/87.* Guilford, Conn.: Duskin Publishing Group.

Suárez, Andrés. 1967. *Cuba: Castroism and Communism, 1959–1966.* Cambridge, Mass.: MIT Press.

———. 1971. "Leadership, Ideology, and Political Party." Pp. 3–21 in Mesa-Lago, ed., 1971.

Sutherland, Elizabeth. 1969. *The Youngest Revolution: A Personal Report on Cuba.* New York: Dial Press.

Szelenyi, Ivan. 1982. "The Intellegentsia in the Class Structure of State-Socialist Societies." Pp. 287–326 in Burawoy and Skocpol 1982.

Taber, Michael, ed. 1983. *Our Power Is That of the Working People: Fidel Castro Speeches,* vol. 2. New York: Pathfinder Press.

Tellería, Evelio. 1973. *Los congresos obreros en Cuba.* Havana: Editorial de Arte y Literatura.

Thomas, Hugh. 1971. *The Cuban Revolution.* New York: Harper.

Toma, Peter. 1979. "The Communist Party of Czechoslovakia." In Fischer-Galati 1979.

Torrado, Fabio 1990. "El diversionismo ideológico y el proceso de rectificación en Cuba." *Cuba socialista,* no. 1 (January–March):92–97.

Trabajadores. Havana.

USSR Academy of Sciences. 1988. *Soviet Economic Reform: Proposals and Solutions.* Moscow: Nauka Publishers.

Valdés, Nelson. 1972a. *Cuba: Socialismo democrático o burocratismo colectivista?* Bogotá: Ediciones Tercer Mundo.

———. 1972b. "The Radical Transformation of Cuban Education." Pp. 422–55 in Bonachea and Valdés 1972a.

———. 1988. "Revolution and Paradigms: A Critical Assessment of Cuban Studies." Pp. 182–211 in Zimbalist 1988.

Veiga, Roberto. 1978. "Informe central presentado al XIV Congreso Nacional de la CTC." *Trabajadores,* special supplement, 29 Nov 78.

———. 1980. "Clausura del octavo curso para directores de empresas, celebrada en la Escuela Nacional de Dirección de la Economía." *Cuestiones de la economía planificada* 3, no. 2 (March–April):24–34.

———. 1984. "Report Presented to the 15th Congress of the CTC."

Vilariño, Andrés. 1980. "Surgimiento del sistema de dirección de la economía socialista en Cuba y sus particularidades." *Cuestiones de la economía planificada* 3, no. 3 (May–June):60–94.

Wainwright, Hilary. 1990. "New Forms of Democracy for Socialist Renewal." *Socialist Review* 20, no. 2 (April–June):31–44.

Walder, Andrew. 1986. *Communist Neo-Traditionalism: Work and Authority in Chinese Industry.* Berkeley: University of California Press.

Weir, Stan. 1983. "On-Going Rank and File Control: The One Effective Weapon Against Bureaucrats in Society." Pp. 175–85 in Shalom 1983.

Wertheimer, Alan. 1975. "In Defense of Compulsory Voting." Pp. 276–96 in Pennock and Chapman 1975.

White, Gordon. 1987. "Cuban Planning in the Mid-1980s: Centralization, Decentralization, and Participation." *World Development* 15, no. 1 (January):153–61.

Williams, Raymond. 1983. *The Year 2000.* New York: Pantheon.

———. 1985. "Towards Many Socialisms." Pp. 294–311 in Nicolić 1985.

Wilson, Jeanne. 1986. "The People's Republic of China." Pp. 219–51 in Pravda and Ruble 1986.

———. 1987. "The Institution of Democratic Reforms in the Chinese Enterprise Since 1978." Pp. 298–328 in Sirianni, ed., 1987.

Wolf, Eric. 1969. *Peasant Wars of the Twentieth Century.* New York: Harper.

Wood, Ellen. 1986. *The Retreat from Class.* London: Verso Editions.

Woodward, Ralph Lee, Jr. 1963. "Union Labor and Communism: Cuba." *Caribbean Studies* 3, no. 3 (October):17–50.

Zeitlin, Maurice. 1970. *Revolutionary Politics and the Cuban Working Class.* Princeton: Princeton University Press.

———. 1977. "Corporate Ownership and Control: The Large Corporation and the Capitalist Class." Pp. 233–79 in Zeitlin, ed., 1977.

———. 1981. "Who Owns America? The Same Old Gang." Pp. 167–72 in Robertson 1981.

Zeitlin, Maurice, ed. 1977. *American Society Inc.* Chicago: Rand McNally.

Zeitlin, Maurice, and Robert Scheer. 1963. *Cuba: Tragedy in Our Hemisphere.* New York: Grove Press.

Zimbalist, Andrew. 1975. "Worker Participation in Cuba." *Challenge* 18, no. 5 (November–December):45–54.

———. 1985. "Cuban Economic Planning: Organization and Performance." Pp. 213–30 in Halebsky and Kirk 1985.

———. 1989. "Incentives and Planning in Cuba." *Latin American Research Review* 24, no. 1:65–93.

———. 1990a. "Does the Economy Work?" *NACLA Report on the Americas* 24, no. 2 (August):16–19.

———. 1990b. "Perspectives on Cuban Development and Prospects for the 1990s." Typescript, January.

Zimbalist, Andrew, ed. 1988. *Cuban Political Economy: Controversies in Cubanology.* Boulder, Colo.: Westview.

Zimbalist, Andrew, and Claes Brundenius. 1989. *The Cuban Economy: Measurement and Analysis of Socialist Performance.* Baltimore. Md.: Johns Hopkins University Press.

Zukin, Sharon. 1981. "The Representation of Working-Class Interest in Socialist Society: Yugoslav Labor Unions." *Politics and Society* 10, no. 3:281–316.

———. 1984. "Yugoslavia: Development and Persistence of the State." Pp. 249–76 in Harding 1984.

Zwerdling, Daniel. 1978. *Workplace Democracy.* New York: Harper Colophon Books.

Index